CHIRON IN LOVE

CHIRON IN LOVE

The Astrology of Envy, Rage, Compassion, and Wisdom

Liz Greene

THE WESSEX ASTROLOGER

Published in 2023 by
The Wessex Astrologer Ltd
PO Box 9307
Swanage
BH19 9BF

For a full list of our titles go to www.wessexastrologer.com

ISBN 9781910531969

Cover design by Fiona Bowring at Bowring Creative
Typeset by Kevin Moore

A catalogue record for this book is available at The British Library

Table of Contents

Introduction

The astrological Chiron is as much an enigma today as it was at the time of the discovery of this heavenly body in 1977. Some excellent books have been published since then which explore Chiron's meaning in the natal chart, and no doubt more will appear in the years to come. But gathering insight into Chiron is necessarily an ongoing process, and perhaps a more than usually difficult one because of the disturbing nature of its symbolism.

It takes a long time after the discovery of any new planet (or in this case, a planetoid-comet) for astrologers to develop a perspective on the psychological dynamics the astrological symbol represents, and an even longer time for those dynamics to make sense on a broader collective level. Uranus was discovered by Sir William Herschel in 1781, an event sandwiched between the American War of Independence in 1776 and the French Revolution in 1789. Yet the successful expression of a nation built on the revolutionary democratic principles declared so eloquently during those great 18th-century upheavals still eludes much of the world two and a half centuries later. Even in nations that have espoused the ideals of democracy, we are still struggling with how we might best navigate its challenges. As Winston Churchill once said:

> Democracy is the worst form of government, except for all those other forms that have been tried from time to time.[1]

And if we are still trying to work out how to cope with Uranus, it is more than likely we will be slow in understanding many dimensions of Chiron for a long time to come.

---

1 Winston Churchill, 11 November 1947, at winstonchurchill.org/resources/quotes/the-worst-form-of-government/.

The material in this book was first given as a seminar entitled 'Chiron in Love' at Regents College, London on 6 November 2005 for the Autumn Programme of the Centre for Psychological Astrology. The theme of Chiron in relationships had intrigued me for many years because of the large number of close relationships I had encountered through my astrological counselling work, not only romantic but also familial, in which major Chiron synastry aspects appeared with surprising frequency, and where people kept hurting each other deeply yet found it hard to fathom the underlying reasons or implement genuinely helpful ways of dealing with their unhappiness. The seminar was recorded and transcribed but never edited, and it lay untouched in my files for fifteen years.[2]

In the autumn of 2020, I decided to give three online seminars on Chiron for students from both the Centre for Psychological Astrology and MISPA, the Mercury Internet School of Psychological Astrology created and run by John Green. I felt Chiron was a disturbingly relevant symbol because in early 2020 the world had begun to experience the full impact of the Covid pandemic, with all the collective bewilderment, anxiety, and anger that erupted as a result. In the global outpourings of helplessness, fear, rage, polarisation, and an apparently obsessive determination to find scapegoats, I could discern the tracks of the mythic Centaur's responses to his unmerited poisoned wound.

The main reason why I felt Chiron was so relevant at the time was that I could see around me everywhere a constant and often extreme expression of the astrological Chiron displayed by the media, by governments, and among individuals in every country. One of the most important among the many threads of Chiron's story is compassion for the suffering of others; but another, equally important thread is the sense of feeling victimised and

---

2 I had already written about Chiron and Saturn as psychological defence mechanisms in a seminar volume called *Barriers and Boundaries*, published by the CPA Press in 1996 and available as an ebook from Amazon. But this volume did not deal with Chiron's dynamics in relationships.

unfairly injured, and the resulting resentment, rage, envy, and impetus to hunt down any culprit who, fairly or unfairly, can be held accountable for the suffering.

No specific planet or planetary configuration can be equated with external events such as pandemics, wars, terrorist attacks, economic crises, and natural disasters, although astrologers have been trying for a few thousand years to find exact correlations and will no doubt go on trying. Hindsight, as the mythic Titan Epimetheus discovered, is always easy. It seems these kinds of happenings can occur under any planetary combination, and if astrological planets are understood as symbols rather than concrete 'causes', they cannot be held accountable for human misery. But our human responses to such events are characterised by the planetary lenses through which we perceive them, and our perceptions lead to choices and actions that have consequences. Certain kinds of events coincide with and bring out certain kinds of responses. In an article in *The Telegraph* published in February 2023, the author, Anita Singh, discusses the idea that the kind of 'witch trial frenzy' currently infecting social media tends to occur at times of political and social dislocation, when people feel particularly anxious and insecure.[3] When we become convinced that life has unexpectedly and unjustifiably made ugly faces at us, personally and as a collective, we tend to see and react to these experiences through Chiron's eyes.

Covid has not finished with us; the virus is still causing hospitalisations and claiming lives. But it has ceased to be the major topic of discussion in the majority of countries. Virtually all the draconian rules and regulations instituted to combat Covid have been abandoned, and the full psychological, physical, and economic costs of the pandemic and the ways it was dealt with are only now being evaluated. But the experience of unfair wounding, central to Chiron's myth, had not yet finished revealing

---

3 'The Witch Trials of JK Rowling, review: a podcast that promises to add more flames to the fire', Anita Singh, *The Telegraph*, 21 February 2023.

its various expressions in the world at the time I completed my seminars on Chiron in late 2020. In the spring of 2022, Russia invaded Ukraine, and as a direct consequence of this event combined with various global political and financial decisions, many countries experienced drastic increases in the price of fuel, energy, and food, along with skyrocketing interest rates: a 'cost of living' crisis that has had severe repercussions on every level of society and has resulted in yet more victims of life's unfairness.

At the time of writing this introduction in the spring of 2023, it seems we are in the throes of an ongoing struggle that increasingly resembles the nine-headed Lernaean Hydra of myth: cut off one head and three more grow in its place. Official responses have tended to prove hopelessly inadequate because they deal with external facts while ignoring inner psychological states. Individuals in positions of power, who make major political and economic decisions for the rest of us, all have Chiron somewhere in their birth charts and a personal agenda to match, whatever their political persuasion. The expression of Chiron's characteristic depression, rage, self-pity, and scapegoat-hunting as a knee-jerk response to a sense of unfair injury and victimisation is erupting everywhere in the media, in politics, in religious institutions, in education, on social media, and in everyday conversation. After many decades of relative peace and prosperity in the West, it seems we have forgotten how to deal with humanity's endemic tendency, when under pressure, to display its least attractive face.

Astrology is a subject to which people often turn when all other avenues have failed. Even the most hardened rationalist can be found secretly trawling astrological websites to make some sense of a world that increasingly resembles the lines from William Butler Yeats' great prophetic poem, *The Second Coming*, written in 1939: 'Things fall apart; the centre cannot hold; mere anarchy is loosed upon the world.'[4] And astrologers are

---

4 William Butler Yeats, *The Second Coming* (1919), first published in *Michael Robartes and the Dancer* (Cuala Press, 1920).

expected to provide solutions to questions they may be unable to answer, like why people suffer unnecessarily and unfairly, why victims so often turn into persecutors, and why it seems that any balanced and reasonable dialogue has become increasingly impossible as the collective polarises over issues linked to personal and ancestral wounds that have not healed. The material in this volume on Chiron, comprised of the original 2005 seminar with additional sections added from the more recent seminars of 2020, seems to me increasingly relevant for any astrological practitioner or student because I feel there is something the astrological community is still failing to understand about this mysterious heavenly body.

Most astrologers are familiar with the myth of the wise King of the Centaurs who is accidentally wounded by an arrow dipped in the poisonous blood of the Lernaean Hydra, and who cannot heal his injury despite all his knowledge and skill. Chiron has become the archetypal figure of the Wounded Healer who develops compassion and the power to help the suffering of others because of his own poisoned wound. But in the original myth, which emerged in preclassical Greece, Chiron doesn't learn to heal because of his wound. He is a healer already, and the incurable injury destroys both his calling and his future. When all remedies and skills have failed, he can only lie in his cave howling in pain. The only escape from his suffering is to relinquish his divinity and die like any mortal being.

It is this difficult mythic theme that forms the focus of the book. Ways of permanently healing Chiron's wound and saving the world are not included. But a deeper understanding of Chiron's nature and its implications in our everyday lives and our close relationships might be a more helpful way each of us as individuals can work with this paradoxical and challenging astrological symbol. The original seminar was entitled 'Chiron in Love' because Chiron's story is most clearly and poignantly enacted, not on the global stage by armies, health organisations, politicians, and politically motivated groups, but in our most personal exchanges with the people closest to us. The core of the book is the dynamic of Chiron in the synastry between two natal horoscopes, although I have included a background of mythic material about Chiron that might help to shed light on the interaction between Chiron in one horoscope and the planets and angles in another.

Unlike some astrologers, I do not believe that Chiron's wound can ever be entirely healed, because it is related to our experience of being mortal, flawed humans, and to the collision between our ideals of a perfect world and the reality of the world as it is and may continue to be. This may be an unpopular view in some circles because it asks each individual to honestly face inner conflicts that are usually projected onto other people and the outside world. Projection, and the divisive polarisation that so often results from it, might initially appear to make Chiron's hurt easier to bear, but ultimately it does little except generate more wounding. Healing Chiron's wound, in my understanding, doesn't lie in fixing the failings of society, creating a perfect world, and never experiencing hurt, rage, and envy again. It lies in each of us coming to terms with the roots and nature of our own individual suffering, bitterness, and sense of victimisation, and finding ways of working with these experiences creatively rather than trying to cure them or finding someone to blame. Jung put it succinctly when he said:

> If things go wrong in the world, this is because something is wrong with the individual, because something is wrong with me. Therefore, if I am sensible, I shall put myself right first. For this I need – because outside authority no longer means anything to me – a knowledge of the innermost foundations of my being, in order that I may base myself firmly on the eternal facts of the human psyche.[5]

---

5 C. G. Jung, 'The Meaning of Psychology for Modern Man', in *Civilisation in Transition*, CW10 (Routledge, 1964), ¶329.

Part One

The Nature of Chiron

The theme of Chiron in love might at first seem like an oxymoron. The archetypal figure of the Wounded Healer, irrevocably injured yet drawing on the wound to offer compassion and healing to others, doesn't usually evoke images of flirtation, romance, and sexual passion. But hopefully during the course of the seminar, the apparently contradictory nature of this juxtaposition might not seem quite as strange as it first appears.

I would like to begin with some general comments about Chiron's status as a heavenly body. Chiron isn't technically designated as a planet. In astronomical circles it's understood to be a hybrid between a planetoid and a comet, and it is classed as a 'centaur', the name given to small bodies with the composition of comets that orbit the Sun chiefly between Jupiter and Neptune. Chiron was first noticed in 1977 by the American astronomer Charles T. Kowal, and many questions remain about the relative newness of its discovery and the relationship, if any, between its name and its astrological significance. The planets known in antiquity earned their names partly through many centuries of observation and partly through the perceptions of cultures that approached the meaning of heavenly bodies with mythic consciousness and an intuitive understanding of symbols.

One of the difficulties that arises with Chiron is the fact that we haven't had that long to observe it, and the astronomers who named it cannot be assumed to possess either mythic consciousness or a grasp of symbols. As a planetoid it's known as 2060 Chiron, and as a comet it's 95P/Chiron. Some excellent books have already been written about the astrological Chiron.[6] But there is still a great deal of ongoing work to be done by astrologers on this mysterious celestial object to develop a sense of what it might mean in an individual chart as well as in synastry, transits, and progressions.

There is consequently a problem for the more rationally inclined astrologer about why, since the name Chiron appears to be completely arbitrary, we should immediately pounce on all the stories and attributes connected with this mysterious figure in myth and assume that it can actually help our interpretation of the astrological Chiron. There is no reason why we should, any more than we should attribute qualities to Uranus that belong to the mythic god of the starry heavens, or assign attributes to Neptune that belong to the mythic ruler of the sea. The process of synchronicity does seem to be at work with the naming of heavenly bodies – at least in the past, although ideological concerns now appear to have superseded what was once a more intuitive process of naming them.

Yet despite our current preoccupation with imposing ideology on imagination, perhaps the names of new heavenly bodies will continue to be mysteriously appropriate. After all, Uranus, when it was discovered in 1781, was initially called 'the Georgian Star' after King George III, and then it was called 'Herschel' after its discoverer. But somehow, despite these efforts, the planet eventually found its right name. We don't really know about Chiron yet. I can only suggest that, having watched its natal placements, transits, progressions, and synastry since its discovery, I have found that the mythic imagery does seem to be strikingly relevant in terms of reflecting the experiences and inner states Chiron symbolises or corresponds to in human life. If we try to apply other myths, they don't

---

6 For literature on Chiron's meaning in the horoscope, see, among others, Melanie Reinhart, *Chiron and the Healing Journey* (Starwalker Press 2010); Barbara Hand Clow, *Chiron: Rainbow Bridge Between the Inner and Outer Planets* (Llewellyn, 1987); Lisa Tahir, *The Chiron Effect: Healing Our Core Wounds Through Astrology, Empathy, and Self-Forgiveness* (Bear & Company, 2021).

appear to work. If any of you have an issue with this, you must simply go home and observe Chiron in as many charts as possible and try to form your own conclusions.

Let's start by looking at Chiron in myth, and what this ancient body of stories might tell us on a psychological level. Then we can begin to explore the question of why Chiron seems to be so extremely important in relationships. Any of you who work with synastry will undoubtedly have noticed that close Chiron aspects between charts are disturbingly common in intense relationships where there is a powerful physical attraction. Initially this frequency might make no sense, any more than the prevalence of Saturn in synastry makes sense unless we start thinking about relationships in terms other than 'and they lived happily ever after'.

Chiron might seem to have little to do with love and attraction. Symbolically, it is connected with the difficult themes of unfair human suffering, unjustified wounding, and the painful question of why so many decent, blameless people are subjected to grossly unfair and apparently arbitrary hurts in life. Chiron also seems to be related to the 'professional victim' psychology which, in a classic reflection of what Jung called *enantiodromia*, results in the paradox of the victim becoming a persecutor who claims a plethora of fresh victims among those perceived as oppressors. Spite and vindictiveness rather than compassion and wisdom thus emerge from the suffering. What has this got to do with love? It might have a great deal to do with it on deeper levels we need to look at more closely when we're trying to understand why we enter relationships that sometimes cause so much pain.

Chiron's iconography

The name Chiron in Greek is properly spelled Cheiron, and it is derived from the word *cheir*, which means 'hand'. From this word we derive the term 'cheiromancy': palmistry, or 'divination by the hand'. Chiron's name refers to the skills inherent in his hands as both a healer and a hunter. He makes one of his earliest mythic appearances in Homer's *Iliad*, in which he is described as 'the most righteous of the *kentauroi*'.[7]

What does 'the most righteous' mean? There is an implication that centaurs in general, being half horse and driven by their animal instincts, don't always have a concept of righteousness. But this centaur is different from the rest because he upholds the idea of doing what is right and just. In other words, he displays reason, which to the Greeks represented one of the most important attributes of divinity. In Greek thought, reason doesn't imply rational analysis alone. It suggests clarity, perspective, balance, a capacity to see connections and implications, and an intuitive grasp of the whole.

We meet Chiron in Greek art dating as far back as the 9th century BCE, where he is portrayed illustrating one or another of the stories associated with him. The interesting thing about this iconography is that during this archaic period, the other centaurs are presented in the way we usually think of them based on art from later centuries: the divine half, depicted naked, ends at the waist, and from that point on, the centaur is a horse. These figures usually have two human arms and four equine legs. But in preclassical Greek art such as this amphora from the 6th century BCE showing Peleus handing his young son Achilles into the care of Chiron, the Centaur is represented wearing a *chiton*, a type of tunic fastened at the shoulder, and he has a complete human form, including two human legs. The horse part is attached at the base of his spine and the two rear legs are equine. This portrayal identifies Chiron as being much closer to humanity than his fellows, even to the point where he's dressed as an ordinary Greek citizen.

Other iconographic evidence identifies Chiron as being different from his fellow centaurs. He is usually shown instructing Achilles or another

---

7 Homer, *Iliad*, 11.832, trans. A. T. Murray (Harvard University Press, 1924).

Amphora dated to c. 520-510 BCE from the school of the painter Antimenes, showing Chiron receiving the young Achilles from the boy's father King Peleus of Phthia. Walters Art Museum, Baltimore.

young prince, because this is one of his main roles in myth. He is the tutor of the young princes of the royal dynasties of the Greek city-states. We can always recognize Chiron in early Greek iconography, first because he's more human than the other centaurs, and second because he's often shown as a mentor or teacher accompanied by a human child.

Chiron's proximity to humanity, and his loneliness, are beautifully portrayed in Mary Renault's novel, *The Bull From the Sea*. He isn't an actual centaur in the novel. Renault evokes archaic Greece in a way that renders it accessible and believable, and the book is firmly rooted in archaeological and literary sources. But it's clear in her portrayal that Chiron belongs to an earlier stream of human evolution – perhaps Neanderthal – of which he and his people are the last surviving remnant. He is called 'Old Handy', a reference to the Greek meaning of the name Cheiron, and he is both king and priest to his people, as well as being a healer. This is how Renault describes him:

> Whatever wild shape his guardian god had put on to beget him, some god was there. You could see it in his eyes. Dark and sad they were, and looked back a long way into the ancient days of the earth, before Zeus ruled in heaven...And I knew the old Kentaur's sadness. He had come further up from the earth than all his people, who feared his wisdom and did not know his mind.[8]

During the classical Greek and Roman periods, the fashion for differentiating Chiron from other centaurs died out, and he is portrayed in the same way they are except for the characteristic symbolism of instructing a human child. This Roman fresco from Herculaneum, dated to the 1st century CE, is quite well known and, like the much older Greek vase painting, portrays the centaur instructing Achilles. Although Chiron is presented in the usual half-horse way, his lyre and the laurel wreath around his head link him with Apollo, the god of prophecy, healing, and music, who in myth raised him after his mother Philyra abandoned him.

This kind of iconography, using symbols to represent specific attributes and meanings, is very similar to the iconography of many of the world's religions. Each symbol contains a story in itself. Chiron is a healer, so he is

---

8 Mary Renault, *The Bull From the Sea* (London: Penguin, 1973), pp. 57-58.

Chiron instructing Achilles in how to play the lyre. Roman fresco from Herculaneum, 1st century CE. Museo Archeologico Nazionale di Napoli.

sometimes portrayed in connection with other healing deities like Apollo and Asclepios. He is also a teacher, so he is shown giving instruction to a child. In the Herculaneum fresco, he's teaching Achilles how to play the lyre. But in most ancient images, he instructs his pupil in the art of the hunt. Astrologers tend to forget the element of hunting that is repeatedly emphasised in portrayals of the mythic Chiron. He's usually perceived as a kind, wise healer, but he shares with his centaur brethren a predilection for the chase and the kill.

Artists have continued to portray Chiron into the modern era, retaining the motif of the teacher of young princes. But it's the hunt that's emphasised, not the healing arts. This pastel drawing from 1862 by Eugène Delacroix is called *The Education of Achilles*, in which Chiron is instructing the young hero-to-be in the art of the chase. The atmosphere is wild and turbulent.

Eugène Delacroix, *The Education of Achilles* (1862).
Getty Center Collections, Los Angeles.

The next painting, dated to 1782, is by Jean-Baptiste Regnault and is also called *The Education of Achilles*. Chiron is demonstrating the use of the bow. The tone isn't agitated like Puget's painting, and Chiron is portrayed as young and beardless rather than the usual 'wise old centaur' figure with grizzled hair and beard. It's his patience and care that are illustrated, rather than his energy and violence, although the theme of hunting is the same. Alongside the image of the wise centaur who teaches and heals, there is a continuity of the idea of centaurs as expressions of wild, primitive nature.

Both facets exist in the symbol of Chiron, and both qualities can arise in relationships when Chiron is constellated by synastry aspects between two charts.

Jean-Baptiste Regnault, *The Education of Achilles by Chiron* (1782). Musée du Louvre, Paris.

Finally, here are two paintings from the late 19th and early 20th centuries that remain faithful to the theme. First is John Singer Sargent's elegant art deco sketch of Chiron teaching Achilles how to use the bow. This was painted in 1921. Rather than hunting in the forest, they are in the heavens, accompanied by Zeus' eagle.

John Singer Sargent, *Chiron Teaching Achilles How to Hunt* (c. 1922-25).
Museum of Fine Arts, Boston.

The second painting is by the Italian artist Eduardo Ettore Forti, dated to the end of the 19ᵗʰ century. It's called *Festival of the Centaurs* and portrays a centaur, who might or might not be Chiron, carrying a *maenad* – a female initiate of the Dionysian mysteries – on his back. This image is a detail; the full painting shows two other centaurs making music for the couple with pipes and flute.

Detail from Eduardo Ettore Forti, *Festival of the Centaurs*, c. 1895. Private collection.

There are not many images, ancient or modern, which relate the centaurs to erotic playfulness and affection rather than abduction and rape. The latter is a more usual theme in centaur art over the centuries, although Chiron himself is never portrayed in this way. A Roman sculpture known as the 'Borghese Centaur' presents a centaur with Eros on his back, but it isn't clear whether this is Chiron. If it is, it's an unusual motif in his early iconography.[9]

In myth, Chiron had a wife called Khariklo, whose name means 'graceful spinner'. She was an Okeanid nymph who lived with him on Mount Pelion and acted as foster-mother to the young princes in Chiron's care. But she is rarely portrayed in ancient art. Khariklo's father is usually referred to as Okeanos, god of the encircling cosmic ocean. As well as being Chiron's father-in-law, Okeanos is also his maternal grandfather through his mother Philyra. The image below, from an Athenian wine-bowl dated to the 6th century BCE, shows Khariklo, furthest on the right, with other deities forming part of the wedding procession of Peleus and the sea-goddess Thetis. Damage to the wine-bowl has erased the lower half of her body as well as the first letters of her name, inscribed over her head. Chiron can be seen on the left, further back in the procession, complete with hunting trophies. He is portrayed in characteristic archaic fashion, with two human legs. Under Khariklo's cloak, figures of horses or centaurs are just visible on her tunic.[10]

Khariklo bore Chiron many children. Among them were the Pelionides nymphs who lived on Mount Pelion, and a son called Karystos. Like his sisters, Karystos bore a human form. He was worshipped as a rustic vegetation-god on the island of Euboea.

---

9   The theme of a *maenad* riding a centaur appears in a fresco at the Villa de Cicerone at Pompeii, dated to the 1st century CE. The *maenads* or Bacchantes, female initiates in the mysteries of the god Dionysos, were known for their wild, ecstatic behaviour during the god's rituals. The Romans seem to have viewed them as the natural companions of the centaurs.

10   The name Chariklo has now been given to a planetoid or 'centaur' orbiting, like Chiron, between Saturn and Uranus (10199 Chariklo). It was discovered by James V. Scotti in 1997. Chariklo, which is larger than Chiron, has rings like those of Saturn.

Khariklo, far right, accompanying other deities including Chiron in the wedding procession of Peleus and Thetis. Greek wine-bowl, 6th century BCE, ©The Trustees of the British Museum.

Images of Chiron have fascinated people for nearly three millennia. So far we have seen three faces of Chiron: the teacher-healer, the hunter and, less common but perhaps equally important, the lover. All three are relevant to the astrological Chiron. When a mythic image continues to live and inspire creative ideas in art over the centuries, it describes something that continues to be of vital importance for us in terms of our psychological expression. It's a never-ending story, an archetypal pattern, not an archaic belief that expired with the demise of ancient cultures.

It's interesting to note which mythic figures from antiquity demonstrate this kind of 'agency' and longevity because they tell us which archetypal patterns have remained most resonant for us over the centuries. We see little of Hera after the fall of Rome, but Orpheus with his lyre remains a constant theme in romantic art. We can still see centaurs today on advertising logos and in fantasy films such as *Harry Potter and the Philosopher's Stone* (2001), in which the CGI centaur Firenze, voiced by Paul Fearon, instructs Harry about the dangers of the Dark Forest, and *The Chronicles of Narnia: The Lion and the Witch and the Wardrobe* (2005), in which Patrick Paul Kake plays the benign centaur Areius. And even

Chiron himself makes a cinematic appearance, played by Pierce Brosnan in the 2010 film, *Percy Jackson and the Olympians: The Lightning Thief*. There is something about the hybrid nature of the centaur – his strange half-horse, half-human shape – that continues to fascinate us.

The meaning of mythic hybrids

The hybrid creatures found in Greek myth as well as in the stories of other cultures are complex and disturbing. They reflect bridges between different spheres of reality or, in human terms, different dimensions of the psyche. They imply that there are two or more worlds that are combined or integrated. Anything that has a composite shape involving both human and animal presents us with some attribute of life that is neither solely human nor solely instinctual. It's a combination of both.

Because the Greek gods are generally anthropomorphised – imaged in human form – human features in these hybrids are also god-features. But the hybrid beings, although usually at least partly divine, are inconsistent in their response toward humans. Some are benign, some are ambivalent, and some are vengeful. The Greek Sphinx who guards the gates of Thebes and poses the famous riddle to Oedipus is a hybrid between a female divinity, a lion, and an eagle. She is an instrument of vengeance for the gods and destroys any human who can't answer her riddle. Pan is a hybrid between a male divinity and a goat, but in contrast to the Sphinx he is the benign face of the natural world and has no intrinsic enmity toward humans. The Minotaur is a hybrid between a human and a bull, but like the Sphinx he is a tool of vengeance for the gods to punish human arrogance and *hubris*. He is unrelentingly destructive and feeds on human flesh.

In the religious iconography of ancient Egypt, the gods are usually shown as hybrids. Very few – Osiris and Isis in particular – are portrayed in entirely human form, but even Osiris, presiding over the cycles of nature, is often portrayed with green skin. We find human figures with animal heads and animal figures with human heads. We can see similar hybrids in the images of Babylonian myth. At the British Museum visitors are confronted by huge winged bulls with human heads in the exhibit of Babylonian artifacts.

In common with these other mythic hybrids, Chiron, who is half horse and half god, bridges worlds. He stands between two dimensions of reality, the divine and the instinctual, and he provides the possibility of integrating them, although in ordinary life they seem irrevocably split. In psychological terms, this merging of human/divine and animal reflects a fluid interchange between the realm of consciousness and the realm of the instinctual unconscious. We are not accustomed to such images in the art of the modern world unless they're meant to be deliberately metaphorical or quirky and tongue-in-cheek – what some might call post-modern pastiche – like the strange hybrids that appear on the decorative ceramic plates created by the Italian artist Piero Fornasetti (1913-1988).[11]

One of Piero Fornasetti's decorative plates, designed for an exhibition in Milan in 1947. The woman in the image is Lina Cavalieri, an Italian operatic soprano from the early 1900s. Fornasetti found a woodcut of her face in a magazine, but never actually met her.

Although a number of Greek deities such as Pan are composite in form, the Olympian gods are not portrayed as hybrids. Although they are often amoral by human standards, they symbolise the divine laws that govern the universe. Zeus transforms himself into various animals and birds to achieve his many seductions, and the Olympians have their associated token animals: Athene her owl, Hera her peacock, Zeus his eagle, Artemis her hind. But the seven planetary gods known to the Greco-

---

11 See www.fornasetti.com for the 'Tema e Variazione' wall plates.

Roman world are fully anthropomorphic. The image of the hybrid reflects a state of oneness between psyche and body, spirit and matter, because these opposites have not yet polarised. In Jung's terminology the hybrids symbolise a completeness that exists before the emergence of the ego and the resulting split between consciousness and the unconscious.

Earlier cultures such as those of Egypt and Babylon present us with creation myths of an emanated universe where forms are constantly emerging and transforming, rather than a cosmos which a transcendent God created once and for all *ex nihilo*, as he does in the Abrahamic religions. Hybrid figures are part of the context of these ancient cultures. But by the Hellenistic period, philosophy began to replace myth, and mythic images were understood as allegories and metaphors rather than realities. Even by Plato's time in the 4th century BCE, the gods were understood in some philosophical circles as psychological forces. The cosmos was perceived as a rational order – the Greek word *kosmos* in fact means 'order' – and hybrids like Chiron and Pan who appear in later Greek iconography are unusual. Their rarity means they're worth paying careful attention to.

Chiron's lineage

The stories about Chiron's lineage can help us to understand more about the possibilities he offers. He is the son of Kronos, whom we know in astrology as Saturn. Kronos seduced a nymph called Philyra, but when his wife Rhea discovered them *in flagrante*, he transformed himself into a stallion and galloped away to escape his wife's ire, leaving Philyra alone and pregnant. When the child was born, Philyra found his centaur form repellent and frightening, and she abandoned him, begging the gods to transform her into any shape other than human so that she could escape her shame. Kronos, out of pity, turned her into a linden tree. The abandoned infant Chiron was rescued by Apollo, who raised him and taught him the arts of healing and music, while Artemis taught him the skills of hunting and the use of the bow.

Philyra's father was Okeanos, the great stream that surrounds and supports the universe. This cosmic stream isn't simply water. It's the primal substance of many mythologies: the raw, fluid, creative 'stuff' out of which everything emerges. Chiron, half-horse and half-divine, is the progeny of our old friend Saturn, whose nature is Titanic or earthy. But Chiron is also the grandson of the boundless, primordial realm of Okeanos: the imaginal world as both the matrix from which all life emanates and the glue that binds it all together.

What kind of combination might this suggest? The astrological Saturn symbolises, among other things, the limits of form. Kronos is the son of Gaia the Earth and Ouranos the Starry Heavens, but he takes after his mother. Once images, inspirations, and ideas have been encased in matter, they are limited and cease to possess fluidity and infinite possibilities. The world of Okeanos, in contrast, might be loosely comparable with the domain of the astrological Neptune. It's the amorphous matrix out of which everything is formed. In alchemy it is called the *prima materia*, from which the seven alchemical metals emerge. In Kabbalistic thought it's called *our*, the primal light which emanates from the unknown godhead and out of which all things are born.

Chiron's hybrid nature seems to seems to suggest that he conjoins Saturn's structured, earthbound perception of reality with the boundless realm of pre-form, where the divine is just beginning to emerge into manifestation. In Platonic thought, this boundless world is understood as the World Soul, which Jung explicitly equated with his idea of the collective unconscious. In the work of Neoplatonists such as Iamblichus, this realm is also understood as the imaginal realm. The imagination, accessed through ritual as well as through dreams, divination, and art, provides humans with a bridge between consciousness and the collective unconscious – the domain of the archetypes or, put another way, the abode of the gods – because it belongs to both.[12]

Chiron is the conduit between the realm of the imagination, in which the soul exists without corporeal limits – the *mundus imaginalis* – and the mortal body with its limits and its inevitable time-locked doom. Chiron combines Okeanos' realm of endless fluid possibilities and the Saturnian world of law, structure, form, and mortality. We don't have many bridges between these two worlds. Ritual and prayer can sometimes briefly conjure it; certain hallucinogenic drugs might provide a temporary crossing; and art, music, and the world of dreams may offer us a transient passage. But the ego is usually torn between them, encased in the limits of mundane life but striving endlessly to find a way across to a dimly glimpsed ideal realm of love, beauty, truth, and unlimited possibilities.

This striving forms the core of what is sometimes called our 'religious instinct'. We create religious images in the hope that they will somehow offer a way to bridge the two worlds, although institutionalised religions often become encased in Saturnian structures, inflexible dogmas, and worldly politics, and lose their capacity to move fluently in the ever-changing waters of the imaginal realm. The story of Chiron's ancestry tells us something important about what this heavenly body might symbolise astrologically. It is related to the human religious instinct – or we might also call it the quest for meaning – because it brings together two separate and apparently irreconcilably divided domains. Like the two worlds of Will Parry and Lyra Belacqua in Philip Pullman's *His Dark Materials*, there may be no awareness in either realm of the existence of the other. One half of Chiron belongs to the suffering world of form, and the other to the world of the Paradise Garden, the divine realm from which we instinctively feel we have come and to which we hope one day to return.

---

12 For the role of the imagination in the work of Iamblichus, see Iamblichus, *De mysteriis*, trans. Emma C. Clarke, John M. Dillon, and Jackson P. Hershbell (Brill, 2004). See also Liz Greene, *Jung's Studies in Astrology*, pp. 73-116.

Another important attribute belonging to the mythic Chiron, perhaps connected to this function as a bridge between the formal and imaginal worlds, is that he's a prophet, a *mantis*. He is a seer, and so are some of his children.

Audience: I didn't realise he married.

Liz: Yes, I mentioned earlier that Chiron married the nymph Khariklo, one of the daughters of Okeanos. Okeanos is therefore both Chiron's maternal grandfather through his mother Philyra, also a daughter of Okeanos, and his father-in-law. We tend to focus on the solitary 'Wounded Healer' theme and forget that in myth, every figure interacts with other figures to create a story. No mythic character functions entirely alone. We don't usually associate the wounded healer with the comforts of conjugal bliss and the responsibilities of parenthood. Chiron fathered many children on Khariklo, and I'm not aware of any story suggesting that this marriage was problematic like that of Zeus and Hera, or Aphrodite and Hephaistos.

According to the late 5th century BCE poet Pindar, Chiron couldn't reproduce his centaur form. His children were born with a human shape, even though they were immortals. One of Chiron's daughters was called Hippe, which means 'horse'. According to Euripides, she was a seer and inherited her father's healing skills, and her cures had the power to release humans from pain. But Zeus, exhibiting his usual animosity toward humanity, turned her into a horse as a punishment for her generosity.

Audience: Why did Zeus hate humans so much?

Liz: To start with, he wasn't responsible for their existence. They were created secretly by Prometheus, who shaped their bodies out of water and earth, and Athene, who breathed life into them. Then, to make matters worse, Prometheus stole Zeus' divine fire and gave it to humans so they could develop their godlike potential through vision and imagination. They now possessed all four elements: the water and earth of which their bodies were made, the divine breath of Athene, and the sacred fire of Zeus. This was not only an offence to Zeus but also a terrible threat. That's why he sent a great flood to drown them all, although this proved unsuccessful because Prometheus, whose name means 'foresight', advised his son Deucalion and his daughter-in-law Pyrrha to build an ark so that humanity could survive.

Audience: In the Biblical story, God punished humans because they were sinful.

Liz: Yes, but they were innocent in the Greek story. However, they could become rivals to Zeus because of their potential to develop godlike powers. We might also interpret it slightly differently: Zeus understood all too well that humanity, once it possessed those godlike abilities, would use them unscrupulously and in violation of divine law, and would destroy the order of the cosmos. I leave it to you to think about the implications of that interpretation.

Let's go back to Chiron's children. Eratosthenes, a Greek mathematician, astronomer, and poet from the 3rd century BCE, offers a different story about Chiron's daughter Hippe. She became pregnant by the wind-god Aeolus, and as the time approached for the birth of her child, she fled into the forest, fearful of Chiron's wrath. While giving birth, she prayed to the gods to be turned into a horse. Artemis took pity on her, and once the child was born, the goddess fulfilled Hippe's wish and placed her in the heavens as the constellation of Hippios.[13]

The wild centaurs, who were fathered on the mares of Mount Pelion by Kentauros, the son of Ixion and Nephele, mated with their own kind, perpetuating their hybrid nature. Some of Chiron's daughters, the Pelionides nymphs, acted as their nursemaids. But Chiron, the child of two

---

13 Hippios is an archaic Greek name for what we now know as the constellation of the winged horse Pegasus, who has a different mythic background. For ancient sources on Hippe, see Timothy Ganz, *Early Greek Myth: A Guide to Literary and Artistic Sources* (John Hopkins University Press, 1993), p. 734.

divinities, could generate progeny only in human form. Whatever Chiron's hybrid nature might symbolise within us, it evidently can't be inherited. Other deities, such as Zeus, Apollo, Ares, and Aphrodite, produce divine or semi-divine children who look like them and who in turn produce their own children and grandchildren who eventually become rulers of city-states or ancestors of great dynasties. The divine inheritance, even if it's diluted and humanised, retains the form of the originating deity.

Most kings in the ancient world claimed descent from an immortal. Alexander the Great believed he was the child of Zeus, conceived while his purported father Philip was off fighting wars. The Romans traced the foundation of their city back to Mars, who fathered the twins Romulus and Remus on the mortal Vestal Virgin Rhea Silvia. Julius Caesar claimed descent from Venus, who mated with the Trojan mortal Anchises and bore

Left, Augustus 'Prima Porta', 1st century CE. Right: Apollo 'Belvedere', 120-140 CE, a Roman copy of a Greek original. Both statues, Musei Vaticani.

a hero called Aeneas, the mythic progenitor of the Roman people. The emperor Augustus, who lived in an age of relative scepticism, circulated rumours that he had two fathers: the politician Gaius Octavius and the Sun-god Apollo. The uneducated populace believed him. Augustus, a genius at political propaganda, portrayed himself on coins and monumental sculptures in the immediately recognisable Apollonian pose of Greek classical art, with one arm outstretched.

Chiron's children inherit some of his gifts. But they don't contain within themselves two dimensions of reality, although their mantic abilities allow them to intuit both dimensions. Perhaps Chiron in the natal chart might denote a place where we can intuit or 'see' the potentials of that other world, but we can't ultimately move beyond our humanness. That in itself is a facet of Chiron's wound. We know how things could be or might have been, but as limited mortals we can't make it happen. Chiron seems to represent something we can't pass on in the way the children of other deities can pass on their divine parent's attributes down the generations. But although Chiron can't confer his hybrid nature genetically, he can teach others about what it means.

The myth of the Wounded Healer

The story that astrologers tend to relate to Chiron is his wounding by Herakles' poisoned arrow. But the way it's usually presented today in astrological and therapeutic circles is significantly different from older versions of the story. According to the updated version, Chiron is wounded and then becomes a healer because he has experienced deep suffering and develops compassion. I'm not suggesting that this idea is 'untrue', as it's a powerful theme connected with the emergence of genuine empathy and the capacity to turn one's own suffering into a creative tool to relate to and alleviate others' pain.

Chiron is thus a potent image of the healer who has acquired wisdom through personal pain. This version of Chiron has learned how to heal others because he has been wounded, and he reflects the process by which life's damage can enhance consciousness and put us on a path connecting us with deeper or higher realities. The fact that Chiron can't heal himself is a necessary part of the story. If we could fully heal our own wounds, we might well lose our compassion for others who are suffering. It's only the ongoing recognition of our frailty and damage that allows the continuance of empathy. There is profound truth in this interpretation. The only problem is that the idea of healing gifts emerging as a product of wounding is not what the myth of Chiron as it has come down to us from antiquity actually tells us.

There are many documentary and iconographic sources for myths, and they inevitably mutate over time according to changing cultural contexts. Many myths are connected in their origins with local nature-deities and heroes as well as heavenly phenomena, and the differences over the centuries reflect the different localities and cultures in which the myth arises. We saw an example of this cultural diversity in the two related but different stories of the Great Flood, the Hebrew and the Greek. But the archetypal core is consistent. Zeus, for example, is the King of Heaven wherever we find him – he's a god of light and thunder, governing from the heights – but different communities worshipped different attributes at different times in the long history of ancient Greek culture. For some, he was the benign and just All-Father. For others he was the turbulent and temperamental hurler of the thunderbolt, feared but not trusted. For yet others, he personified the restless, promiscuous creative spirit, changing his shape to seduce countless women and fathering heroes and demigods wherever he passed. Zeus had many epithets and stories, depending on the cultural context.

Sophokles mentions Chiron's immortality, as he is the child of two immortals, a Titan and a nymph. But the familiar story of his wounding and the offering of his immortality to Prometheus isn't consistent in early sources. Apollodorus describes the battle between Herakles and the Centaurs, during which an arrow, aimed elsewhere, accidentally penetrated Chiron's knee.[14] Pausanias echoes this.[15] Diodorus Siculus describes the accidental injury by Herakles' arrow but states that Herakles actually killed Chiron.[16] As Chiron is usually described as an immortal, this is a curious contradiction. Ovid, in *Fasti*, doesn't speak of a battle between Herakles and the Centaurs, but states instead that while Chiron and the young Achilles were entertaining Herakles on Mount Pelion after the hero's battle with the Lernaean Hydra, Chiron fingered the poisoned arrows out of curiosity. One of them accidentally fell out of the quiver and landed on his left foot.[17] This version is also offered by Hyginus.[18]

Ovid describes the exchange of immortality between Chiron and Prometheus, but Apollodorus informs us that it was to Herakles that Chiron offered his immortality. Prometheus, as a divine Titan, didn't need it, but Herakles, who was only a mortal hero, did: 'And he [Herakles] offered Zeus Cheiron, who was willing to die in Herakles' place'.[19] In the *Metamorphoses*, Ovid makes a brief allusion to the wounding and the death but unfortunately doesn't give us details, although what he does say is beautifully evocative:

> Cheiron, you, immortal now and destined by your birthright to live on through all eternity, will long to die when you are tortured by the serpent's blood, that agonizing poison in your wounds; and, saved from immortality, the gods shall put you

14 Apollodorus, *The Library*, 2.983-87.
15 Pausanias, *Guide to Greece*, 5.5.9-10.
16 Diodorus Siculus, *Library of History*, 4.12.3-12.
17 Ovid, *Fasti*, 5.379.
18 Hyginus, *Astronomica*, 2.38.
19 Apollodorus, *ApB* 2.5.4, 2.5.11, in Ganz, *Early Greek Myth*, p. 147; also see Apollodorus, *The Library*, 2.119-120.

in death's power, and the Three Goddesses shall unloose your threads of fate.[20]

It seems that different cultures – and different individuals within a single culture – select and develop various versions of a story to reflect particular perceptions of the archetypal pattern. I'm not suggesting that only the earliest rendition of a mythic story is the 'right' one. Myths are living entities and, because they are symbolic, many meanings may be simultaneously 'right', and different readings of a story may be especially applicable at different epochs of history. But when we're seeking astrological insights, it's always worth looking at versions of the story different to the ones we're most attached to, because they can offer us a new perspective on the pattern.

Herakles the solar hero

Whatever version of the story we consider, the most striking difference between the one given in ancient sources and the one told in contemporary astrological circles is that in earlier sources, Chiron doesn't become a healer because he's wounded. He's already a healer, and his wounding not only puts an end to his career but also results in the relinquishing of his immortality. There seems to be agreement about the fact that the wounding occurs accidentally through the agency of Herakles, the Greek version of the Roman Hercules: the tough, brawny superhero of Greek myth who is given twelve Labours to perform as a penance for the inadvertent murder of his wife and children, and manages to complete all of them through a combination of luck, cunning, aid from divinities who favour him, and simple brute force. Despite his lack of reflection, he is the quintessential hero, whom the mythological scholar Carl Kerényi calls 'the god among the heroes'.[21]

---

20 Ovid, *Metamorphoses*, 2.649-54.
21 Carl Kerényi, *The Heroes of the Greeks*, trans. H. J. Rose (Thames & Hudson, 1974), p. 127.

Herakles' twelve Labours are sometimes understood to reflect the solar cycle through the twelve zodiacal signs. The numerical correlation between the Labours and the zodiac was taken up and developed along Theosophical lines in Alice Bailey's commentary on the myth, which she used as an illustration of the spiritual challenges facing each sign.[22] From a psychological perspective, Herakles might be seen as the courageous albeit often brutish ego-consciousness that attempts to develop an individuality through mastering the instinctual world, with all the benefits and problems of this inevitable stage in human development.

The Labours are mythic images of the struggle against archaic instinctual forces inimical to human development. Several of these tasks, such as stealing the golden apples from the Garden of the Hesperides and capturing the Mares of Diomedes, require the cunning and deftness of the thief. All the creatures Herakles must physically fight are wild, and some are monstrous and vicious, such as the Nemean Lion, the Lernaean Hydra, the Erymanthian Boar, and the Stymphalean Birds who eat human flesh. The Labour of cleaning out the Augean Stables involves a confrontation with vast amounts of animal dung, requiring endless patience and humility.

All these tasks might be seen as the various ways in which the ego emerges from the matrix of the unconscious psyche. Jung equated the Labours of Herakles with the process of freeing the soul from the grip of fate or *Heimarmene*, which he defined as unconscious compulsion or the 'fate in the stars'.[23] Herakles is a pivotal figure in the myth of Chiron's wounding. And the role of the ego in this story may be deeply relevant to the theme of Chiron in relationship because it's the ambivalent interaction between Herakles and the wild centaurs – echoed in our own ambivalent

---

22 Alice A. Bailey, *The Labors of Hercules* (Lucis Publishing, 1974).
23 C. G. Jung, *Psychology and Alchemy*, CW12, trans. R. F. C. Hull (Routledge & Kegan Paul, 1968), para. 457. For Jung on *Heimarmene* or astral fate, see Liz Greene, *Jung's Studies in Astrology* (Routledge, 2018), pp. 117-150.

relationship with our instincts – which results in Chiron's wounding and death.

The battle between Herakles and the centaurs

Herakles had just finished the second of his twelve Labours: the fight with the Lernaean Hydra, a poisonous snakelike monster with nine self-regenerating heads. All the hero's spent arrows were covered in the Hydra's deadly blood. After he put the arrows back in their quiver, he set off to visit his friend Pholos, the wisest and most benign of the wild centaurs. Pholos had a sealed jar of wine hidden in his cave which he had vowed to never touch because he knew that wine could drive centaurs mad. This gives us an interesting insight into the nature of centaurs. Intoxication turns them savage and brutal, and they begin to destroy everything in their path. It presents us with a rather unattractive aspect of our instinctual nature in relation to alcohol, which can be witnessed at any football match or pub brawl.

Pholos, modelling himself on the wise King Chiron, was determined to be civilised and loyal to his vow. Despite Herakles' insistence, he refused to open the jar of wine. But Herakles, being somewhat pushy as the human ego often is, finally bullied Pholos into opening the wine. The other centaurs, who were all hanging about outside the cave eavesdropping, caught a whiff of it. They went mad from the mere scent of it, seized the jar, and started drinking. They began to tear up trees and smash boulders and hurl rocks, shooting arrows at each other and also at Herakles. Chiron, their King, rushed out of his own cave to stop the madness, because these were his people and he was responsible for them. Herakles meanwhile was pulling arrows out of his quiver and shooting them in every direction, killing many of the centaurs.

In the midst of the *mêlée*, an arrow passed through the arm of one of the centaurs and accidentally struck Chiron. The arrow lodged in Chiron's hip, knee, or foot/hoof (depending on which myth you read), all three of which belonged to the horse part of him. Because the arrowhead was coated in the Hydra's virulently poisonous blood, the wound it inflicted couldn't be healed. Chiron rushed back into his cave howling in agony. No matter what remedy he tried, his skills couldn't heal the injury. Because he was immortal, he couldn't die the way the other centaurs did. His situation was impossible and tragic. He couldn't function because of his agony, so he lay in his cave screaming in pain. Then a divine intervention occurred.

The Titan Prometheus, who had offended Zeus by stealing the god's fire to give to humans, had been punished by being chained to a rock in the Caucasus mountains, where Zeus' eagle visited every day to devour Prometheus' liver. But this torture didn't quite kill the Titan because every night the liver miraculously regenerated and heralded another day of agony. Zeus, displaying his most spiteful face, decreed that this misery had to go on until some divine being was willing to surrender the gift of immortality to Prometheus. There had been no volunteers. Herakles, who felt guilty because Chiron was his friend, said to his father Zeus, 'I know someone who might be willing to do it.' Thus Chiron relinquished his immortality to take the place of Prometheus in the underworld, freeing the Titan from suffering and at the same time freeing himself from his own pain.

Before his wounding, Chiron was already a healer and teacher, good and wise, gifted and kind. But through no fault of his own, he is caught in the crossfire between the solar hero and the rampaging centaurs who have gone mad at the scent of wine. He blunders into the middle of the conflict to stop it, but although he is a noble ruler and an immortal, he doesn't have the power to tame an instinctual collective gone berserk. He is accidentally and unfairly wounded. He can do nothing to heal himself despite all his wisdom and all his arts, because the Hydra's poison is an eternal poison – a kind of collective evil that has no antidote.

Some collective evils, like that which spawned the Holocaust, cannot be 'cured'. They tend to erupt again and again in different cultures at different epochs of history, sometimes with different scapegoats and different methods, but with the same archetypal core. We often fail to recognise them at their inception and also often fail to learn from them, and we need to do our utmost as individuals to ensure we don't repeat them. Yet we may repeatedly fail to mitigate this human problem because no individual, however dedicated and wise, possesses the capacity to heal the entire collective. That kind of healing depends on every one of us dealing with the poison inside ourselves and in our own individual lives. As long as any individual remains wilfully unconscious – and the likelihood is that there will always be multitudes – we will inevitably meet our own potential evil again and again in the outer world.

It's only when Chiron is ready to relinquish his immortality that he is granted release from his suffering. This is a disturbing *dénouement*, and it's understandable that it has been reinterpreted so that Chiron's wounding results in compassion and healing gifts. But I think it's important to explore the myth in its original form as well as acknowledging the value of the later version, rather than trying to convince ourselves there will always be a happy ending to this story.

Chiron can't keep his immortality without eternal misery and wretchedness and the loss of his purpose in the world. He can't remain a god. He isn't to blame, and his blamelessness seems to be one of the major themes of the astrological Chiron. Whatever injury, suffering, pain, or wounding is implied, it isn't connected with individual culpability. It has nothing to do with sin or karma or divine retribution or punishment for personal faults or failings. The mythic Chiron might be accused of *hubris* in his belief that he alone can redeem his drunken tribe of centaurs, but the *hubris* springs from a deep sense of responsibility and caring. It's because he aspires to a high ideal that he suffers. Yet he can't do otherwise because he is 'the most righteous of the *kentauroi*'.

Chiron's story doesn't belong to the paradigm of divine rewards and punishments in which we have been brought up in the Abrahamic ambience of our culture. It's completely outside that framework and challenges our reluctance to countenance paradox. If we want insight into Chiron, we might start by relinquishing preconceived notions about rewards and punishments. Chiron's myth speaks of terrible accidents that happen when our idealism collides with human reality, and when two dimensions of human nature, both equally part of us, come into conflict.

Chiron's story also points to what can happen when something good and noble in us attempts to resolve a conflict which is so much larger than any individual. Every one of us suffers collateral damage, and it casts doubt on the idea that only a special few are genuine victims of persecution and oppression. As we all have Chiron somewhere in the birth chart, as individuals we are all victims of life in one way or another. What makes us truly individual is how constructively we deal with it, and whether we're able to get out of the cave.

The nature of Chiron's wound isn't parental in the ordinary reductive sense. It's not the direct result of unpleasant childhood experiences. Early hurts can and usually do act as triggers for a much older collective history and are embedded in a much larger framework than the problems of the immediate family or any individual sins of commission or omission. This larger framework concerns the nature of the world that humans have created during our aeons-long struggle between our instinctual nature, itself divine, and our solar aspiration, equally divine, to individuate as a species within the greater living fabric of the planet itself.

It can be helpful to consider all the major characters in a mythic story about a planetary archetype, rather than isolating one single figure and trying to define the planet through keywords. All the characters are interrelated and depend on each other to bring the story to fruition. In the Stoic philosophy which has permeated our astrological worldview since Greek times, all the dimensions of life are interconnected through chains of *sumpatheia* or correspondences. Life is a unity and no single component exists independent of the others. Body and psyche are not separate, and soul and fate, as the Romantic poet Novalis once wrote, are two names for the same principle.

To the Stoics, these chains of correspondences, sympathies, and symbolic resonances were called 'causes', but not in the sense we usually think of causality. Our modern understanding of causality is that if we drive at 70mph in a 20mph zone, the speed camera will record our misdemeanour and we will receive a fine or the loss of our driving licence. *A* causes *B* which results in *C*. But a 'cause' in Stoic thought is a relationship, which generates energy that in turn results in movement, choices, and consequences that in turn result in further relationships, movement, choices, and consequences. It's an unfolding chain of threads like the creative weaving of a tapestry. Every character in Chiron's myth is a 'cause' in this sense, and we might see Herakles, Pholus, Prometheus, Zeus, the wild centaurs, and even the jar of wine as dimensions of Chiron.

Herakles seems to symbolise something in us, and perhaps in the astrological Chiron, that aspires to be heroic. The word hero comes from the Greek *heros*, which means 'protector' or 'defender', and it is not limited solely to male figures or those who perform superhuman physical feats. Herakles is the brave, shining impulse to fulfil an individual destiny by overcoming or mastering – on behalf of others as well as ourselves – the compulsive power of our unconscious complexes, our family inheritance, our bodily frailty, our heredity, and our victimisation at the hands of life. Herakles is our human challenge to *Heimarmene*, the 'fate in the stars'. As the son of Zeus, he seeks to achieve this through boldness, courage, strength, cunning, and persistence. He often fails, and he sometimes displays considerable arrogance as well as stupidity – as does the human ego – but he isn't a villain. *Hubris* comes with the hero kit.

Herakles is the main catalyst in the story, and he must do what he does because that's what heroes do. There isn't a lot of point in taking an ideological stance and saying, 'Herakles is evil because he's egocentric, insensitive, and narcissistic. He has no social conscience. What about the damaging effects of his exploits on nature? What about the Hydra's rights? What about the way he bullies Pholus?' Herakles isn't well suited to political and sociological debates and isn't interested in becoming a 'team player'. He faithfully lives the individual solar hero's mythic role.

The wild centaurs are also essential characters in the story, and they are also part of Chiron, who, despite his wisdom and immortal lineage, is their King. They are neither better nor worse than Herakles, just different. They seem to symbolise a facet of us which is raw animal: primordial physical power guided by intelligent instinct, with a constant vulnerability to losing the plot and abandoning all civilised behaviour when intoxicated by either wine or the enticing inebriation of mass movements with their collective abrogation of individual responsibility.

Nature has vast intelligence, but it's a different kind of intelligence from the ego-consciousness that Herakles symbolises. Both Herakles and the centaurs are hunters for different reasons. Herakles hunts creatures like the Hydra and the Nemean Lion to protect others because these creatures are destroying villages and taking innocent human lives. The centaurs hunt to eat and protect themselves rather than to fulfil a task or show off trophies or demonstrate superiority over other species. If they take the life of an animal, it's to sustain their own lives, and not out of a need to assert power or fulfil a hero's destiny.

The centaurs can be incredibly destructive, and if they're drunk it means that whatever capacity for ethical choice they might possess in their human half is lost. They become an unthinking, destructive force which is as real and as present in life, and in us, as Herakles is. Left alone, they are an intrinsic part of the fabric of the instinctual world, the link between ourselves and other species. The conflict between the hero and the wild centaurs is archetypal. It goes on in us all the time and forms the basis of Freud's psychoanalytic theories, which are built on the idea that the *ego* must reveal and master the *id*. This is the nature of our duality and is perhaps one of the reasons why we envy and idealise the animals while at the same time projecting our own despised instinctual needs on them and attempting to harm or destroy them. We take one side or the other, because we don't know how to deal with this conflict in ourselves.

Chiron embodies the integration of both dimensions because he is a hybrid. His duality is encompassed in a single body. There is no conflict between the horse and the god. He is both the hunter who destroys life and the healer who saves life. We don't really understand what this kind of integration might look like in everyday life. We get little glimpses of it, but every time we get near it, we begin to polarise and embrace divisive ideologies. We say, 'This side is good and the other side is evil. This side is the right one and the other side is the enemy.' Chiron's hybrid nature exists within us, so we possess the innate capacity to intuit a potential bridge between these two aspects of ourselves. But our efforts to build the bridge will inevitably take a battering. We are born into an imperfect world, full of other humans who are as ignorant and insensitive as we ourselves are, who still think that the only way to solve the conflict is through a war, a change in the law, a march, a riot, a different government, or the stifling of any ideas that might disagree with our own.

Whatever it is in us that senses the possibility of a state where the two dimensions can coexist in some kind of balance, it will inevitably be wounded by something we encounter in the outer world – in our family life, our school, our society, our culture, or our own bodies. Something is guaranteed to wound that fragile, delicate, paradoxical ability to integrate two aspects of reality. And once it's wounded, it crawls back into its cave and lies there howling in pain and begging for death.

Relinquishing immortality

Whenever I've discussed Chiron's myth in a seminar, someone usually gets agitated and says, 'Can't you talk about the good side of it?' But that *is* the good side of it. If we want to make sense of Chiron in its sign, house, and aspects to other planets, as well as in the synastry between two birth charts, we need to recognise that this astrological symbol points to something in us which has been painfully damaged by a collision into which we have been born, of which we are a part, which is going on in the world outside us and which is also going on in our inner world. The collision is much bigger than we are as individuals, but we experience it in a deeply personal way. If we want to work with this dilemma, we might need to take very seriously the necessity in the myth to 'relinquish immortality'. What might this mean?

Some people protect themselves from Chiron's reality by insisting that they aren't suffering and don't feel wounded or damaged in any way. They don't have a natal Chiron; it's been cancelled. Perhaps it's understandable that although a lot of work has been done on the astrological Chiron, many astrologers still won't use it in chart interpretation. They believe it's not relevant. It isn't a proper planet, after all; it's a hybrid between a comet and a planetoid, and it's a relative newcomer to our solar system. Pluto isn't a proper planet either. In 2006 it was demoted to the category of planetoid. But it's not a good idea to assume that Pluto is insignificant. Chiron is a heavenly body within our solar system, and it's odd that many people who will happily plot Lilith in the chart won't consider Chiron. The Moon's Nodes are also not planets, yet many astrologers place great importance on them. Try doing your own research and look at Chiron in as many charts as you can before you come to the conclusion that Chiron is unimportant.

Some of the difficulty may lie in Chiron's implication of something we really don't want to look at within ourselves. This 'something', if we reflect on the myth, is that we're all in pain because we are human. We long for a state of enlightened perfection that we dimly sense is our potential as individuals and as a collective. But this requires a godlike vision and wisdom we can never achieve, and a self-control which, if exercised, would inevitably violate another dimension of us which is equally real and true

– the side of us that needs to function in harmony with our instincts and with the natural world. This is an essential human duality, and we usually make a mess when we try to resolve it because it's a paradox. It means we can't categorise other people neatly as 'good' or 'evil' and we have to take responsibility for which seeds we cultivate in ourselves.

Wherever Chiron is placed in the birth chart, we will experience the paradox of human nature in a painful way through our own individual experiences, and it can be hard to know how to alleviate the pain. Understandably, no one wants to focus on the image of the wounded centaur howling in his cave. We're drawn to the wonderfully optimistic belief that if we could just find the right formula, we could heal anything. There must be a system of belief, a method of prayer, a philosophy, a meditation technique, a herbal or homeopathic remedy, a school of psychotherapy, or an antidepressant that will do the trick and heal the wound.

Perhaps what we are seeking is a cure rather than healing. If so, we may be doomed to failure. A cure is like the scene at the end of *Indiana Jones and the Holy Grail,* when Indiana pours the magical water from the Grail onto his father's mortal injury and presto! the wound is gone. But healing might involve something subtler, like an internal shift in our attitude toward the pain. Healing may sometimes encompass the release of some of the pain, but this resolution in the myth is paid for by the relinquishing of immortality, which carries with it a different kind of pain. The myth tells us that Chiron's wound can never be cured. But perhaps we can try to transform our way of responding to it and turn it into something more creative and life-affirming than a display of vindictive spite and envy or a lifetime's membership in Victims Unite. That effort might itself constitute healing.

Innocence and experience

The poisoned wound might be healed rather than cured, but in its place comes the pain of accepting mortality: being human rather than divine. The wound leaves a scar because it has robbed us of our innocence. If we smash a precious vase, we can glue it back together again very skilfully, and it might still hold water. But the cracks might always leak a bit and make it vulnerable to being broken again.

Wherever Chiron is placed in the chart, we can't get away with wilful naivete, because our psychological virginity has been violated and there isn't any way we can reclaim it. We can't unlearn what we have learned. We might be able to move beyond bitterness, but the scar will always twinge when the weather changes. Is that a bad thing? Not necessarily. Perhaps that's why the image of Chiron teaching a child is so relevant. The fact that we can't get our innocence back doesn't preclude treasuring innocence where we find it, in ourselves and in others, and assisting in the process of its gentle growth into maturity.

This doesn't include the kind of impossible idealisation that we often project on children when we try to freeze them in aspic and shield them from life, refusing to allow them to make their own mistakes and develop as individuals. Chiron's task of teaching his young human pupils to hunt as well as heal involves respecting innocence while recognising that it can't remain the same forever. The theme of innocence lost is relevant not just to Chiron individually, but also to what is constellated in relationships when Chiron is involved in the synastry between two charts.

In 1964, James Hillman published an essay entitled *Betrayal*.[24] It's one of the most powerful works he ever produced. He suggests that the experience of being betrayed, with all its shock and hurt and disillusionment, is an essential step on the road toward individuation According to Hillman,

24 James Hillman, *Betrayal* (Guild of Pastoral Psychology, 1964). The essay is available online at static1.squarespace.com.

betrayal shatters the childlike fantasy of perfect fusion, and we must all undergo it if we are ever to relate deeply and authentically to other humans. Chiron's wound is often about betrayal, although there are many other experiences that involve the loss of innocence. This doesn't mean we must lose our idealism. But childlike innocence may need to transform into something subtler.

Everyone is robbed of their innocence sooner or later in some sphere of life because Chiron is in everyone's chart. We're given a window, usually unwillingly, into how that ferocious battle between Herakles and the wild centaurs is enacted in everyday reality. It's inarguable that human destructiveness is always with us. What do we with do with the poisonous bitterness which is one of the central motifs of this myth? When Chiron is lying in his cave howling, between the wounding and the relinquishing of his immortality, he is in extreme agony. He's incoherent and incapacitated. He's not likely to greet visitors by inviting them in for a cup of tea and asking them to talk about their problems. He will be savage toward anyone who intrudes on his agony. Horses, when injured, kick and bite or run away. Chiron's reaction to extreme pain is an instinctive, visceral reaction, and it's sometimes savage.

Perhaps some of you have experienced this state yourselves at some time in your lives. It may be a crushingly painful migraine or a raging tooth abscess or a broken bone. Someone comes in and says, 'Would you like a nice cup of tea? You'll feel so much better!', and you want to bash their head in. You don't want determinedly cheerful company. You just want the pain to stop. The last thing in the world you can tolerate is somebody telling you that everything will be alright, because it feels as though it will never be alright again. You want to strike them, verbally if not physically, not least because they are up and walking and you are not.

Rage, self-pity, and a terrible envy toward those who appear not to be hurting reflect Chiron's poisoned wound. The pain of disillusionment and shattered dreams is the psychological equivalent of the broken bone or the abscessed tooth. With prolonged painful and disabling illness, the response may be long and drawn out, and it isn't unusual for a chronically ill person to suffer an apparent change in personality and become unpleasant, spiteful, and demanding when they were once warm, responsive, and sensitive to the feelings of others. It's entirely understandable, but it's highly distressing for everyone involved and may ultimately destroy relationships and families. Something like this can occur on subtler levels when natal Chiron is triggered in synastry.

Of course it must be someone's fault. As a society, we currently seem to be wallowing in a blame culture. Someone must be made responsible for our suffering as individuals and as a collective – a partner, a family member, a company, an author, a social group, a political party, a government minister who can be vilified in the newspapers and threatened on social media, or a sociopathic dictator who, like the mythic Scapegoat, carries the entirety of human evil for us so that we don't have to stare our own banal, everyday evil in the face. Witch-hunts and scapegoating are directly related to Chiron's complex response to suffering. Any disaster that happens to us in life means that someone must be culpable. We can't bear to contemplate the possibility that life is unfair, humans are fallible and imperfect and often unashamedly awful, and terrible things sometimes just happen.

We might blame the cause of our inner pain as well as our physical suffering on someone or something outside ourselves. We might try to make ourselves feel better by extracting as much money as we can from the purported culprit. Or we might do our best to destroy their reputation and career. We might vilify a social or racial or religious group and load them up with 'sins' in the same way ancient communities loaded an actual goat with the sins of the community and drove the animal into the desert to die. We might also invert the rage and then blame ourselves, feeling shame and self-loathing because we believe the wound is entirely our own fault. But Chiron's suffering tends to be impervious to the kind of treatment that utilises blame as a painkiller. The suffering can't be alleviated simply by turning a perceived persecutor into another victim.

A sense of justice being done may be necessary on a worldly level. We may even have to fight a war or assist another country in defending its autonomy in the face of a destructive threat. Sometimes someone really is to blame in the mundane world, although even Hitler could never have risen to power without the conscious or unconscious collusion of a collective already primed to receive his message. A public apology coerced from the person we believe has wronged us might give us a momentary flicker of satisfaction. But after that initial flash of triumph, we still won't really feel any better because the wound still hasn't healed and the innocence hasn't been reclaimed. If we deny this, we may seek yet more scapegoats to persecute in a perpetuating spiral.

We can recognise displays of this kind of bitterness on social media and in any newspaper every day. But it can be worked with more creatively. It's a stage in a process; it isn't the place where Chiron's story finishes. It's a liminal zone, a place in between. Some people get stuck in that interim place and can't move beyond it. Because they don't acknowledge the inner pain and paralysis in the cave, they may remain oblivious to it until someone else comes into their lives with a planet that aspects their natal Chiron. Then the unconscious well of poison starts to bubble and rise to the surface, often in the last place we would ever expect or want it: a close relationship with someone we love and admire.

Chiron, like the other heavenly bodies, reflects a series of stages in a story rather than a static set of characteristics. These stories are like alchemical processes that are ongoing over a lifetime. Chiron's story involves lots of characters and several phases of development. The good Centaur who teaches and heals and enjoys a blameless and fulfilling life is an ideal that belongs to all of us. It allows us to envision a better world. But at some point along the way, usually when we're young and perhaps before we're even aware of it, we experience wounding. The wound is nourished by the fertile soil of a family history of similar wounding, and the injury begins to assume huge proportions because it's so much larger than us. Like a giant magnet, it draws in every small experience of unfairness and injustice, real or imagined, swelling the fund of bitterness and envy. It's a kind of energy vortex which, if it's not made conscious, remains raw and unhealed, waiting to be triggered by an external event or a deep bond with another human being.

In the cave

I've used the metaphor of Chiron's cave to highlight one of the most challenging aspects of working with the pain of the Centaur's wound. Where is this cave in which some part of us huddles up in pain? What might it look like astrologically? What form does it take in an individual life? Is it entirely unconscious, or do we sometimes get glimpses of it? Or do we persistently project it onto others?

Chiron's house placement and sign can point to the sphere of life and the manner in which we're likely to experience the story, and its aspects to other planets suggest the ways in which our wounds affect other dimensions of our lives. Chiron stands at the interface between Saturn's ego-boundaries and the collective realm of the outer planets. Experiences of universal suffering seep through the cracks of Saturn's defences and make us aware of larger collective issues through our personal pain. Bringing light into the cave requires a slow, patient, and determined effort to achieve self-honesty, and an acceptance of the fact that it won't come all at once.

In the story, Herakles informs Zeus that Chiron is the right candidate for the trade-off because no other divinity is willing to give up immortality. And why would they? Relinquishing immortality means relinquishing power over life and death and giving up immunity to all the woes that flew out of Pandora's box. The only reason Chiron is willing to do it is because his misery is so great that he has no other option. Herakles, not Chiron, initiates the exchange because the Centaur is too paralysed with pain to think of a way forward. The heroic solar hero, who can be so unreflective in so many ways, can at least recognise that a sacrifice of some kind is required.

Audience: I think the relinquishment of immortality means a kind of humility in life, and an acceptance of your own death.

Liz: Yes, I agree. The sacrifice suggests an acceptance of life's imperfections, the limits of our power as individuals, and our inevitable mortality. In ancient Greek thought, it would have been similar to accepting one's *moira*. Although Moira as a goddess later became the personification of Fate, the word means 'allotment': the boundaries set by the living organism of the universe for the nature, development, demise, and ultimate purpose of each living thing.

Chiron's sacrifice certainly involves humility as well as an acceptance of physical mortality. But this kind of acceptance doesn't come from cynicism or the abandonment of ideals. Imperfections and limits are an integral part of life to the Saturnian realist, who knows how the world works: there are no free lunches, you get what you pay for, and if you can't take the heat, stay out of the kitchen. If you want to achieve anything in life, work hard, take responsibility for your actions, discharge your duties honourably and without complaint, don't expect handouts, and get over yourself. Saturn builds strength through self-sufficiency and heals its own pain through discovering inner authenticity. As Winston Churchill once said, 'If you're going through hell, keep going.' From Saturn's perspective, if you can't bear reality, go to a monastery or an ashram, but don't waste other people's time and taxpayers' money moaning. That's Saturn's form of acceptance and, in its own domain, it often works very well.

Chiron's realism is more complex because of his hybrid nature. His father Kronos is himself fathered by Ouranos, the Starry Heavens, and the earthbound Titan has inherited Ouranos' attributes of reason and planning. Kronos can look ahead, not as a visionary but as an engineer and an astute observer of cause and effect. He can envisage and implement the order necessary for the efficient running of the world, including the natural cycles of sowing and reaping. In Hesiod's poem *Works and Days*, Kronos presides over a Golden Age when humans respect and live their lives in obedience to the cycles and laws of the earth-world. Kronos' mother is Gaia, the Earth itself. He has no grandparents other than primal Chaos.

But Chiron has inherited not only the practical wisdom of his father – hence his name, 'he who works with his hands' – but also the boundless realm of the imaginal world through his maternal grandfather Okeanos, the primordial substance of creation. Chiron is at one with the natural world, but he also possesses a social conscience and a respect for the law which reflects the ancient symbolism of the King as a divine vessel bridging heaven and earth. He is a priest-healer. He takes responsibility for his fellow creatures as an act of love as well as an act of duty. Chiron is the ultimate idealist because he knows that a deep and genuine sense of interconnectedness and shared suffering is the only antidote to destructive polarisation and fragmentation. His relinquishment of divinity is especially poignant because of this idealism. Acceptance of limits is far more painful if we glimpse the unity but lack the power to implement it in the world, and if the world has wounded us and thwarted our efforts because every human has a shadow.

Chiron's painful acceptance of mortality, unlike Saturn's canny accommodation with it, costs a great deal because we need to remain loyal to our ideals while at the same time recognising that whatever we're able to achieve, personally and collectively, will always be limited. Even worse, we may not be thanked for our efforts. Victim and persecutor are interchangeable because they are both part of an imperfect, suffering world struggling to unfold, and no amount of scapegoating, self-blame, passive bitterness, or violent protest will make the struggle go away. There are problems that we will never solve in our lifetimes, and perhaps not in our children's or grandchildren's either. We won't be able to save the world, let alone stop a simple battle between drunken centaurs, and it's likely that we will be injured if we try.

How can we live by the values of what is essentially a religious vision – and I'm using the word 'religious' in the broadest sense and not in the doctrinal or dogmatic sense – and yet at the same time recognise that it will never be manifested on earth in the way we envisage it, in our personal lives or in the world? Chiron requires loyalty to our aspirations. They mustn't be sacrificed on the altar of cynicism. Yet life is often unfair and brutal, and human nature is complex and sometimes frighteningly ugly. It isn't easy to relinquish the illusion that we have the power to achieve perfection, bully others into accepting our definitions of what is right and true, and transform evil in the world while failing to recognise our own petty personal evil. If we manage to achieve even a tiny crumb of illumination or pass an even tinier crumb on to someone else, we will still suffer because so much will remain unhealed and unchanged. Yet paradoxically, this kind of humility may be the most profound aspect of Chiron's healing.

The blame game

Audience: What about the issue of blame?

Liz: The relinquishing of immortality may require us to give up the luxury of blame. Blame belongs to Saturn's world, which relies on cause and effect. Saturn is the great lawmaker of the divine pantheon. Jupiter is also known in myth as a lawgiver, but he has a tendency to change his mind a lot, and sometimes he shamelessly espouses a double standard. Saturn remains loyal to his principles, even if they're harsh. Traditionally this planet is exalted in Libra, the sign most concerned with justice and balance. The image of Justice, which has been with us for many centuries and still adorns our law courts, is portrayed wearing a blindfold. Justice must be impartial because feelings – including compassion – can cloud clear and objective judgement.

In our courts there is an attorney for the prosecution and an attorney for the defence. In theory, everyone is entitled to a fair trial, although reality, as usual, often contradicts the ideal. Is the accused person guilty or innocent? If they're innocent, someone else must be guilty. Someone must have committed the crime and must be found and punished. This is entirely appropriate for the material and social levels of reality that Saturn, ruler of Capricorn and Aquarius, governs. But it isn't Chiron's reality.

Recently I was given a digital camera by a friend, and in the very long list of instructions for what to do and not do, I read the following warning: 'Do not eat the camera'. I thought about that for quite a while. Why would anyone eat a camera? But if some unfortunate person did eat the camera and became ill, they could sue the manufacturer if no specific warning was included in the instruction booklet. This is the instrumental causality of Saturn's world: *A* makes *B* happen, and *C* is the result. *A* is clearly to blame.

One of the issues around relinquishing immortality is that it may be pointless to look for someone or something that's ultimately responsible for the existence of human suffering, historically, socially, or personally. I know several academics who blame Plato for the entrenched dualism that has resulted in modern Western society's destructive split between body and spirit. But unlike St. Augustine and the Christian Fathers who followed him, Plato never described the material world as evil, or the human body – especially a woman's body – as the bearer of Original Sin. Nor was he a misogynist, unlike so many in the hierarchies of the world's religions or, for that matter, the hierarchies of our universities. These academics have evidently also forgotten that no author has the power to make people adopt a viewpoint or an idea over so many centuries unless they are already inclined that way to begin with. Doctrinal religions have always attempted to define the nature of evil and tell us what we must avoid if we wish to enter a promised afterlife free from suffering. Life itself, in some religious perspectives, is essentially a write-off because the mortal body is corrupt and doomed to suffering and death.

One of the least attractive examples of this vision of life is the medieval interpretation of the Seven Deadly Sins. Envy, Gluttony, Pride, Wrath, Lust, Deceit, and Sloth are proclaimed as the sources of our suffering, and if we can refrain from committing them, we will receive a get-into-heaven-free card. The Sins have their origin in the characters of the seven planetary gods, which were appropriated and transformed by the Gnostics of late antiquity into evil compulsions which the planetary archons impose on the human soul as it descends from its pure spiritual home into corrupt earthly incarnation. Augustine, by the way, was a Gnostic before he converted to Christianity, so we know where he acquired his loathing of the human body and the material world. He certainly didn't get it from Plato. But the so-called Sins, like the planetary gods, are archetypal elements in life itself, with dark and light dimensions that are creative as well as destructive.

There is some affinity between these dualistic ideas and the emphasis in some Hindu and Buddhist teachings on non-attachment as the path that can lead us out of suffering. But non-attachment is also alien to Chiron's world. For Chiron, attachment, rooted in love and a sense of responsibility, is a fundamental dimension of life. Non-attachment might spare us the pain of rejection and loss, but it also means relinquishing both passion and compassion.

When we have tried unsuccessfully to blame our parents, grandparents, great-grandparents, society, and the whole of human history, do we move on to blaming a mythic Adam? The blame can fall on anything from wars and pandemics to sleazy political leaders or militant trade unions, to the political right or the political left, to a social, religious, racial, or gender group, or to a friend, lover, or family member whom we feel has injured us. If a relationship fails, it can't possibly be the case that the two of you really did try but were fundamentally incompatible. A wounded Chiron is often emotionally withdrawn, resentful, envious, and manipulative, and we might not always be either loving or lovable. Yet it's the other person who is accused of being unable to love. It must always be someone else's fault.

This does *not* mean we 'deserve' the unfair wounds inflicted on us. Of course we don't. We are often blameless victims of other people's malice, envy, spite, and displaced rage. And we may need to spend a long time being enraged at the sheer injustice of it. Anger may be an entirely healthy, appropriate response, for a while. For some people who have problems with Mars and never seem capable of expressing anger, it's a necessity. But those people who have harmed us because they are eaten up by malice, envy, fear, or a desperate need for control are themselves victims. That doesn't excuse them, and some of them might need to be prosecuted and put in jail; Chiron may need to call on his father Saturn for assistance in the mundane world. But the people who hurt us are themselves collateral damage, not the source of human suffering. Who are we going to blame then?

Audience: But when you're dealing with violence or intentional abuse, where clearly the other person has inflicted harm although you've done nothing to deserve it, surely it's right to blame the person.

Liz: Yes, it is, for a while. And we may need to seek justice and try to ensure that such individuals can't harm us or anyone else in the future, even if the serious flaws in our policing and justice system sometimes make us feel even more abused and victimised. In Saturn's world this kind of blame might be entirely appropriate, and our own rage and pain should never be ignored or denied or rationalised away. In Saturn's world an eye for an eye, if confined within the limits of the law, is sometimes a better response than meekly turning the other cheek. It can be healthier psychologically.

But every planet has its own nature and domain, and what is appropriate in Saturn's world might simultaneously be deeply inappropriate in the domains of the other planets. Each of us has all the planets in our birth chart, and we need to be able to navigate all these different levels of reality with as much insight as we can cultivate. Saturn's world is reassuring because it deals in concrete realities. But if you step out of Saturn's world and into Chiron's, you might recognise that the person who is abusing you was probably abused in childhood. Chiron's wounds are infectious and are often passed down from one generation to the next. It's a truism that people who act out violence tend to have a history of being subjected to violence in early life.

On this theme I would recommend a film made in 2005 by David Cronenberg and starring Vigo Mortensen, called *A History of Violence*. It presents a subtle and terrifying picture of the infectious nature of violence. Growing up in a violent culture, whether national or local, can even numb us to personal experiences of violence within the family. I'm not suggesting that you shouldn't feel rage and pain and, if appropriate, seek justice through legal channels. But understanding Chiron's perspective might help you to refrain from distorting or inventing facts, perpetuating the destructiveness, spewing poison over anyone who might vaguely resemble your idea of a persecutor, and becoming as cruel and abusive as the person whom you believe has harmed you.

It's a tricky business navigating between what actually happens in concrete reality and how we perceive and interpret what happens. There's sometimes a blurred line between victim and perpetrator. Sometimes the exploitation of this can lead to horrible abuse within the legal system. How many cases of rape have been dismissed by blaming the victim for being allegedly 'provocative'? How many cases of prosecution resulting in the destruction of a reputation and a career have arisen from an angry person taking revenge for a past rejection through a fictitious or grossly amplified accusation of sexual harassment? Which cases are truly abuse, and which are, like beauty, in the eye of the beholder? Are we always objective enough to discern the difference? Sometimes the blame game can become a hall of mirrors in which we lose our moral compass and become the very thing we hate.

In recent times it's become fashionable to rewrite history in stark monochromatic terms, or to cancel uncomfortable aspects of it altogether. But in Chiron's domain the colours are rich and subtle, and there is no 'delete' key. It would be absurd to suggest that no feelings of blame should be permitted when we feel our lives have been unfairly violated. But blaming without genuine reflection can be destructive to our ability to walk out of the cave upright, make peace with ourselves and the world in which we live, and move on with our lives.

The coherence of any society depends on Saturn's laws and the sense of safety that every individual feels within the protective structure of those laws. There are injuries to which we, as individuals and as a society, may be subjected where it's essential to find the culprit and punish them. Suggesting that a tough childhood or economic deprivation excuses the perpetrator may not be very convincing in such situations. Every human has choices, however difficult their background and circumstances. But in Chiron's world, Saturn's approach tends to fail because even the achievement of a just verdict in the outer world won't heal the wound in the inner world. Something else is required. When Chiron is involved in the synastry between two people in relationship, it's often counterproductive and even destructive to approach the mutually painful dynamic through Saturn's definitions of blame. External justice may be necessary in the external world. But it won't alleviate Chiron's inner suffering.

To understand the meaning of any planet, we need to be able to imagine where the planet wants to go and what teleology it needs to fulfil. Chiron aspects between two charts are often suggestive of deep hurt inflicted in a relationship, although sometimes subtly and usually unconsciously. But we may need to let go of the hope that we can reclaim our innocence through assigning blame. We may reclaim something, but it won't be the same as what we lost. And we will reclaim nothing if we engage in scapegoating.

Genuine forgiveness isn't available on tap like lager, and how it happens is a mystery. Some might say it's an act of grace rather than an act of will.

Stifling justifiable outrage can be immensely self-destructive. Anger and a demand for recompense – or at the very least, a genuine, heartfelt apology – may be important, for a time. But you might not succeed in getting either the justice or the apology. After you've gone through all the raging and the blaming, it might become possible to adopt a different perspective. The abuse may have been cold and calculating. But it's more likely to reflect a terrible compulsion that the individual tried to fight but failed to master. With such aspects, you will usually find a history of abuse in the family, going back many generations. Merely recognising this can sometimes shift the paralysis of the wound.

What we perceive as a destructive injury unfairly inflicted on us might have been inflicted by individuals or groups who have themselves been subjected to unfair suffering. If we can understand this, our way of dealing with such people may subtly alter. With great reluctance we might have to recognise our similarity to them as both perpetrator and victim, especially if we pursue them in court. The acknowledgement of mutual suffering may not preclude utilising the blunt instrument of the law. But it might take us beyond an endless self-pity party and an unthinking assumption that 'everyone' belonging to the perpetrator's social, racial, economic, gender, or religious group is equally culpable. The larger causes may still need to be addressed, but our perspective will have changed and our methods of trying to alter things may become less spiteful and therefore more effective.

Audience: But what about what they are discovering now about the huge numbers of abused children that have slipped through the net of social services?

Liz: I can't tell you how to handle these situations in worldly terms. As a collective and as individuals we need to deal with such problems within the range of the laws that are available, always ensuring that our own perceptions are as clear as possible and not coloured by an internal propensity for feeling victimised or projecting our own sense of victimisation on others.

The Cleveland child abuse scandal ought to have taught us something about this. [25]

I'm not saying, 'Forgive them, for they know not what they do.' Usually they know perfectly well what they're doing and they do it anyway, even if they struggle against it. And sometimes they don't struggle, and merely justify their behaviour. But this is a seminar on Chiron, not on how to deal with social injustice in practical terms. I do understand your question, but I'm not a lawyer and I can't offer any answers about practical action. In exploring Chiron, sooner or later – and sooner is usually better – we need to move beyond the endless circle of blame and retaliation. Otherwise the wound won't heal, and we may carry the poison in us for a lifetime and pass it down to the next generation.

Audience: Are we bound to carry it on to the next generation?

Liz: Sadly, yes, unless we can work with it creatively. It isn't the sins of the parents that are imposed on the children; it's their unconscious complexes and unresolved inner conflicts. Chiron can't pass on his hybrid form, but he can teach his pupils about its meaning. And if he remains stuck in a cycle of blame and self-pity, he can also teach them how to hate. Even if

---

25   The Cleveland child abuse scandal took place in the West Midlands in 1987. It involved a sudden huge increase in purported child abuse cases, the majority of which were eventually disproven after over a hundred innocent families had suffered unnecessarily and unfairly. The accusations were based not on disclosure but on a new and controversial diagnostic test by a group of paediatricians at Middlesborough General Hospital. 121 children were abruptly and forcibly taken away from their parents without explanation and placed in foster homes, care centres, or hospitals; 94 were subsequently returned after the accusations had proven to be false. The chief instigator, Dr. Marietta Higgs, refused to accept that she had been overzealous and viewed any disagreement as 'denial'. The episode, which has continued to arouse controversy many decades later, is a disturbing example of a number of themes linked with the astrological Chiron, including good intentions coupled with distorted perceptions, the inclination to blame indiscriminately without sufficient evidence, cruelty masked as solicitous concern, and the urgent need for sensitivity and careful self-reflection when dealing with such a highly charged sphere of human suffering. See 'The Cleveland Report by Judge Elizabeth Butler-Sloss', *The Therapeutic Care Journal*, 1 August 2011.

we manage to resolve some issues within ourselves, new forms of the same archetypal dilemma will emerge for the next generation to deal with.

In families, close Chiron contacts between charts are as ubiquitous as they are in romantic relationships. The wounded wound their children, and the wounded children wound their parents and their own children. And so it goes on. Chiron's natal sign signifies a generation group, just as the outer planets' signs do, although its elliptical orbit means that some Chiron generations span quite a short period of time. I'll be talking more about this generational aspect of Chiron later. But generational or not, it seems that each of us must find a way to deal with our own dilemma. We might not be able to pass our individual solutions on to our children, but we can pass on more constructive ways of thinking, and we might refrain from passing on our unresolved bitterness.

Audience: Can it really be worked with?

Liz: With difficulty, and slowly, but yes, I believe so. That's what I've been trying to say from the beginning of the seminar. We need first to understand the nature of our wound. Then we need to find a way to move through the swamp of rage, blame and self-blame, hate, envy, and self-pity to a place where we can begin to discover a profound sense of how difficult it is to be human, and how these kinds of things emerge from a condition that all of us are in some way contributing to as well as suffering from. This is the beginning of compassion, which is very different from both pity and self-pity.

Audience: And after the compassion comes the question, 'How do I not end up abusing someone else?'

Liz: The moment we begin to feel compassion, we're less inclined to cruelty, although we may have to constantly renew the exploration to avoid repetition. If there is any antidote to human evil, it's the capacity for human love, and love, in contrast to being 'in love' or obsessed with an object of desire, is probably 95% compassion and only 5% passion. Compassion comes from a Latin root, *com* + *passio*, meaning 'to feel with'. The word 'empathy' comes from a Greek root, *en* + *pathos*, meaning 'to feel into'. The most effective antidote to the poison is a combination of empathy and compassion, but we don't discover these things without first recognising how and where we feel we've been injured and what we have allowed the injury to do to our own development.

Audience: Earlier on, you said that Chiron wasn't related to the idea of karma. But now you seem to be saying that a person will pass the wound on if they haven't dealt with it.

Liz: Passing it on doesn't mean karma in the sense that what you did in your last life will determine what happens to you in this life. A parent or a teacher may pass on knowledge, insight, loving behaviour, bigotry, or hatred to a student or a child, but this doesn't depend on former lives. What I mean by passing it on is that we can't offer our children what we ourselves have no comprehension of. It's a bit like the old question: How do you explain an orgasm to someone if you've never experienced one? You can discuss the physiological responses in great detail, but not the experience itself. We can't teach our children realities of which we are ignorant. And we can't communicate a forward path that is creative rather than destructive if we're unconsciously trapped in our own darkness.

Our children inherit our complexes, just as we have inherited our parents' complexes. This seems to be psychological rather than genetic, although I'm not sure the two are really that separate; we know very little about the mystery of genes and what levels of body and psyche they might encompass. A family is a collective psyche as well as a group of distinct individuals, and family issues can't be compartmentalised and hidden away behind locked doors. Children always intuit their parents' secrets, especially if any discussion about them is forbidden.

If there is an unresolved conflict in the family, it doesn't mean the parents are bad or have done something wrong. But despite their good intentions – and sometimes *because* of those good intentions – an unconscious conflict can be passed on to the children because it remains unresolved and still festers. You might try reading Frances G. Wickes' excellent book, *The Inner World of Childhood*, first published in 1927 but still entirely relevant. She wrote about the way in which children intuit their parents' unconscious conflicts and hidden secrets, and the damage that can be caused by well-meaning parental deceit and silence.

Chiron and karma

Audience: So how would you understand karma?

Liz: I don't really understand it. But I think it's important to differentiate between the idea in Hindu philosophy and the idea as it has come to us filtered through Madame Blavatsky's Theosophical writings in the late 19th century. I can't pretend to have any real grasp of the concept in Hinduism. But I believe the word *karma* implies 'substance' – the stuff we are made of. Our birth charts describe a particular mix of psychic and physical substance which forms the individuals we are and are meant to become. On the basis of our substance, we attract its like in the outer world. Goethe called this 'elective affinities', and it's like a tuning fork resonating with a note on the piano.

This doesn't 'fate' the future. Our choices and actions alter and generate further psychic and physical substance, and this developing substance in turn attracts further situations and people who are made of similar substance. These encounters in turn result in further choices and actions, resulting in yet more substance. When the soul incarnates in a new body, the substance we have accrued in the past draws to itself in the present those external situations and people who resonate with it. So we reap what we sow and hopefully we learn from it, not because of some irascible cosmic judge who has decided we were naughty, but because substance can only draw similar substance to itself. Fate and soul, as Novalis wrote, are two words for the same principle.

Karma in Theosophical thought, which has influenced many astrologers from the late 19th century onward and is still very much alive today, is embedded in a rewards-and-punishments framework. There is an unmistakable Abrahamic morality infusing the idea as it appears in the work of Theosophically inclined astrologers such as Alan Leo. It's sometimes affectionately known as the 'ding-dong' theory. If you were a good person in your last life, you'll be rewarded in this one and have lots of trines and sextiles in the birth chart. If you were a bad person in your last life, you'll be punished in this one and have lots of squares and oppositions, especially to nasty planets like Saturn or Pluto. If you are suffering, it must be because you did something cruel or selfish or immoral in a former incarnation and now you are having to expiate your actions so that you will learn and evolve.

There are many problems with this interpretation of karma, including definitions of 'good' and 'bad', who or what establishes these criteria, what cultural context they're embedded in, and whether it's even possible to draw such an uncompromising line between such sharply defined opposites. We also need to think about what is known as the 'doctrine of subsumption', an idea that has ancient origins and is still important in mundane astrology: the individual's chart may be 'subsumed' by the chart of a nation or even the chart of the nation's ruler.[26] Viewed from a psychological perspective, this concept is deeply relevant to Chiron. If a collective has become mindlessly destructive and goes on the rampage, or a natural disaster overwhelms a village or a country, individual lives, however blameless, are subsumed in the fate of the collective. The destiny reflected in the individual horoscope

---

26 For the 'doctrine of subsumption', see C. E O. Carter, *An Introduction to Political Astrology* (L. N. Fowler, 1951); Charles Harvey, *Anima Mundi: The Astrology of the Individual and the Collective* (CPA Press, 2002).

could be subsumed by such collective events. It's the essence of what we call 'unfair'.

Trying to apply the 'ding-dong' theory to Chiron's suffering won't get us very far. Blavatsky was deeply interested in Hindu philosophy. But although she vigorously repudiated her Russian Orthodox background, she wasn't known for a capacity for self-reflection, and her lack of awareness of herself made it virtually impossible for her to write about karma without being influenced by an entrenched idea of divine judgement based on a rigid Abrahamic interpretation of morality.

Chiron's tendency to pass on the wound points to what we find too painful to deal with, rather than what we have deliberately done 'wrong'. Our children can certainly wind up carrying unresolved Chiron issues for us, but blame may be entirely inappropriate. Every individual's story is different. Often secrets are kept because of a genuine desire to protect a child's feelings. Families don't usually inflict Chiron's wounds on purpose; we don't often meet Lionel Luthor from *Smallville* in real life. Even when violence and abuse are part of the picture, they're more often compulsive than calculated.

The further back across the generations we go, the more we're forced to confront the same conundrum. How can we extract our ancestors from the context of their historical and cultural matrix and demand to know why they didn't behave in accord with our current values? It's simply not possible, particularly if we look at the constantly shifting cultural 'norms' colouring each individual's perceptions, including our own. Exploring Chiron creatively doesn't require either a belief in reincarnation or the successful identification of a culprit, current or historical.

Audience: Everyone is born with Chiron somewhere in their chart, in every historical era. Let's say you manage to resolve a family issue. There will still be another one.

Liz: Yes, there will always be another one. The unfair poisoned wound may change its outer shape and external triggers, but it's the same archetypal wound. We might, over a few more decades or perhaps centuries, learn to handle it slightly better, but then again, we might not. When the outer planets were discovered, new issues emerged into collective consciousness that had always been there but hadn't been named or acknowledged. Since these discoveries – Uranus in 1781, Neptune in 1846, and Pluto in 1930 – we've been struggling to work with the collective dynamics these planets symbolise. We've made a mess of it a lot of the time, but I would like to believe that bit by bit, tiny crumbs of understanding keep appearing, even when concerted efforts are made to stamp them out.

Chiron was discovered in 1977. In terms of the time it takes for an archetypal pattern to reveal itself in collective awareness, that's only the blink of an eye. Long into the future, beyond any of our individual lifetimes, we may deal differently with Chiron, just as we're dealing slightly more creatively with Uranus, Neptune, and Pluto. Chiron's wounds may always exist simply because we're mortal and we will all die one day. If we eventually evolve into entirely spiritual, incorporeal beings as the Theosophists believe we will, then fine – we won't have natal charts, in which case we won't have to worry. But as long as we are mortal creatures, there will always be Chiron issues.

The idea that Chiron's pain can be healed once and for all by any individual or group, however hard they work at it, is a beautiful dream. But as you say, people will continue to be born with Chiron in the natal chart. We would all like an end to war, but people will continue to be born with Mars in the chart, and the fighting spirit will still erupt in destructive as well as creative ways in one form or another. Wars aren't limited to bloody battlefields. They can also occur within families and on social media. We might get better at avoiding hair-trigger responses, and wiser at understanding the roots of anger and aggression, personal and collective. But Mars will never transform into Venus, and Venus can be pretty troublesome too. Each of us might be able to heal to the extent that we're able to work more positively with something that's an innate part of the fabric of our mortal life. What we contribute to life might contain a bit less poison and a bit more wisdom and compassion. But being human means being hurt.

Audience: Would the parents' unsolved problems show up in the Chiron placement in a child's chart?

Liz: Up to a point, yes. Chiron is a bridge-builder and its history is also our familial and cultural history, so it reflects a collective inheritance as well as personal experience. Chiron's natal placement might suggest a certain kind of parental pattern, although not specific concrete circumstances. For a fuller picture, we would also need to look at the parental significators – the 4th and 10th houses and the Sun and Moon – to see whether Chiron is involved.

Themes of suffering and victimisation as a dominant motif in the family background might be emphasised if Chiron is strongly linked with parental significators. We might also need to look at the synastry between Chiron in our own and our parents' charts. I will talk more about Chiron in family charts later. If Chiron is in the 4th or 10th house or makes a strong aspect to Sun or Moon, we tend to perceive our parents through Chiron's eyes, and they will often provide an easy hook for our projections through their own behaviour and experiences. We might also find similar Chiron aspects and house placements in their charts. But astrological planets are modes of perception. They're symbols, not concrete facts. Our parents didn't put Chiron into our charts.

Perception, fate, and repetition

If we view a sphere of life through Saturn's eyes, we will develop certain values, attitudes, and responses which reflect that Saturnian perception. If Saturn is in the 10th house, the arena of vocation, social position, and involvement in public life will be the place where those perceptions are reflected in our experiences. Put another way, our perceptions are synchronous with our experiences. Inner and outer coincide in a way that Jung called 'meaningful coincidence', which was his definition of synchronicity. As the 10th house is also related to the mother, we may also perceive and experience her through Saturn's lens. We can't throw away the lens because it's an intrinsic part of us. But we can reflect on the difference between mother as a real person and our perception of mother as an archetypal figure.

If Jupiter is in the 10th house, we'll view that same sphere of life through Jupiter's lens, and we will develop an entirely different set of values, attitudes, and responses because we perceive and experience an entirely different reality. Jupiter's and Saturn's lenses are both real, but they contradict each other. Viewing life through both at once – which is necessary when they form an aspect in the natal chart – can require a lot of hard work.

Sometimes two siblings perceive their parents through completely different lenses. The elder sibling with a 4th house Saturn perceives a Saturnian father, while the younger with a 4th house Jupiter perceives a Jupiterian one. Sometimes this difference is synchronous with external circumstances through the parent's changing attitudes during the time gap between the two births. Things like financial pressures, illness, greater confidence in raising a child, or the breakup of the parental relationship can alter parents' attitudes. But these are triggers, not causes, and ultimately it's the individual's perception that constitutes their reality.

It's a mystery why and how the external world matches our unconscious perceptions and expectations. Although we can always try to find a rational explanation, in the end there doesn't appear to be any causality involved. We might draw qualities and behaviour patterns out of others if we persist in seeing them in a particular way. For example, if we're convinced that a partner will reject us and we try to pre-empt the rejection by behaving in defensive ways, our own actions could help to bring about the rejection we fear. But the rejection may happen whatever we try to do or not do, not least because we tend to be drawn to people who mirror our perceptions back to us through their own perceptions and attitudes. I know this is a tricky concept to take on board, and possibly even an unpleasant one for some because causes are always easier for the rational mind to accept than synchronicities. But it highlights the difference between understanding astrological significators as symbols and treating them as literal facts.

Events do often coincide with planetary symbols. But the precise nature of the event usually eludes accurate prediction. It's the *kind* of event that we glimpse in the chart, reflected by its archetypal core, rather than the literal details, and that archetypal core will resonate with something inside us. As an example, let's consider Richard Nixon. In his natal chart, Pluto is at 28° Gemini in the 10th house. It opposes a conjunction of Mars at 29° Sagittarius, Mercury at 0° Capricorn, and Jupiter at 1° Capricorn in the 4th house. It also trines the Moon in late Aquarius in the 6th house and trines a Venus-Chiron conjunction in early Pisces, also in the 6th house.

Pluto in the 10th house is often interpreted as an ambitious person, perhaps motivated by positive goals and perhaps not, who may achieve considerable power but tends to suffer the misfortune of attracting powerful, ruthless enemies who ensure the person's downfall. Does this mean Nixon was fated to experience his humiliating fall from power following Watergate, whatever he did? Does it mean he looked out at the world through Pluto's lens and, given this planet's obsession with ensuring survival at any cost, believed there were ruthless enemies everywhere and defended himself through ruthless means, thereby invoking his own fate?

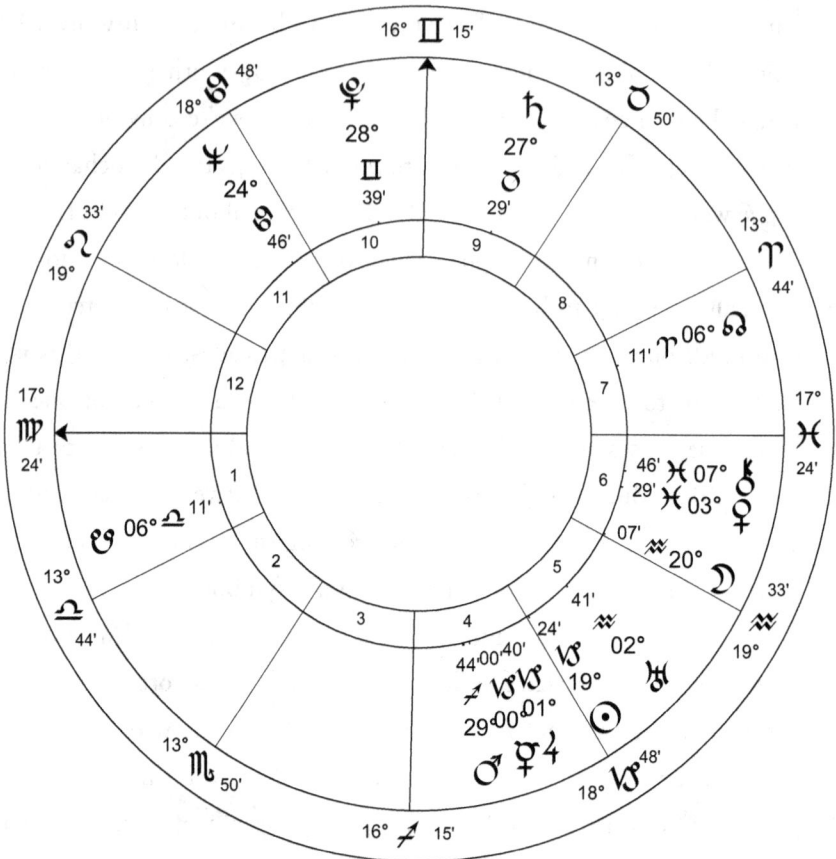

Richard Nixon
9 January 1913, 9.35 pm, Yorba Linda, California[27]

If we consider the 10th house in relation to the mother, might it also suggest that Nixon's experience of a possessive and controlling mother inclined him to defensive and perhaps deceitful behaviour from childhood as a means of survival? If so, can he be blamed for this? Should we blame his mother? How much of his downfall was fated and how much was made inevitable through his own perceptions and consequent actions? Did he

27 See www.astro.com/astro.databank for the birth data for this chart and all the other charts used in this seminar volume.

fall, did he jump, or was he pushed? Or all of the above? This takes us straight into the conundrum of the nature of fate.

Every planetary symbol, including Chiron, has a spectrum of meanings from dark to light and from inner to outer, with all the shades in between. How we perceive and interpret reality, how we respond to events, and whether we seek to enlarge our self-awareness so we can develop as individuals and claim at least some genuine freedom of choice, are certainly half the equation. But we don't really know what the other half is. Jung put it elegantly when he declared that free will is 'the ability to do gladly that which I must do', the operative word being 'gladly'.

Astrological predictions can sometimes be terribly literal. As Mark Twain was purported to have said, 'It is difficult to make predictions, especially about the future.' If we interpret every chart component in solely external terms, these predictions doom us to focus on one dimension of a planet rather than exploring its entire range of inner as well as outer possibilities. Then we are far more limited in our choices and responses, and we may inadvertently create our own fate or turn it darker than it needs to be, as well as narrowing our lives unnecessarily. We can't change the archetypal background of our perceptions. It's innate and it will usually be mirrored by external reality on some level. If natal Chiron is in the 4th house, we can't send it back and order a Venus replacement from Amazon. Family, home, and roots will always be coloured by Chiron themes, externally as well as internally. But we can move across Chiron's spectrum and the different levels of expression it describes, and deal with the wound in a different way. We can learn to work consciously with suffering. It's meaningless suffering that destroys us.

The range of wounds that humans can experience is limitless. We can be rejected emotionally in lots of different ways; we can be abandoned on many levels; we can be marginalised or scapegoated for a multitude of reasons; we can be physically injured or brutalised deliberately or accidentally; we can be intellectually stifled or forced to pursue a life we didn't choose; we can suffer from genetic illness or disability; we can lose those dearest to us; and we can be betrayed or humiliated on many possible levels. All these forms of pain can be interpreted through different planetary lenses. The injuries that happen to, us, whether through the agency of others, self-inflicted, or through what insurance companies used to call 'acts of God', are infinite in terms of concrete events. But when we perceive our injuries through Chiron's lens, they take on a special quality that has the same voice, whoever is speaking.

Think about your last trip to the dentist. If you view the experience through Saturn's lens, it's an uncomfortable but necessary part of keeping your body healthy. It's unpleasant but you put up with it stoically and leave the dental surgery quite pleased with yourself because you've discharged your duty to your oral hygiene for another year. And if you have to lose a tooth or be fitted with a denture, well, that's just the hard reality of life. Viewed through Venus' lens, the important issue is having a beautiful smile, and it's worth putting up with just about anything and paying any amount of money to achieve it. And it's even more rewarding if you happen to fancy the dentist.

But viewed through Chiron's lens, it's a terrifying experience because of the expectation of suffering. You'll put off the visit for as long as possible, and the delay may worsen the condition of your teeth. The hygienist becomes a sociopathic sadist and the dentist transforms into the slasher from *The Nightmare on Elm Street*. If you must have a tooth extracted, it confirms your conviction that life is brutally unfair, because surely they could have saved the tooth if they had cared about you enough or if you could have afforded a top-quality private dental clinic. You leave the dental surgery feeling as though you're suffering from PTSD because it was so traumatic.

We can bring many different archetypal perceptions to our experience of injury. When we bring Chiron's perception to it, the experience carries all the connotations of Chiron's myth. It isn't really an issue of 'objectivity', as there is probably no such thing. But we may need to recognise the agendas we bring to our experiences and try to learn to view life through more than one lens. The archetypal Scapegoat is a powerful mythic theme, as is the poison that won't fully leave the system. The ineradicable poison is a motif that often surfaces in therapeutic work as a repetitive compulsion, or a painful emotional experience that returns cyclically in long-term psychotherapy. We go over the same ground again and again but the wound never seems to change, and we feel we will never be free of it.

Repetition and cyclical return to the place of suffering are characteristic of the inner world of Chiron. People who are in analysis for many years, and feel they have understood and worked through a lot, often become aware that there is something that just won't shift. They have gone over the same ground again and again and extracted more and more insight each time, yet the pattern doesn't seem to alter. Or perhaps we might say that the perception doesn't alter, because they keep looking through the same planetary lens.

Greek myths of the underworld present us with this motif in figures like Sisyphus eternally pushing his rock up the hill, Ixion eternally tied to his burning wheel, and Tantalus eternally hungering for the fruit just out of reach. These mythic characters must undergo the same suffering over and over with no release. They are all being punished for their *hubris*, their belief – or, if you like, their perception – that they are equal or even superior to the gods. We're back to the theme of relinquishing immortality. The arrogance of *hubris* is relevant if we believe we can fix everything. Ixion, Sisyphus, and Tantalus, locked in their endless cycles of pain in Tartarus, had in common a conviction that they could outwit the gods, who might be understood as the natural forces or laws of life – the *moira* or set of boundaries, limits, nature, and purpose which forms the teleology of all living things.

Part Two

Chiron in Synastry

I've offered that very long description of Chiron's myths and meaning because I feel it's important that we try to deepen our understanding of the many levels of Chiron's symbolism before we explore its dynamics in relationship. Understanding synastry involves recognising each planet as a living archetypal pattern. Otherwise we won't really comprehend what happens when our natal Chiron is 'triggered' or constellated by another person's planets, or what happens when a planet in our own chart is constellated by someone else's Chiron.

Chiron is often found forming close synastry aspects in the charts of people involved in significant relationships of every kind. These might be romantic or familial, but Chiron's involvement also turns up in important working relationships as well as relationships between nations and their leaders. Any of you who do a lot of synastry work will have recognised this already. The frequency might seem surprising in love relationships if we believe love to be identical with romance, especially when the aspects have very tight orbs. Like Saturn, Chiron in synastry reflects subtle, often deeply unconscious issues activated in the relationship that could lead to creative transformation or profound hurt and disillusionment, and frequently both.

Also like Saturn in synastry, Chiron requires effort, honesty, and consciousness on the part of both people to express its most creative dimensions. The onus lies not only with the Chiron person but also with the other person, since both are participants in the story. One of the most important creative possibilities in this kind of exchange is the experience of mutual compassion. Another is acceptance of reality – not the pragmatic realism of Saturn, but the wisdom to recognise suffering as an inevitable dimension of human life and a potential stage in a process of individuation. Without consciousness, Chiron aspects can be hurtful and destructive in relationships through the unleashing of envy, anger, resentment, self-pity, feelings of inadequacy and, at worst, emotional and physical abuse. But these aspects can also lead us to a profound level of self-understanding that allows us to accept ourselves as fallible humans, and to accept others with the same genuine wisdom and compassion.

It's sometimes helpful to think of natal planets that are triggered by someone else's chart as parts of ourselves that need to be awakened, given shape, or offered new modes of expression in order to fulfil their potential. We need other people to precipitate this kind of awakening; it doesn't happen in a vacuum. Even the most profoundly introverted and misanthropic artist working in solitude recognises, at some level, that the work of art is ultimately meant for an audience, even if an invisible one, and that art in all its forms is a mode of communication that, at its best, forms relationships that endure across generations, cultures, and centuries.

While sexual attraction and mutual interests may provide the spark between people who fall in love, these factors don't apply to family bonds. Yet Chiron is usually involved in both settings. We might consider that there is a teleology, an ultimate meaning and purpose at work which, however painful, aims to fulfil a particular requirement or 'destiny' in the two individuals to develop into what they need to become.

People who trigger our natal charts tend to wake our planets up whether or not we recognise it and regardless of whether we find it pleasant. In a similar way, no important transit to a natal planet happens in a vacuum. Other people are usually involved in the ways we experience a transit because the natal planet is kicked into life through a cast of characters who act as catalysts and mirrors. Even if we are well related to the part of ourselves symbolised by the natal planet, there are always new levels that can be developed. In relationships involving close aspects to Chiron, we can sometimes feel the hand of the *daimon* at work.

The natal planet or angle, sometimes with considerable struggle and pain and often unwillingly, is woken up, stimulated, and sometimes transformed. In other words, it's given the opportunity to find fuller expression. It's placed in a kind of alembic or alchemical vessel with another person's planet. No alchemical work can be performed with just one substance; there must always be two. It's the chemical reaction between them that generates change and development. As Jung observed: 'The meeting of two personalities is like the contact of two chemical substances: if there is any reaction, both are transformed.'[28]

Given the often painful themes connected with Chiron, of course we are going to need other people to awaken our consciousness of this story within ourselves. We're hardly likely to enter Chiron's cave voluntarily with a big smile and a feeling of pleasurable anticipation. We will be attracted to, or born into proximity with, people who bring Chiron to life in us and offer us a chance of undergoing a process of change rather than languishing in a static place of suffering. If we are locked into the pattern of a succession of relationships in which natal Chiron is repeatedly involved in strong aspects with another person's planets, it may be a way in which the psyche is trying to come to terms with something that's too difficult to deal with on our own. Humans only seem to discover the unconscious if it delivers a hard kick. We may need the alchemical process of another person's planets activating natal Chiron to release both the poison and the creative potential.

---

28   C. G. Jung, *Modern Man in Search of a Soul*, (Kegan Paul, 1933), p. 49.

Moon-Chiron aspects in synastry

I've been focusing mainly on natal Chiron constellated by a planet in someone else's chart. But what about the other way around? What if it's our planet making an aspect to someone else's Chiron?

Audience: I would be doing the same thing to them.

Liz: Yes, in a general sense – there is an activation of something within you too. But the planet is different, so it's not quite 'the same thing'. They aren't triggering your wound; you're triggering theirs. A planet in your natal chart is stirred by the other person's Chiron, which means that their complexity, defensiveness, pain, and perhaps also wisdom and compassion will activate something within your own psyche and help bring it to life in a new way. The way might be difficult and you might decide you would rather be elsewhere, but there is a meaningful pattern at work.

Let's take the Moon as an example. How does the Moon respond to another person's Chiron? How many of you are or have been in a close relationship with someone where there's a strong Moon-Chiron link between your two charts? I see a lot of hands raised. What does the Moon respond to, and how does it respond?

Audience: My Moon conjuncts Chiron in the chart of someone I was involved with for a long time, and it was incredibly painful. Every time I saw this person, I would cry. I couldn't stop crying. I couldn't find any reason for feeling like that.

Liz: When we consider any close planetary aspect in synastry, it can help to think of a planet as a deity. It's a kind of god, a living archetypal pattern in ourselves and in the whole of life. It has its own nature, needs, fears, strengths, and weaknesses, and its own path to fulfilment. When it's involved in synastry, it must interact with another god. The two deities are locked in a room together for the duration of the relationship, and sometimes for a long time afterward if the relationship ends. Within families, that room may remain locked for more than one generation. There will be a reaction in both planets. Neither emerges untouched.

Deities in myth sometimes like each other and sometimes they don't. Sometimes they're bitter enemies. Sometimes they fall in love, as Ares and Aphrodite do, and sometimes they quarrel incessantly, like Zeus and Hera. Sometimes they're envious of each other. And sometimes they do all these things. In Homer's *Iliad*, the gods, during the Trojan War, find themselves on opposite sides, some favouring the Greeks and some the Trojans. Deities who are otherwise fond of each other wind up exchanging violent blows on the battlefield.[29] The planets in that locked room may begin their sojourn with good will or they may begin with an already full-blown antipathy.

Try to use your imagination, rather than relying on keywords. What does the Moon symbolise in us?

Audience: The Moon tries to help, to nurture.

Liz: Yes, that's an important dimension of it. The Moon is our organ of connection with all the nonrational domains of life, and this includes not only emotions and bodily feelings but also imagination and instinct. In myth the lunar goddess Artemis is the protector of nature, animals, and children, although she is also a hunter. She embodies the instinctual cycles of the natural world reflected in the cycle of the Moon in the heavens. Lunar deities in the myths of many cultures guard the young, the helpless, and the wild. They also preside over the unknown depths of the sea, the underworld, and the realm of magic. Although we associate the sea with Poseidon-Neptune, before the rule of the Olympians it was the domain of Tethys, the Titan daughter of Ouranos and Gaia, sister-wife of Okeanos

---

29 Ares, Aphrodite, Apollo, and Artemis, each for their own reasons, sided with the Trojans, while Hera, Athene, Poseidon, Hermes, and Hephaistos – Aphrodite's long-suffering husband – sided with the Greeks. Zeus kept his options open and offered aid to both sides.

and mother of all the river-deities. And the underworld belongs not only to Hades-Pluto but also to triple-headed Hekate, mistress of magic.

Through the Moon we experience a feeling of connection, belonging, community, family, safety and security, home, and containment within the natural world through the fulfilment of our instinctual and emotional needs. We reach out to other people through our Moon. We also make a relationship with the imaginal world, from which we may draw creative inspiration as well as immersing ourselves in the brooding darkness and mystery of the underworld. The Moon is the organ of nourishment, and we achieve this through relationships.

Lunar relationships aren't limited to other humans, as Artemis and Hekate both demonstrate. They may also include animals, plants, water, memory, music, art, poetry, drama, and the world of dreams. The emphasis in any individual will reflect the Moon's natal sign, aspects, and house placement. The Moon reflects what we most need in order to feel connected.

Audience: What about Venus and relationships?

Liz: I've been using the words 'need' and 'feel'. Neither belongs to Venus' domain. Venus is concerned with a different dimension of relationship, one which isn't based on needs and feelings. We assume that love is always an emotional experience, but there are other equally important levels. The astrological Venus desires, values, admires, appreciates, and recognises and nurtures beauty. But Venus doesn't need or empathise in the way the Moon does.

Think about the signs Venus rules: Taurus, an earth sign, and Libra, an air sign. Neither of these signs is known for its emotional vulnerability or neediness, although both value relationships highly. Even when Venus is placed in water signs, it's still an active planet, just as the goddess in myth is active rather than receptive. In ancient Sparta Aphrodite was worshipped in full battle armour, and in Babylon Ishtar was a war-goddess. Venus doesn't mirror anyone, although she spends a lot of time looking in the mirror. She mates but doesn't become dependent, which is why she's a far better *hetaira* than she is a wife. She's certainly fertile; in myth she gives birth to fifteen children by seven different fathers. But like Jupiter, she doesn't stay around long enough to nurture them.

The Moon is like a set of antennae. It picks up subliminal emotional signals and impels us to connect and bond, which is why we talk about it in relation to the mother, who is usually the first living being with whom we form an instinctual bond. The psychoanalyst D. W. Winnicott, one of the most insightful researchers into child psychology, calls the mirroring of the child in the mother's face

> ...the beginning of a significant exchange with the world, a two-way process in which self-enrichment alternates with the discovery of meaning in the world of seen things.[30]

The natal Moon is not, of course, literally one's mother. It's our Moon, not hers. But we perceive mother and express our own mothering inclinations and our need for a particular kind of mothering through the lens of our natal Moon.

The Moon reaches out from the very beginning of life and bonds with the primary caretaker, and our emotional perception of relationship is built on the foundations of what we experience through that early lunar exchange. That's why we look at the natal lunar sign, aspects, and house to get a sense of what kind of mothering we feel we have experienced. We will interpret our early experiences of bonding through our lunar house, sign, and aspects. Throughout life we express the Moon to reach out to other living beings. Then we feel we belong. We aren't alone and we haven't been abandoned.

---

30   D. W. Winnicott, 'Mirror-role of Mother and Family in Child Development', in P. Lomas (ed.), *The Predicament of the Family: A Psycho-analytical Symposium* (Hogarth Press and the Institute of Psychoanalysis, 1967).

The Moon needs an Other to come alive, just as the Moon in the heavens needs the light of the Sun and the infant needs the mirror of the mother's face. The Other, hopefully, can provide us with a sense that life is safe, nourishing, and supportive. But sometimes the Moon reaches out to another person and encounters Chiron. Why would anyone feel that Chiron is safe? Perhaps the Moon is seeing the kind, wise Centaur who teaches and heals. Perhaps it's the wildness of the hunter that draws lunar empathy; in myth, after Chiron was abandoned by his mother, Apollo taught him music and the arts of healing, but it was Artemis who taught him how to use the bow. But more importantly, the Moon may sense the depth of hurt, despair, and potential wisdom in the Chiron person and feels needed. When we're needed, our own needs are fulfilled. They are, in a sense, the same thing.

Think about what binds us to other people. Do we perceive them as beautiful and exciting, or idealise them in some way? Is that what is meant by loving someone? That might certainly describe the experience of falling in love, and the perception of beauty and value in another person may be related to our experience of Venus. But for the Moon to bond, we need to feel compassion for someone. We need to feel connected through our shared vulnerability. The archetypal mother offers unconditional love to a tiny, frail infant. If we're relating through the Moon, we don't want a superhero or someone who appears so wonderful that we have to struggle to be wonderful ourselves to merit their love. We want another frail, vulnerable human. Our most enduring emotional bonds with others are built on shared suffering.

Compassion doesn't just bind us emotionally and make us feel needed. It also opens the gates to the imagination, beginning with the capacity to imagine ourselves in the other person's shoes. We're no longer trapped within our own private loneliness. Think about what happens when people are grieving, whether it's an individual, a family, or a whole society. Shared suffering makes people care for each other in ways they might not ordinarily experience. Collective disasters like the Twin Towers or the Southeast Asian tsunami of 2004, or the deaths of greatly loved figures such as Princess Diana or Queen Elizabeth, draw people together through shared grief in ways that don't happen in other circumstances. What else makes us empty our wallets, which we might ordinarily never consider doing, except suffering on a grand scale? Why do so many people contribute so generously to charities when a collective disaster hits, when at other times they might resent any financial demand, even from people close to them?

Compassion obscures our differences, just as the light of the Moon blends colours and blurs different elements of the landscape. When we look at things at night, we see their similarities rather than what sets them apart. We can see every hair in the animal's coat in Albrecht Dürer's watercolour, *Young Hare*. That's typical of the sunlit art of the Northern European Renaissance. But Monet's *Waterlilies* looks best when our vision is blurred. No surprise that in Monet's natal chart the Moon is in its own sign of Cancer. In one of Mary Stewart's early novels, she describes the legend of the Moon-Spinners. I don't know whether this legend has ancient roots or whether the author invented it. If it's the latter, she tapped into an archetypal theme that faithfully reflects lunar mythology.

> Sometimes, when you're deep in the countryside, you meet three girls, walking along the hill tracks in the dusk, spinning. They each have a spindle, and onto these they are spinning their wool, milk-white, like the moonlight. In fact, it is the moonlight, the moon itself...all they have to do is to see that the world gets its hours of darkness, and they do this by spinning the moon down out of the sky.[31]

---

31 Mary Stewart, *The Moon-Spinners* (Hodder & Stoughton, 1962).

These figures are related to the three Fates, but in the novel they're entirely benign and they protect the vulnerable. At the dark of the Moon, all innocent hunted creatures are given their chance to escape the hunter.

In light of all this, the frequency of Moon-Chiron contacts in synastry isn't at all surprising. We all need to feel we are needed by someone. If we don't feel needed, we are alone. We are outsiders, excluded from the human family, and there is nothing more frightening or painful to the Moon. Need provides the foundation for many relationships, and a lot of people choose partners who need them rather than partners whom they passionately desire. And a wounded Chiron is deeply needy, although not always very gracious about showing it.

Audience: I wonder if you could talk a bit about close relationships where one person might want to heal the gloom of the other, but the feeling isn't reciprocal.

Liz: By gloom, I assume you mean depression or, as it was called in earlier centuries, melancholy?

Audience: Yes.

Liz: Apparent lack of reciprocity is a frequent theme in Moon-Chiron relationships. The Chiron person may not be receptive when we try to offer compassion, or they may accept the offering but resent it at the same time. Or they may fear our intervention because it exposes a helplessness they don't want to acknowledge. Extreme pain also has a way of making people oblivious to the pain in others as well as envious of others' power to help. Chiron may bite and kick – usually metaphorically, but sometimes literally – and try to undermine or injure us or shut us out to compensate for feelings of weakness. This is especially the case if the person can't acknowledge their own suffering.

Audience: I have a natal Moon-Chiron square. My Moon is in the 4th house. All the work I 've done on myself in my own life seems to be linked with that 4th house. Although I started out with a Bed and Breakfast house where others came for a brief stay, it's amazing how my life and theirs have changed by sharing my Moon. I've been there so long, and they are all staying!

Liz: So you're working out a difficult natal Moon-Chiron aspect by being a healer, and by creating a home which reflects the positive side of Chiron rather than the destructive side which may be part of your family background.

Audience: Yes.

Liz: With difficult natal Moon-Chiron aspects, working with others' pain can be a fruitful way of working with the aspect. But acknowledgement and understanding of your own wound, and compassion for yourself rather than self-pity, are necessary to get the best from it. The same applies to Moon-Chiron contacts in synastry. The potential with close Moon-Chiron contacts, natally and in synastry, involves opening up the heart through compassion and the experience of shared suffering.

In synastry, problems in the relationship often appear to lie with the Chiron person, who may wear the mantle of the 'identified patient' or the 'unloving' one. But a defensive Chiron is often gifted at 'gaslighting' and may work to convince the other person that they are the one with the problem. And the Moon may fail to understand the nature of Chiron's defences because it's so needy itself and can easily interpret those defences as lack of love. The Moon can sulk and feel unappreciated and resentful, especially if it's under siege in the person's own birth chart. If we have a Moon-Chiron square ourselves, or hard aspects between Moon and Saturn or one of the outer planets, another person's Chiron aspecting our Moon will trigger the natal configuration and wake us up to our own internal distress in uncomfortable ways that we might not want to face. Then we might need to work hard to be conscious of when we're projecting our own defences and difficulties on the Chiron person, who will often provide an easy hook for the projection.

A sad but not unusual example of this dynamic is the synastry between King Charles III and the late Diana, Princess of Wales. Charles' natal Chiron is at 28° Scorpio, square Diana's Moon at 25° Aquarius. In her chart, natal Moon opposes Uranus at 23° Aquarius and Mars at 1° Virgo, and squares Venus at 24° Taurus. His Chiron triggered that difficult natal T-cross. Although many people cast him as the villain during their acrimonious divorce, the reality was far more complex.

In theory, the process of working with our natal Chiron through the empathy of someone else's Moon is very positive. We become aware of our own hurt and vulnerability through the other person. We realise they can offer a quality of emotional support and empathy we badly need. This can facilitate a depth of understanding in both people which results in a deeply compassionate bond. That's the potential of Moon-Chiron aspects in synastry. But the problem in actual life is that we don't always want to have Chiron woken up. We long for it but we bitterly resent it when it happens because of the ambivalent feelings it arouses.

Chiron and cultural stereotypes

Audience: Do you think women might find it easier to accept having their pain seen than men do?

Liz: I would be careful about that kind of generalisation. Some individuals are more able to tolerate having their vulnerability seen than others, and it reflects particular placements in the birth chart rather than gender. Sometimes a complex, defensive natal aspect like Moon-Chiron can make it hard for a person to tolerate being seen as vulnerable, regardless of their sex. Sometimes defensiveness arises from the fierce pride and self-sufficiency inherent in certain zodiacal signs, especially if the Moon is in Leo, Scorpio, or Capricorn.

There are many mysteries about the human personality that the natal horoscope can't shed any light on. The birth chart tells us nothing about gender, any more than it tells us about sexual preferences, the degree of intelligence, the extent of a talent, or whether a person will choose to use abilities and gifts in life-enhancing or destructive ways. In fact, the chart alone doesn't even tell us whether we're looking at a human, a cat, an institution, a business venture, or a country. The natal chart reflects a moment in time and provides us with an insightful map of how attributes such as gender, intelligence, and talent will express themselves through the patterns at the moment of birth, within the limits of the nature of the entity that has been born. But the chart can't tell us what the entity or the attributes actually are.

Some might say that the chart can't tell us about the soul of the individual who has incarnated at that birth moment, but only about the patterns of expression and development in that incarnation. We also need to bear in mind the alchemical mix between the individual chart and the environment, including family and cultural context, which may overemphasise some attributes and stifle others. Every individual needs to be understood as an individual, and not as a statistical component in a generic group.

Having said that, it certainly seems to be the case that social expectations and assumptions might make it difficult for many men to cope with a partner who sees that heart-rending suffering in the cave. Chiron rolling about howling and begging for death doesn't exactly accord with a macho image of masculinity, although the mythic Chiron is always presented as a male deity. But pride and defensiveness, and the fear that weakness and vulnerability will be exploited, are not in themselves gender-related. They're basic human reactions when life makes ugly faces at us.

Also, many parents, unconsciously – and because they can't avoid being cast in an archetypal role by their children – may find it intolerable if their child senses vulnerability and suffering in a parent who is expected to be a confident authority figure or a strong and unconditionally loving nurturer. We haven't looked at Chiron in parent-child relationships, but everything I've said about romantic relationships will apply here just as much, with the added difficulty of the archetypal parent-child dynamic. Once the mythic Chiron has been wounded, he can no longer mentor children.

Cultural stereotypes are changing, although perhaps more quickly on paper than on the emotional level. Ideas and ideologies, which belong to the realm of Uranus, always fail to take human emotions and instincts into account. However urgently some people might wish to define or redefine masculine and feminine, archetypes are like everything living. They grow at their own rate of speed and alter over time according to their own teleology, not the conceptions of the human intellect. They are always moving toward what they might eventually become, but they unfold in their own way regardless of how hard we try to hurry them along or stop them in their tracks. We don't know what they might become in the future, any more than we know what humans might become. We have only a snapshot of ourselves embedded in a particular time, a particular historical epoch, a particular society, and a particular family. The old argument about nature versus nurture is rather like the argument about the chicken and the egg. When we consider Chiron, it might, in the end, be the wrong question to ask.

Current statistics, if they are to be trusted – which is highly questionable – suggest that many women are much quicker to seek a doctor's help when they're in physical pain than many men are. This is sometimes offered as one of the reasons why statistically, women tend to live longer. I don't know whether this statistical picture is really true or, if so, whether it will continue as it is or change over time. Nor do I feel there's a simple explanation. It may be a cultural issue or a biological one, or a combination of the two; or it may be a matter of individual choice.

The first experiences of physical and emotional pain, for many men, come through unpredictable illness or accident, or a devastating emotional loss. But for most women it's inevitable unless there is deliberate intervention, and it occurs no later than the onset of the menstrual cycle. It's cyclical rather than incidental. Cyclical menstrual pain and its concomitant emotional lability are part of the organic experience of most women from puberty until menopause. So is childbirth. This may result in greater awareness of the body because there isn't any escape from its vulnerability. The irrevocable nature of biological cycles is linked with the symbolism of the Moon's phases, which in myth are often portrayed in the triad of the maiden, the fruitful wife, and the old crone. I don't know whether heightened sensitivity to and acceptance of the vulnerability of physical embodiment, resulting in a greater willingness to seek medical as well as emotional help, can be attributed solely to social attitudes. I've seen so many exceptions that I'm not sure whether there is even a rule.

If social stereotypes pose a problem for us personally, it might be helpful to consider the extent to which our conscious or unconscious allegiance to, or rebellion against, preconceived notions and assumptions is a factor in our experience of wounding. That means it's probably related to natal Chiron. But sensitivity to this kind of issue might not be the case for everyone. Some people might feel wounded in other ways. Identity politics doesn't provide much help in working with Chiron and may even make matters worse. For some people, issues of gender have nothing to do with Chiron's place of pain. For others, gender and the social assumptions regarding it are experienced as the source of the wound. I'm wary of any single, literal, external explanation for Chiron's suffering, because it's our own perceptions combined with external reality that comprise Chiron's experience of injury. The external world provides us with a catalyst rather than a cause.

As the late Queen put it so delicately, recollections may vary. A particular experience can make one person feel victimised, humiliated, and helpless while the same experience may inspire another person to make more of themselves and their potential gifts. Focusing solely on external influences such as social expectations won't really help us to understand and work with Chiron on deeper levels. However we might choose to identify ourselves, we all long for someone who will perceive and feel compassion for our secret suffering, and who will accept, love, and value us even if we give up our immortality – which might perhaps be understood as giving up our need to be seen as perfect, and relinquishing our expectation that the world will always be just and fair according to our personal definitions of justice and fairness.

It takes a lot of courage to deal honestly with our reactions to someone constellating our Chiron. We desperately want the other person to understand us, yet we may resent them because they do, and we may find subtle ways of punishing them, especially if we're unconscious of where we're hurting and why. We might not thank them for the compassion they're offering because we are afraid of being loved as we are. We would rather be loved as the person we would like to be. And offering help to someone else's Chiron will not invariably earn us the just reward we hope for.

It can be very tricky to handle Chiron aspects in synastry. Yet if we're willing to try, it can be profoundly healing because we have actually let another human being see the place inside where we feel unfairly and irrevocably damaged. The effort to share that with another person without identifying with the archetypal victim – and without turning it into a tawdry public spectacle for a faceless audience while claiming a tidy sum from the media – might be a major component in what we call healing.

The various definitions that people have of healing are interesting to explore. The idea that we can wave a wand like Professor Snape, recite a magical spell, and make Draco Malfoy's wounds vanish as if they had never existed is a hopelessly naïve image of Chiron's healing. The idea that we can heal Chiron's wound by injuring the person or group we believe has injured us is equally naïve. Understanding and accepting a wound makes a difference in terms of how we cope with the pain. It isn't meaningless pain any more. We may still hurt, but our perception of ourselves is transformed if we can allow ourselves to be loved on that level. And when the Moon feels compassion for the Chiron person, it forms a profound bond. It can be uncomfortable because the Moon can't remain unaffected. We can't easily get up and walk away, and even if we do, we will have changed because we've suffered with the other person. The Moon has woken up. And it has a long memory.

Audience: You are assuming that the Moon person has the will to help the Chiron person.

Liz: No, I'm not assuming that. None of us is obligated to feel what we don't feel, even if governments or pressure groups try to insist that we should. I'm suggesting that the potential is there if genuine love can grow between the two people.

Audience: If the Chiron person has issues with power and control, and they sense your lunar vulnerability, it can go badly wrong.

Liz: Yes, it can go badly wrong, for many reasons. I did say that working with Chiron in synastry is tricky. There isn't any guarantee that things will end well, and they sometimes end very badly. Pride is one reason and, as you say, so are addiction to power and the need to control. You can't expect a wounded animal to behave according to genteel dinner party rules. If you feel you can't cope with this kind of situation, fair enough; then you're better off not getting involved, or getting out as quickly as possible. Chiron's wounds are one of the major sources of cruelty and the desire to harm and humiliate others. All too often, the wounded becomes the wounder. This is the *enantiodromia* of the victim and the persecutor, the reversal of the opposites. All these issues spring from the same source, which is our terror of being seen as the vulnerable and imperfect humans we actually are.

Audience: But the Moon person can also feel afraid. It's the fear of rejection, of hurt, even of violence.

Liz: Yes, and the fear may sometimes be justified. We might need to ask ourselves why we're drawn to a particular relationship or a repeating pattern in relationships. Is it what Freud called 'repetition compulsion' – the unconscious need to constantly return to parental surrogates who treat us as we were once treated, but whom we hope against all hope will one day change and show us the longed-for love and understanding we were denied in early life? Is it the belief that our own devotion and sacrifice will somehow draw compassion from the other person to provide the compassion for ourselves that we can't find? Is it the *daimon* that requires us to undergo a certain kind of experience so we can develop as individuals? Or might it be all these things?

Whatever planet is involved with Chiron in synastry, consciousness in both people is needed to work with the aspect constructively. Both need to be willing to look inward with honesty. It can't be entirely one-sided or it will fail. That's asking a lot, but there are no free lunches in Chiron's world. If we are the Moon person and are unconscious of our feelings, a big mess can develop because we have failed to understand the underlying pain and anger of the Chiron person, and have also failed to understand our own emotional needs. The Moon can feel depressed, pummelled, self-pitying, and crushingly lonely in the face of Chiron's metaphorical kicking and biting. I'm certainly not suggesting that you 'ought' to take this kind of challenge on board simply because it looks compassionate and noble on paper. Although compassion and emotional generosity are among the very best qualities in human nature, a compulsion for self-martyrdom may point to something far more destructive.

Nor am I suggesting that you should remain in an emotionally or physically abusive relationship because it might be 'meaningful'. If the Chiron person stubbornly refuses to leave the cave, you might be better off moving on, unless you're hoping for eventual beatification. Close Chiron synastry aspects can feel like hell at times. Not everyone is suited to this kind of complexity or introspection in their relationships, nor wants to make the sacrifices required. I'm only suggesting that if you do find yourself in such a relationship and you genuinely love each other, there are creative ways of working with the aspect that can make it deeply worthwhile for both people, whether or not you wind up growing grey and old together.

Sun-Chiron aspects in synastry

Audience: What about the Sun and Chiron if the Sun isn't being expressed? What if your Chiron contacts someone's Sun in the 12th house, or if the Sun isn't well aspected, or not aspected at all?

Liz: When you say 'isn't being expressed', I assume you mean not fully conscious.

Audience: Yes. Like when you talk about Chiron or Saturn not being conscious. You've said in the past that any planet can be unconscious.

Liz: I don't believe the full potential of the birth chart is instantly available at birth. It's an unfolding story. We develop it over a lifetime and discover the different dimensions of ourselves symbolised by the planets bit by bit. This is especially true of the Sun, which reflects the core of the individual and can take a lifetime to unfold. Some parts of the chart are slower to emerge than others. Some might never really emerge at all, except in compulsive ways or through projection on others. Conflicts within the chart, sometimes reflected by difficult aspects and sometimes by the balance of elements, suggest that some planets will remain unconscious for a long time and emerge with difficulty. Others will be developed early because they're flexible, comfortable, and well adapted.

Chiron and Saturn can take a very long time because the psychological dimensions they symbolise are usually painful. Both planets describe areas where we feel restricted and deprived. Also, environment plays a big role. A particular kind of family dynamic, educational bias, or cultural background can make it harder to express attributes that are unacceptable to family members, peers, teachers, and social group. This uneven unfolding of the chart occurs in everyone and doesn't imply that something has gone 'wrong'.

The natal Sun's house placement and aspects, or lack of aspects, don't necessarily tell us whether it's being consciously expressed. Sometimes the balance of elements can be important. Lots of planets in earth, for example, with only the Sun in a fire sign, can suggest a conflict between different modes of perception – sensation and intuition – and the Sun-sign might be displayed in more erratic, extreme, or inflexible ways because the intuitive function isn't as sophisticated and socially adapted as the sensation function. The Sun might make lots of aspects, but that doesn't guarantee easy expression.

Sometimes the Sun in an undeveloped element can display striking gifts. But the gifts might not be subject to the person's conscious control, and they may come and go in spontaneous and arbitrary ways. An undeveloped feeling function, for example, may reflect deep, intense feelings, but they aren't available on tap, and a fraught emotional situation can cause the person to disconnect even if they don't wish to. Also, consciousness isn't just a matter of what's in the chart. An equally important factor may be our willingness to recognise all of what we are, rather than clinging to a self-image that deletes big chunks of ourselves because we're afraid those bits won't be acceptable or don't match the image of the person we want to be.

If the Sun is less accessible to consciousness – in other words, if we aren't yet fully able to recognise and value our uniqueness and our individual goals and aspirations – then we aren't likely to enjoy an encounter with another person's Chiron because the relationship will demand that we recognise our individuality. That involves an experience of separateness, which is why some people find it hard to express the Sun. They fear the loneliness of being an individual, and they may also fear the destructive envy which many people display toward someone who is managing to fulfil an individual destiny in a creative way. The Sun in the 12th, immersed in the collective psyche, can have a hard time embracing solar separateness because it feels so isolating.

The Sun in the 12th has the potential to serve as a kind of conduit, communicating the images and feelings of the collective psyche in creative forms. Those forms are often in the arts or the helping professions, but a surprising number of people with a 12th house Sun wind up in politics because they're able to serve as a voice for their collective. The danger lies in being a passive medium and a victim of collective currents rather than shaping those currents according to individual values. That requires consciousness and the courage to express an individuality, which can be deeply painful for someone who has spent life trying to please, placate, and belong. But a submerged Sun will still be woken up by another person's Chiron, even if it's dragged kicking and screaming into the light. Nothing wakes us up to a sense of self with greater force than someone telling us we shouldn't be ourselves, especially if we haven't yet recognised the self that is under attack.

The Sun not only needs to become self-aware; it also needs to shine and inspire. It hints at our vocation, our calling in life. The Sun is often imaged as the archetypal Divine Child, the symbol of a deeper or higher reality in nascent form. In Egyptian myth, Horus, the god of the rising Sun, is portrayed as a child. The card of the Sun in the Major Arcana of A. E. Waite's Tarot deck portrays a radiant, laughing child on a white horse. And, of course, the newborn Christ-child as a symbol of hope and redemption dominates the iconography of Christian religious expression. The astrological Sun reflects that part of us which strives to fulfil the design of the Self, the transpersonal inner spark we sense but can't rationalise or pin down in concrete terms. The Divine Child reminds us that there is always a future and a potential for renewal.

The Sun person may respond to the Chiron person by feeling a powerful desire to offer encouragement and support. The attraction lies in the Sun's recognition of Chiron's potentials – the Centaur could heal and emerge from the cave renewed and able to fulfil a brighter destiny. The Sun person can work generously to help the Chiron person develop their talents. It isn't quite the same as the Moon's empathy. It's more an intuitive recognition of the Chiron person's specialness and future possibilities. Apollo in myth is the god of prophecy, and the Sun can intuit the teleology of Chiron's wound. And the Sun might discover a new sense of its own purpose through the relationship.

That's the good news. As for the bad news, an envious Chiron might do its best to undermine the Sun's efforts to shine, especially through criticism of every creative idea the Sun tries to express. Chiron may also try too strenuously to play the mythic role of teaching Achilles how to hunt and play the lyre, and can attempt to shape and control the Sun's direction in life. Because of Chiron's envy and resentment, this mentoring, which is not always entirely generous, can feel suffocating, controlling, and imprisoning to the Sun. The relationship might fail because of Chiron's corrosive envy, and the Sun may react destructively out of hurt pride. Apollo is a god of light and healing, but when he's offended and angry, he has no qualms about unleashing his deadly arrows.

This synastry aspect is usually less emotionally fraught than Moon-Chiron because it isn't rooted in instinctual needs. It has the potential to generate a mutual inspiration that results in both people discovering and developing abilities, talents, and renewed faith in the future, provided there is enough honesty between them. Apollo raised Chiron and taught him music and the healing arts. Although the Sun-god plays no part in the story of Chiron's wounding and sacrifice, there is a deep affinity between them because Chiron is Apollo's foster-child.

What nudges us into self-awareness might not always be someone's love and appreciation. It can be a person who appears to reject who we are, especially if we haven't yet recognised that essential core ourselves. Then we begin to discover something vitally important to our sense of identity that we've been unaware of or have undervalued. The Chiron person might not, in reality, truly reject who we are; they might be all too aware of it but may find it painful because it arouses such powerful feelings of deficiency and envy alongside the admiration.

Joni Mitchell's song *Big Yellow Taxi* tells us that we don't know what we've got until it's gone. Someone else's Chiron aspecting our Sun may tell us that we don't know what we've got until we've been told we shouldn't have it. We might not realise that we have been unconscious of a particular dimension of ourselves until someone injures it, accidentally or deliberately. Even if the Sun is unexpressed, the Chiron person can still be envious because they can sense the Sun's potential. But the Sun person might not recognise envy as the source of Chiron's hurtful behaviour because they don't perceive themselves as enviable.

Envy is usually the chief problem with Sun-Chiron aspects across two charts because the Sun shines so brightly, even when it's submerged in the 12th house or isolated through a lack of aspects. A wounded Chiron secretly envies Apollo, who is youthful, radiant, and apparently impervious to bruising. The degree to which this synastry aspect can become destructive matches the degree to which it can unlock creative potentials in both people. If the capacity didn't exist for the one, it wouldn't exist for the other. Everything depends on how the two individuals deal with the two planets in their own and each other's charts.

Audience: What about a natal Sun-Chiron aspect? I'm trying to see how envy could play a part.

Liz: Envy is always a danger with Chiron, natally and in synastry, just as it is with Saturn. If we feel we've been deprived of something we need and idealise, it's hard not to envy people who seem to have what we feel we lack or have been denied. When the Sun is involved with Chiron in the natal chart, the wound is felt in our sense of self and our faith in a destiny that will allow us to become the unique individual we were always meant to become. Another person's apparent self-confidence and capacity for self-expression can easily trigger envy in a person with a hard natal Sun-Chiron aspect.

Just as another person's Chiron can injure, stifle, or undermine our solar confidence, Chiron's wound to the Sun in the natal chart can make us feel our self-expression is worthless and will always be unappreciated. It might not always appear that way because Sun-Chiron people can be ferociously proud and often work hard to compensate for their feelings of inadequacy. They can excel and gain acclamation for their special gifts. But sadly, some Sun-Chiron people give up before the struggle begins, and through their own choices they crystallise the feeling of being one of life's failures. They shoot themselves in the foot with the poisoned arrow because it seems less frightening than being shot down by others who might despise what they try to offer. Even in the face of success, the sense of being deficient and inadequate may continue to gnaw away at self-confidence and faith in the future.

This feeling of inadequacy can be triggered in early life by a lack of real recognition of our unique individuality by family, teachers, or peer group. But the aspect is present at birth, not inserted into the chart by external circumstances. It can be helpful to recognise that parental obliviousness to or rejection of one's individuality is a catalyst rather than a cause. The cause, if we understand it from the Stoics' perspective, may be connected with the special destiny or *daimon* that our life is meant to fulfil, and the wound is a necessary part of that destiny. What would Chiron look like as a symbol of vocation?

Audience: A healer of some kind. A teacher.

Liz: Yes, that's often how it works out. But healing and teaching aren't limited to the helping professions. Chiron is also a musician, and the ancient Greeks believed music was a paradigm of the harmonious order of the cosmos and could soothe the soul and reconnect it with its divine origin. Teaching and healing can be expressed through creative work like music, literature, poetry, interior and fashion design, and the visual arts, including film as well as painting and sculpture. It can also be expressed through 'mantic' arts such as astrology. Every creative act we offer that brings us and other people joy and helps us to experience what Plato referred to as the 'recollection' of the life of the soul – no matter how humble the form – can reflect the domain of the Sun. And the artist is often a prophet, seeing far ahead into the future and offering a vision that continues to affect the lives of others long after the artist has shuffled off the mortal coil.

Sun-Chiron people are often secretly convinced that no one will appreciate or want what they have to offer as individuals. The resulting anger may be turned inward: the rejection has happened because we just aren't good enough. Or the rage and pain may be directed against the world, which appears as a hostile place full of fools who are too stupid, callous, and insensitive to appreciate the truth of our vision. That's the dark face of the aspect. But natal Sun-Chiron can also reflect a courageous commitment to an individual destiny that is catalysed by the chronic feeling of being an outsider. Our wounds can lead us to compensate for the pain, just as the mythic Chiron initially tries every skill in his arsenal to heal his poisoned wound. Sun-Chiron's compensation for loneliness, isolation, and low self-esteem may be to offer something to others that is special, unique, and often visionary. And they often succeed at it. That's the teleology of the aspect.

The outsider may be a healer, a teacher, a prophet, an artist, or a lone voice that sees further than others and understands the nature of human imperfection, suffering, and darkness. Often people with a strong natal Sun-Chiron aspect feel both damaged and chosen. This is the archetypal Scapegoat, who is both despised and recognised as a vessel for a deeper or higher reality. The ancient symbol of the priest-king, which is part of Chiron's myth, reflects this theme. Later in the seminar I'm going to explore Sun-Chiron in the charts of some members of the British royal family, and we'll see how this natal aspect appears with surprising frequency down the generations.

In Jung's chart the Sun forms an out-of-sign square with Chiron. Chiron is at 26° Aries in the 3rd house, conjunct Neptune in early Taurus and square the Sun at 3° Leo in the 7th. Jung wrote at length about the loneliness of increased consciousness and the suffering of the outsider burdened with being able to see too much yet unable to communicate it to those who can't comprehend it. Freud, who didn't have a natal Sun-Chiron aspect, was born an outsider through being a Jew in the deeply antisemitic culture of *fin-de-siècle* Catholic Vienna. Freud could never 'belong' no matter what he might have tried to become. And he certainly suffered, not only because of his Jewish background but also for expressing ideas that were perceived as deeply unpalatable and even unspeakable. He could be domineering, intractable, and authoritarian. But he never backed away from expressing confidently and openly his vision of the hidden dimensions of the human psyche.

Jung, in contrast, was socially acceptable within the framework of his Swiss Protestant culture. He came from a middle-class family with respectable parents. He wasn't judged an outsider by his collective. But he inexplicably felt like an outsider from early childhood and experienced a lifelong sense of isolation and rejection, by others and by himself, of the individual he really was – a prophet, an artist, and a visionary as well as a scientist. His visionary gifts may, in part, reflect his natal Sun-Neptune square, but the painful and enduring sense of isolation belongs to Chiron. In consequence Jung was often less than honest about his real views, especially the importance of the esoteric world in which he was so deeply involved. Through most of his life, Jung lacked Freud's courage to face a potentially critical public. But he exhibited a different kind of courage by working doggedly with his inner wounds in a ruthlessly honest way, as he demonstrated in *The Red Book*. He is a good example of the erratic and painful but immensely creative journey Sun-Chiron can pursue if the individual remains loyal to the *daimon*.

Chiron in synastry, Example 1: King Edward VIII and Wallis Simpson

These are the birth charts of King Edward VIII and his wife Wallis Simpson, known to history as the Duke and Duchess of Windsor. Their story is well-documented and has provided fuel for several film and television documentaries and dramatizations, most recently the first two series of the Netflix production, *The Crown*. For those of you who might not be familiar with the story, here is a brief synopsis.

King Edward VIII abdicated the British throne in 1936, not long after the death of his father King George V. Although he became King at the moment of his father's demise, he hadn't yet been ceremonially crowned. He walked away from his royal destiny because he wasn't permitted to marry Wallis Simpson, an American divorcée, and still remain on the throne. The marriage was opposed by Parliament and the Church of England as well as by the royal family. Wallis had been divorced twice, and her abrasive manner made her deeply disliked by almost everyone of any importance. Although Edward's charm and popularity had won over large segments of the public, it ultimately made no difference. His insistence on marrying 'the woman I love' resulted in his exile and the loss of most of his titles, as well as a radical diminishing of his income and the collapse of his family relationships.

The couple eventually settled in France, where various members of the royal family visited him shortly before his death in May 1972. But he was *persona non grata* in Britain. It's likely that Edward often felt bitter regret about his decision to abdicate. At first he continued to hope that his brother, now King George VI, would relent and acknowledge Wallis, and he tried various machinations to get back into the country. After his brother's death Edward tried to persuade his niece, now Queen Elizabeth II, to increase his income and grant Wallis the official honour and titles he felt she deserved. He insisted that Wallis be known as 'Her Royal Highness' in recognition of her marriage to a former king. But this wish was never granted.

Edward's family never forgave him for the repudiation of his royal responsibilities and the scandal and emotional pain it caused. His brother George, a shy and introverted man, had wanted and expected a quiet family life as the 'spare', rather than suddenly being thrust onto the throne as Edward's successor at a time when Hitler had risen to power and another war with Germany loomed on the horizon. But the Windsors' involvement

Wallis, Duchess of Windsor and Prince Edward, Duke of Windsor (King Edward VIII). Photo by Dorothy Wilding, 2 June 1943, ©National Portrait Gallery.

with the Nazis during the Second World War was a far deeper offence. Documents discovered in Germany after the war, known as the Marburg Files, provided strong evidence that Edward had made a pact with Hitler to reinstate him on the British throne once his country had been bombed into submission. Popular history has cast Wallis Simpson as the evil temptress and Edward the pliable victim snared by her wiles. Her dominance over him was reputed to be sexual. This photograph appears to confirm the popular view through their expressions and postures. But the reality may have been far more complex. Relationship dynamics, especially those involving Chiron, usually are.

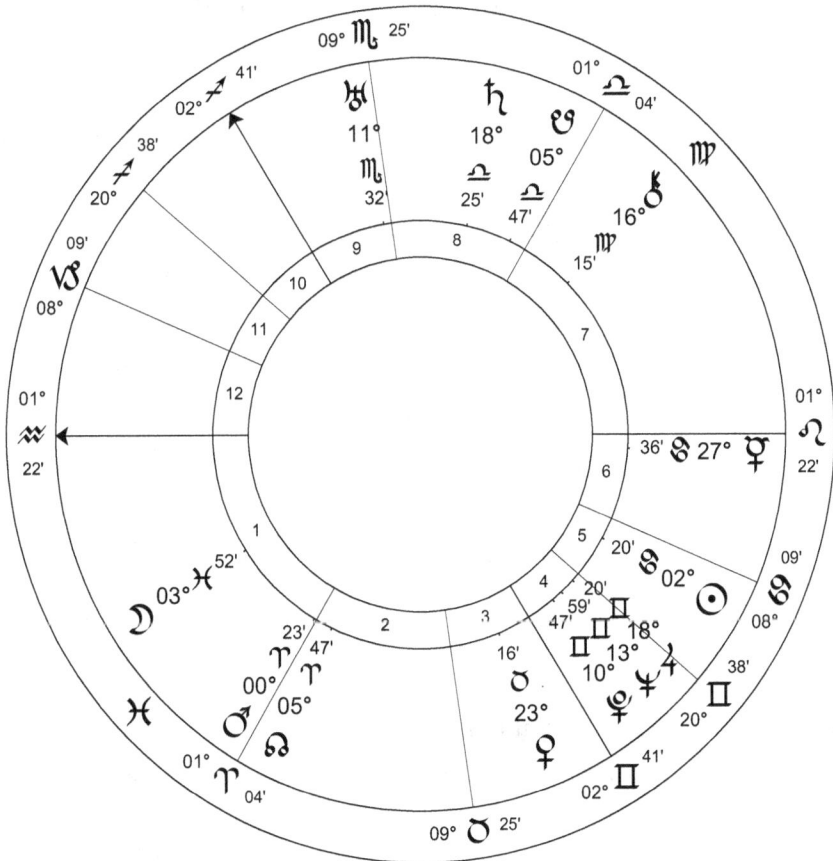

King Edward VIII
23 June 1894, 9.55 pm, Richmond Park, UK

Let's look at Chiron in each natal chart before we consider the synastry. In Edward's chart, Chiron is at 16° Virgo in the 7th house. It squares a
Pluto-Jupiter-Neptune conjunction in Gemini which straddles the 4th and
5th houses, makes a wide trine to Venus in Taurus in the 3rd house, and
sextiles Uranus in Scorpio in the 9th house. It forms no aspects to either
the Sun or the Moon, nor is it on an angle. Placed in the 7th, we might
expect Chiron's themes to be projected onto partners and experienced
through relationships with individuals and with the public.

In Wallis Simpson's chart, natal Chiron is at 20° Libra in the 8th house,
within a degree of exact conjunction with the Moon at 21° Libra. It closely
opposes Mars at 21° Aries in the 2nd house and forms trines to a stellium
in Gemini: Pluto at 12°, Mercury at 16°, Neptune at 18°, Venus at 23° –
all in the 4th house – and Sun at 29° Gemini in the 5th. It's also trine the
Ascendant at 18° Aquarius. Chiron dominates this chart, aspecting both
luminaries, the Ascendant, and the chart ruler, Saturn, as well as every
personal planet except Jupiter and every outer planet including Uranus,
with which it forms a semi-sextile. If Edward was seeking a partner who
could offer him a Chiron experience, he certainly found one.

Would anyone like to comment on Chiron in either of these
natal charts?

Audience: I'm having trouble understanding Chiron in the signs. Would
Chiron in Virgo mean that he would feel wounded through his body
or his work?

Liz: Think of Chiron's natal sign as the sphere of life in which the mythic
Centaur, before his injury, expressed his skills most creatively and fruitfully.
This sphere reflects his ideal of a perfect world, now irrevocably lost. The
possibility of experiencing that ideal world has been torn away from him
through hard, painful experience, and that constitutes the wound. The
domain of Chiron's natal sign is a kind of lost paradise, an idealised vision
of what might and should have been. It's coupled with a profound feeling of

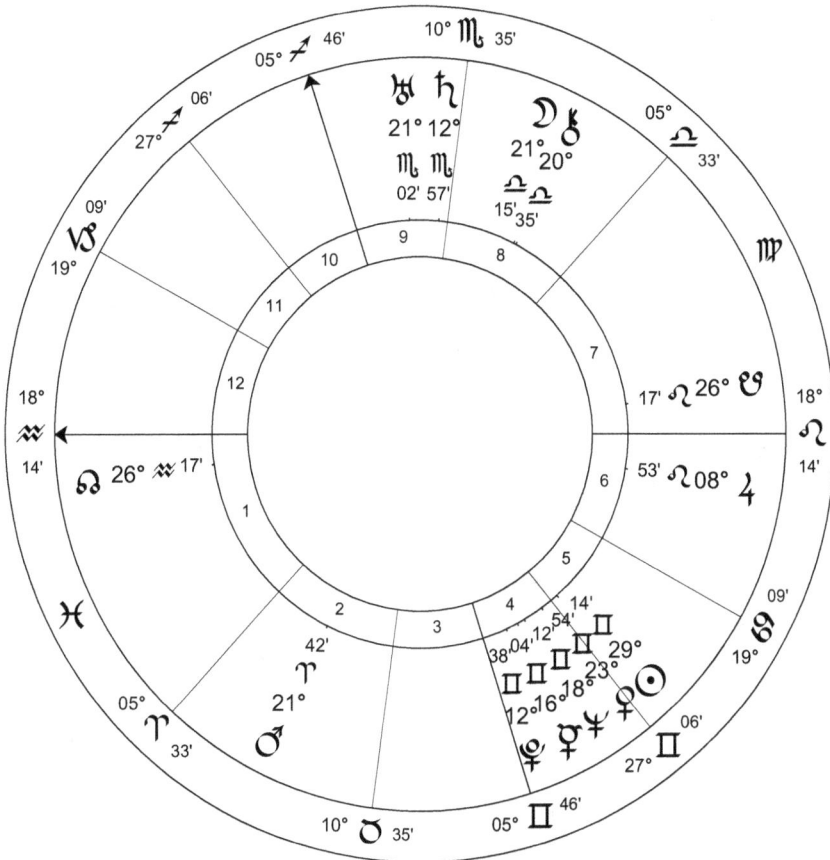

Wallis Simpson
19 June 1896, 10.30 pm, Blue Ridge Summit, Pennsylvania

unmerited injury, deprivation, and disillusionment. It's as though we dimly sense what we could have become, but life's unfairness has ensured that we can never achieve it in its ideal form. It's damaged beyond repair.

Audience: So are you suggesting that with Chiron, we remember a former life?

Liz: No, I'm not suggesting that. I'm speaking metaphorically, not literally. Even if you embrace the idea of reincarnation, all the people born with Chiron in a particular sign – not to mention all the animals, trees, insects, and companies born at that moment under the same configuration – are unlikely to have had former lives with identical wounds. I'm not saying that reincarnation isn't a valid worldview. But if it is, looking at one planet's zodiacal sign is unlikely to tell us much. It's too simplistic and literal an approach.

Chiron's lost paradise is personal, but it's also the crushed dream of a generation group, reflecting the collective events and psychological currents synchronous with the moment of birth. Chiron, like the outer planets, can symbolise generation groups, although some of them are small ones. Chiron takes fifty years to move through the zodiac, but its orbit, like that of Pluto, is elliptical, and it travels very quickly through some of the signs. Its fastest sojourns take place in Virgo and Libra, while it moves most slowly through Pisces and Aries.

Generation groups: Chiron in Virgo and Libra

Planetary generation groups are obviously not the same as biological generation groups. A planetary generation encompasses patterns, meanings, and experiences reflected in the collective psyche by a planet's position in a particular zodiacal sign at the moment of birth. It's a _psychological_ generation group characterised by certain attitudes and responses, rather than a specific age group such as 'Baby Boomers' or 'Millennials'. A Pluto generation, as it moves through Taurus, encompasses thirty years of births; a Chiron generation, as it moves through Virgo, encompasses births occurring during a period of a little over two years. But the fact that these are small groups doesn't diminish their importance.

Collective attitudes, experiences, responses, and interpretations of events occurring during that transit are encapsulated within the individuals born under the transit. We all have a little piece of history within us. The best way to gain insight into our Chiron generation is to look at what was happening in the world, on both concrete and psychological levels, during the time Chiron moved through the sign in which it's placed natally. Think about the political landscape, the moral climate, the social values, the trends in fashion, music, and film, the scientific and technological discoveries, the natural disasters, and the religious attitudes of the time; and then think about the ways in which these collective currents and trends might have been unfair, hypocritical, disillusioning, and destructive. We all bear within us the qualities of our moment of birth. We might say that during the course of Chiron's transit through each sign, a sense of collective wounding is experienced in a specific arena of life according to Chiron's natal house placement and aspects.

Chiron generation groups reflect a certain set of ideals – our very own vision of a lost paradise – and an acutely sensitive response to experiences of suffering and unfairness, both personal and collective, that shatter that paradise in the sphere symbolised by natal Chiron's sign. We might not always be conscious of our collective Chiron responses, especially if natal Chiron collides with the individual values represented by the personal planets in the chart. That can be true of any planet when we aren't conscious of it within ourselves. Chiron is often deeply buried because it's so uncomfortable to look into the wounded Centaur's cave.

Think about what Virgo values most. What does this sign idealise above all else?

Audience: Service.

Liz: Yes, Virgo aspires to be useful in a world that cries out for order, knowledge, common sense, service to others, and respect for natural cycles. This is the lost paradise of Chiron in Virgo. It's painfully attuned to the ignorance, squalor, and indolence of society and the chaos, mess, and arrogant self-entitlement of human nature. Competence, skill, and learning are idealised, but the chronic expectation of failure and the fear of collective criticism can undermine the person's confidence and well-being, physically and psychologically. Chiron in Virgo wants to contribute something of value that can help to create a well-functioning, orderly world. But it seems as though the world always stamps on this dream and berates the skills and abilities the person tries to bring to it. Chiron in Virgo longs to be of service, but no one appears to want the service it offers.

Audience: So he was a very sensitive man, especially with Sun in Cancer and Moon in Pisces.

Liz: Yes, I believe he was. But the sensitivity of the water signs doesn't automatically include a moral conscience, especially if that sensitivity is primarily about one's own feelings and doesn't include acknowledgement of the feelings of others. Nothing in a natal chart can tell us about whether the individual possesses a moral conscience, or whether they will choose to utilise their abilities in creative or destructive ways.

Some years ago, during a seminar I gave on the ambiguous nature of trines, I put up a chart without revealing the name of the individual. The element of water is dominant in that chart, with a grand trine between Sun and Mercury in Pisces in the 10th house, Neptune in the 1st house in Cancer conjunct a Cancer Ascendant, and Jupiter in the 5th house in Scorpio. Chiron is also in Pisces, in the 9th house and out of orb of conjunction with the Sun and Mercury. Chiron makes no aspects to the inner planets. It's sextile Saturn in Taurus in the 11th house, in an out-of-sign trine to Pluto in Gemini in the 12th, and sesquiquadrate Neptune in Cancer in the 1st.

When I asked for comments, most people talked about the sensitivity, compassion, and kindness indicated by all those trines in water, and the spirituality of all those planets in Pisces. The chart we were exploring was that of Josef Mengele, known as the Angel of Death: Hitler's chief medical officer, who performed sadistic experiments on Jewish prisoners at Auschwitz, especially children. After I revealed the name of the individual, there was a long, horrified silence among the seminar participants. I wasn't trying to make anyone feel foolish. But I did want to make the point that a birth chart can't tell us whether an individual will choose to become a force for good or evil. It can only symbolise the ways in which that individual will express whatever lies latent in the soul. Mengele, according to one Auschwitz survivor, was exceptionally kind and empathetic to the children whom he was about to butcher. He would bring them their favourite ice cream and tell them charming stories, before the surgical instruments came out.

Chiron disconnected

Audience: What do you think it means if Chiron is unaspected or weakly aspected? Or when it doesn't aspect any personal planets, like Mengele's Chiron?

Liz: Any planet that is excluded from relationships with other planets, especially the personal planets, tends to be deeply unconscious. That planet is the outsider who can never join the club. Sometimes it reflects a creative gift that seems to erupt autonomously, like someone normally pragmatic and rational who suddenly begins to write exquisite, deeply moving mystical poetry but can never explain how and can't produce it on demand. Sometimes what erupts is not so pleasant and may reveal the darker face of the planet. Sometimes it's a combination of both.

A lot depends on the nature of the planet. If the autonomous planet is Chiron, it may, at its best, reflect a surprising and remarkable healing or teaching gift that seems to have come out of nowhere. Mengele was a gifted physician who had won many academic awards. The sextile between his Chiron in Pisces and Saturn in Taurus might suggest the ability to harness Chiron's skills in practical ways, which he certainly did, albeit cruelly and viciously. But equally, a disconnected Chiron can become a destroyer out of unconscious rage and envy, without the person ever being aware of how deeply embittered and poisonous they are. It's the personal planets that encourage us to recognise and integrate such corrosive feelings. But unconscious compulsions, when they erupt, have a way of feeling like absolute truths, even while they are eroding the last vestiges of our individual values.

A weakly aspected Chiron doesn't mean it's weak; it will still reflect an intractable wound. It's still Chiron. But the wound may lie on the level of the collective unconscious and hasn't been processed consciously through reflection on painful personal experiences. It seems to symbolise an unconscious complex, rooted in the pain and rage of the collective psyche, that can invade and take over the personality without the individual realising it. An unintegrated Chiron may draw heavily on the collective psyche for its fuel, and it can be triggered and brought to life by a major transit or by planets in another person's chart.

Our individual Chiron placements are always open to collective as well as personal feelings of wounding, hurt, and damage. The first usually underpins and inflames the second, heightening the sense of a pain that isn't entirely, or even primarily, our own. Chiron occupies a unique place in the solar system, with an elliptical path that first crosses Saturn's orbit and then swings just inside Uranus' orbit during the course of its cycle. True to the hybrid nature of the Centaur, it symbolically bridges the personal domain of Saturn and the collective domain of Uranus. Mythically, this is entirely appropriate, since Chiron is the son of Kronos and the grandson of Ouranos, and he partakes of both.

The astrological Chiron carries a long past behind it, and it's important to distinguish between our own individual experiences and those which are 'inherited' from the family and the collective psyche of our cultural background. Understanding history – our own, that of our family, and that of our culture – is vitally important. But we can distort and misinterpret history because our personal feelings of injury cloud the lens through which we view and interpret it. There is an academic field of study called historiography, which explores the different agendas that historians have brought to their purportedly objective accounts of the past. Even the historiographers themselves have agendas. But without some effort at discernment, we can easily slide into a kind of mob mentality of catalogued grievances that distort history, erode personal values, undermine the fruits of individual experience, and make any genuine healing virtually impossible.

The self-inflicted wound

By mentioning the water sign emphasis in both Edward's and Mengele's charts earlier, I hope you all realise that I'm not suggesting King Edward VIII was remotely like Josef Mengele, who was a sociopath of the most malignant kind. Edward, by all accounts, was a man capable of deep and genuine love and kindness, and he was greatly loved by many people. But he didn't always display a moral conscience. Perhaps there were times when he just chose to ignore it. He *was* highly sensitive, but primarily about his own feelings. He never really understood the emotional as well as material impact of his actions on his brother and his brother's children, nor comprehend why they couldn't forgive him. In his youth he had a reputation as a callous womaniser. He was adept at emotional blackmail. He could be cunning, deceitful, avaricious, spiteful, and manipulative, and he made some very bad choices, not least in allying himself with the Third Reich while his country was suffering and at war.

If Hitler had won and the evidence of the Marburg Files is valid, Edward's brother King George VI, his sister-in-law Queen Elizabeth, and his nieces, the princesses Elizabeth and Margaret, would probably have been imprisoned and executed by the Nazi regime. Edward either refused to acknowledge this possibility or found himself able to countenance it if it meant he could be King again with Wallis as his Queen. That's rather frightening. But it doesn't mean he wasn't also capable of being a sensitive and often decent man.

Edward believed he couldn't fulfil his role as King without Wallis at his side. He relied on her to provide him with the confidence he lacked.

Natal Chiron in the 7ᵗʰ house suggests that he perceived Wallis as the blameless victim of a malign conspiracy, and felt personally scapegoated and victimised himself when Church, State, and family united to thwart his wishes. Traditionally the 7ᵗʰ house can describe 'open enemies' as well as partnerships, and Edward made many enemies. He categorically refused to accept the suggestion of a morganatic marriage, a union in which he could wed Wallis and remain King but couldn't pass his title and privileges to his wife or to any children by the marriage. He insisted that Wallis be fully recognised as his Queen Consort. His choice of partner was problematic enough, but the inflexibility and bitter outrage with which he tossed aside this reasonable compromise ensured that he couldn't avoid the experience of permanent wounding. In that sense, he created his own fate.

What do you think about Wallis' Chiron in Libra?

Audience: The lost ideal would be justice and fairness.

Liz: I agree, that's a big part of it. Libra is the perfectionist of the zodiac. Some astrologers see Virgo as a perfectionist, but as an earthy sign, Virgo is interested in making things work, including the warts, and not in an ideal of perfection. For Chiron in Libra, the lost paradise is a realm of perfect harmony, beauty, civilised behaviour, and friendly cooperation among individuals and between nations. In Libra's ideal world, no one has a shadow. The complexity and ambiguity of human emotions, especially cruelty, boorishness, and spite, are perceived as a constant wound to the ideal. Wallis felt the behaviour of Edward's family toward her was cruel and vindictive. She failed to notice these same qualities in Hitler and his acolytes, or in Edward's mocking and contemptuous behaviour toward his family.

With all Chiron placements, we may project the real source of the wound: our inability to reconcile our ideals with the realities of life and of ourselves. We may turn our rage toward those we perceive as the villains, rather than looking within at the ways in which we unconsciously amplify and even create our own misery. Edward viewed the royal establishment as a cold, dreary, soulless machine that ground down individual feelings and imagination. He projected his natal Chiron on them, rather than recognizing his criticisms as a distorted image of his own feelings of mediocrity and incompetence. Wallis perceived the royal family as a nest of poisonous vipers, full of ugly emotions as well as appalling bad taste. She projected her natal Chiron on them, rather than facing her own feelings of coarseness, ugliness, and social inferiority.

Chiron in Libra generation groups are acutely attuned to the brutishness and aggression in other people. It feels as though life perpetually smashes the ideal, dragging cherished dreams through the dirt and spoiling everything gracious and elegant with unfairness, cruelty, and incomprehensible emotional demands. Wallis' natal Chiron is in the 8th, so she probably experienced a sense of damage through her intimate relationships, not only sexual but also parental. Her previous two marriages as well as her family history may have taught her that emotional and sexual vulnerability leads to misery, loneliness, and abandonment. She lost her father shortly after her birth. Her first marriage to Earl Winfield Spencer, a heavy drinker, was punctuated by long periods of separation and ended in divorce. Her second marriage to Ernest Aldrich Simpson seems to have been based more on financial benefit than on any deep emotional bond. She met and became involved with Edward while she was still married to Simpson, whom she divorced in the hope that her third marriage might bring her the longed-for happiness that had always eluded her.

Now let's look at the Chiron aspects between the charts. Edward's natal Saturn at 18° 25' Libra in the 8th house is in close conjunction with Wallis' Moon-Chiron conjunction in Libra in her 8th house. What do you make of these two difficult planets, Saturn and Chiron, in conjunction across the charts and also involving her natal Moon? And in the most obscure and mysterious of all the houses in the horoscope?

Saturn–Chiron aspects in synastry

Audience: It looks really unpleasant, but I don't understand what it means. You said earlier that it was their sexual relationship that was rumoured to be the thing that bound them.

Liz: Yes, the general belief at the time, and even today, is that Wallis dominated Edward sexually and he became addicted to this aspect of the relationship. There may be some truth in that interpretation, but it isn't likely to be the only one. Edward's Saturn is conjunct Wallis' Moon as well as her Chiron, and it also opposes her Mars. We need to consider these aspects as part of the dynamic. What does a Moon–Saturn contact in synastry suggest?

Audience: It's very binding. Very loyal. He would dominate her emotions, and maybe reject them or show coldness sometimes, but he would also give her emotional stability.

Liz: Yes, I agree. The question of dominance isn't one-sided, and it may have more to do with mutual dependency than with control. Edward's Saturn in Libra in the 8th suggests that, like Wallis, he feared deep emotional intimacy, especially if it unleashed powerful emotions inimical to Libra's longing for civilised refinement. He might have created barriers against any exposure of intense feeling, particularly in sexual relationships. This could be connected with his reputation as a womaniser; this behaviour pattern is often a defence against intimacy because it provides protection against Saturn's vulnerability. Shallow encounters with lots of people are less threatening than one deep encounter with someone who could penetrate the protective shell.

Audience: So she did penetrate the shell, with her Moon and Chiron on his Saturn and her Mars opposing it.

Liz: Yes, she certainly did. Both these people probably experienced profound feelings of wounding and deprivation in the sphere of deep emotional bonds, including early experiences with family members. Their mutual needs reflect Libra's longing to be appreciated and valued in a world where unpleasant emotions, dark undercurrents, and sudden loss or abandonment can't intrude. Wallis' Moon-Chiron in the 8th suggests that although she badly needed emotional and sexual closeness as a form of security, like Edward she also feared it and preferred to disconnect from her feelings – a skill at which Moon in Libra often excels – rather than experiencing the suffering of disappointed needs. It's helpful to keep in mind the early loss of the father she never knew and probably idealised, suggested by the stellium of Pluto, Neptune, Mercury, and Venus in her 4th house.

For Wallis, emotional dependency was fraught with the danger of rejection, humiliation, and abandonment. In her first marriage she was often literally abandoned because her husband travelled constantly for his work, and his alcoholism may have resulted in periodic bouts of impotence. I don't know whether he was ever violent toward her, but it's a possibility; or he may have exhibited emotional violence, which can be devastating in a different way because it's less recognisable and more insidious. Perhaps Edward and Wallis could understand and empathise with each other's defensiveness and fear of injury in intimate relationships.

Saturn-Chiron synastry aspects are certainly difficult, but perhaps not as negative as we might expect. Outsiders can often bond through shared loneliness and shared grievances. The dependency was mutual, as was the terrible vulnerability. With her natal Chiron and Moon in Libra, Wallis was a perfectionist not only in her need to find beauty and elegance in life, but also in her longing to feel beautiful herself. Although she enjoyed many affairs during and between her prior two marriages, Wallis was not an attractive woman according to the standards of the time. The press was often unkind about her appearance, especially as she was approaching middle age and couldn't compete with the fresh young beauties with whom

Edward had habitually surrounded himself. Her ability to bear him a healthy child was also called into question, as forty was at that time considered a dangerous age to become a mother. If Edward found her beautiful, it would have gone a long way toward helping her find greater confidence.

It isn't possible to know the truth about who dominated whom, or whether domination was really the core component in the relationship. I'm not convinced it was. It's an easy default interpretation that offers the luxury of clearly differentiating the villain from the victim. But as the saying goes, it takes two to tango, and collusion – conscious or unconscious – always needs to be considered in an enduring relationship like this one.

Various film and television portrayals have presented Wallis' demands as the relentless force behind Edward's insistence that she be given full recognition as his Queen. Since this was never going to happen and everybody knew it, it was a self-destructive path to take. Wallis is often portrayed as ruthlessly ambitious and determined to defeat her perceived enemies. But her chart is overweighted in the element of air and doesn't display overt ambition in any obvious way. There are no planets in the 10th house, no planets in Capricorn, and no aspects between Saturn and either the Sun or Jupiter, the ruler of the 10th house. These are the most obvious significators of a desire to be someone important and effectual in the world.

I don't believe Wallis was motivated by the prospect of winning a crown. She longed for emotional constancy, kindness, and security, the three things she had been denied since childhood. But her Saturn is in Scorpio, a placement not known for its ability to forgive or forget emotional wounds. Sometimes Saturn in Scorpio can reflect relentlessly spiteful behaviour as a way of taking vengeance on perceived enemies. And Edward's Saturn on her Moon-Chiron may have reflected his own determined effort to offer fatherly protection to someone he perceived as terribly vulnerable. Offering that protection made him feel strong. The stubborn intractability Edward displayed may have been more his own contribution than hers.

Moon-Saturn contacts can be deeply binding, but they aren't always easy. A conjunction between charts might be easier to work with than a square or opposition, both of which can highlight Saturn's tendency to be critical or cold toward the Moon as a defence against the fear of rejection. And Saturn can envy the Moon's ability to express in a natural way qualities that are much more difficult for Saturn to display without self-consciousness. It's not a comfortable synastry aspect because the emotional chill can infect both people, sometimes due to Saturnian pride concealing vulnerable feelings and sometimes due to Saturn's envy arousing a desire to hurt, undermine, and control.

Saturn can also find it hard to let the Moon enjoy any spontaneous emotional expression. It will happily spoil the party if the Moon seems to be having too much fun in activities Saturn can't participate in. Yet the aspect in synastry, including the square and opposition, often appears in close, enduring friendships. I believe Edward and Wallis, both badly damaged by backgrounds they felt had trampled on their emotional needs and dreams, were enduring friends as much as they were passionate lovers, especially as they got older and had to accept the humiliation of defeat and exile.

This couple's Chiron synastry isn't all doom and gloom and heavy emotional baggage. Edward's natal Jupiter at 18° 21' Gemini, trine his natal Saturn, is also trine Wallis' Moon-Chiron conjunction. He could make her laugh and brought an element of humour and wit into the relationship. Jupiter in Gemini can sparkle with charm and sophistication, and it conjuncts most of the planets in Wallis' stellium, including her Mercury and Venus. They both loved living in beautiful, luxurious surroundings with a crowd of cultured, sophisticated people around them.

With natal Mercury conjunct Pluto as well as Moon conjunct Chiron, Wallis may have been inclined to bouts of severe depression, although she might not always have been aware of it. She may have simply drunk too much or hurled herself into extravagant shopping and lavish parties to escape what Winston Churchill, who had Mercury opposite Pluto, used to refer to as his 'black dog'. Edward could lighten the darkness and bring genuine fun into her life, even if his Saturn spoiled it later. The trine between his Jupiter and her Chiron may have led them to indulge in a lifelong self-pity party. But Jupiter can also bring out the philosophical inclinations latent in Chiron, helping to foster a broader perspective with less focus on personal grievances. It seems that Edward could infuse the relationship with a quality of hopefulness that allowed Wallis to believe she wasn't as dreadful and damaged as she sometimes felt.

Mercury-Chiron aspects in synastry

Edward's Chiron in Virgo squares most of Wallis' stellium in Gemini. The square between his Chiron and her Mercury is exact. What do you make of this square?

Audience: Maybe he sometimes felt unintelligent around her. He had Mercury in Cancer, so his way of communicating wasn't as sharp as hers. And maybe her Venus in Gemini did the same thing. She could be flirtatious and fickle. He had Venus in Taurus, so once his heart was given, he was loyal.

Liz: Yes, all that makes a lot of sense. But try to be clear about how you define 'loyalty'. Different signs have different definitions of it. Sexual loyalty may be essential for some people but not for others. Emotional loyalty, of the kind where you need to know that someone will always take your side and watch your back, is also a requirement for some people but not others. Venus in Gemini can be deeply loyal, although it might not display the possessive intensity of Venus in Scorpio or the chivalrous nobility of Venus in Leo. And there's nothing in the cosmic rulebook that says that Venus in Taurus is always sexually faithful. But you made a very good point earlier.

The Chiron person can often feel intellectually inferior to the Mercury person if these two planets form a strong aspect in synastry.

Mercury isn't only about intellect. It's also about our style of communicating and the way in which we learn and process information. Mercury in Gemini isn't necessarily academically brilliant, but it has the capacity to find the right word at the right moment, and it can be gifted at repartee. There is also often an ease of learning, including practical things like how to change a tyre or replace a fuse. Chiron in Virgo can reflect a gnawing sense of incompetence, not only about practical things but also in terms of learning. There's often a feeling that one has to struggle to understand things, or that what one says will come across to others as stupid, silly, or dull.

In the best of worlds, the Chiron person could learn a great deal from the Mercury person about engaging with others in a fluent and light-hearted way. Gemini is often a master of the art of 'small talk' and the ability to say everything while revealing nothing. Mercury can learn a lot from Chiron about depth of thought and the importance of valuing those who aren't naturally chatty or comfortable engaging in superficial conversation. It's like a union between a historian and a journalist: they can enhance each other's self-expression if they understand the value of each other's contribution.

Sadly, we don't live in the best of worlds. This synastry aspect can often reflect nasty spats and vituperative exchanges if Chiron verbally attacks Mercury and projects its own feelings of being tongue-tied and incompetent to try to make Mercury feel slow or useless. A defensive Chiron can also wilfully misunderstand Mercury's motives and cling to the assumption that everything Mercury says is meant to hurt, and that there is a deliberate and malicious intent to diminish Chiron's confidence.

This rather paranoid response might have no basis whatsoever in reality, but the perceptions of the wounded Centaur aren't always objective and reasonable. Chiron's envy and expectation of being under permanent attack can destroy the fabric of the relationship, and Mercury isn't known for its staying power in the face of complicated emotional demands. The Mercury person is capable of biting repartee and a quick exit, literally by packing a bag and vanishing or metaphorically by simply cutting off communication. Edward and Wallis did stick together, and other synastry aspects, especially all the trines in air signs, must have helped to dilute the acid. But I don't think I would have enjoyed being in the room when they began to argue. It would have been like a scene from Edward Albee's *Who's Afraid of Virginia Woolf.*

When Chiron and Mercury form an aspect in the natal chart, this dynamic can take place internally. The feeling of being unintelligent or inarticulate may be extremely painful, especially if it's triggered by difficulties in early education or by a sibling who's noticeably quicker and cleverer by conventional standards. If anger and envy build up enough heat inside, words can become the vehicle for a defensive attack on anyone who is perceived as condescending, patronising, or even just smarter or more capable than oneself. Depression can also be an unwelcome but regular visitor. If Mercury-Chiron unfailingly displays cheerful optimism, it's probably a performance. But there is also the potential to dig deeply, think out of the box, and develop a rich understanding of the inner patterns that underpin human suffering.

Not surprisingly, Freud is a good example of the creative use of the aspect. Freud's Mercury is at 27° Taurus in the 7th house in an out-of-sign trine to Chiron at 5° Aquarius in the 3rd house. This Chiron-Mercury aspect echoes the placement of natal Chiron in the 3rd house, traditionally associated with Mercury. The wound of being a permanent outsider unable to easily communicate with others helped to fuel his determination to understand the motives behind human behaviour. Whatever more esoterically inclined astrologers might feel about Freud's intellectual dogmatism and apparent antipathy toward the spiritual realm, depth psychology wouldn't exist without him, and Jung's work would never have fully flowered if they hadn't worked together.

The Chiron synastry aspects between Freud's chart and Jung's are worth exploring. Here are the charts, although I'll only touch on them briefly.

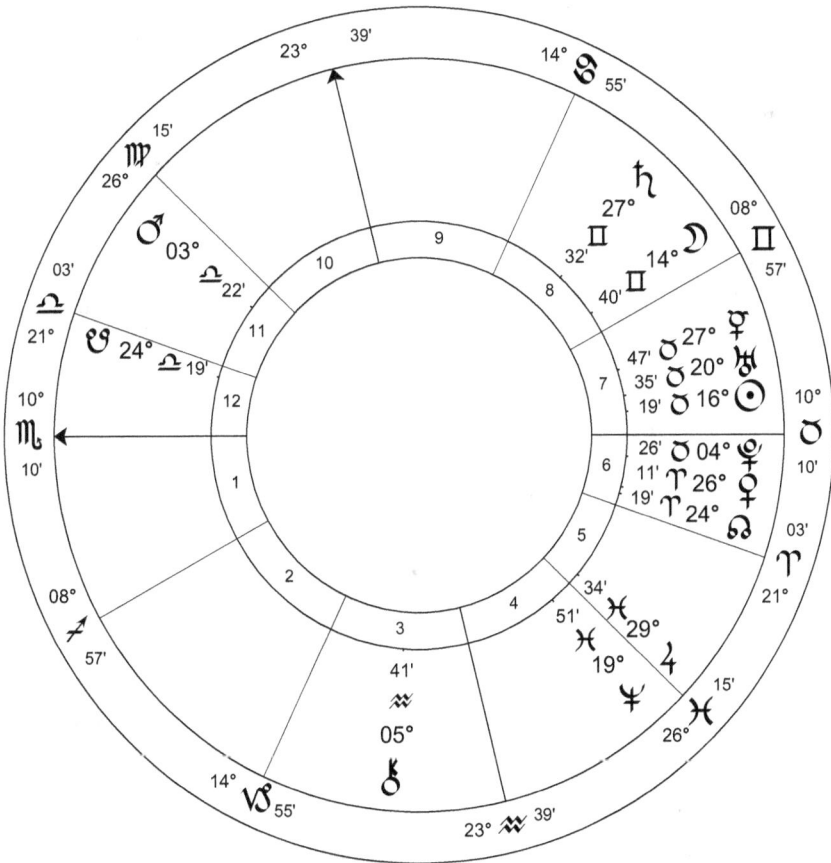

Sigmund Freud
6 May 1856, 6.30 pm, Freiberg/Mähren, CZ

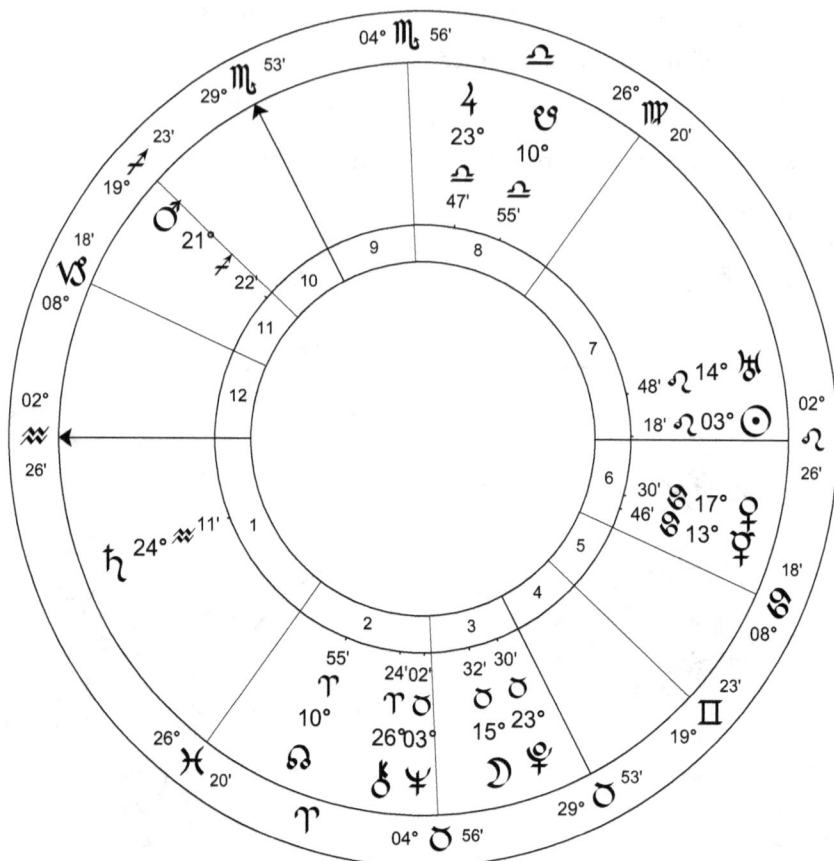

C. G. Jung
26 July 1875, 7.24 pm, Kesswil, CH

Although this wasn't a love relationship in any erotic sense, it was close, intense, inspiring, challenging, and shaped the futures of both men. In Jung's chart there is no natal aspect between Mercury and Chiron as there is in Freud's. But Jung's natal Sun at 3° Leo is in close opposition to Freud's Chiron, Jung's Ascendant at 1° Aquarius conjuncts it, and Jung's Neptune at 3° Taurus squares it. I have no doubt that Freud felt bitter envy as well as deep admiration and affection toward his wayward disciple. Their Sun-Chiron aspect illustrates what I described earlier about these planets in synastry. Freud started off as Jung's mentor, but he was determined to stop Jung from becoming what he actually was – a mystic as well as a scientist – and in the end this repudiation of an essential aspect of Jung's nature helped to push Jung into affirming that he was both. The relationship ended in acrimony, which was probably necessary for Jung to define his own psychological vision. Because of both the relationship and its fracturing, both men grew in stature and in the sophistication and breadth of their work.

Freud (first row, left) and Jung (first row, right) at Clark University, Worcester, Massachusetts in September 1909. Library of Congress.

Venus-Chiron aspects in synastry

Let's go back to the Windsors and look at the square between Edward's Chiron and Wallis' Venus. Venus, unlike the Moon, doesn't reflect instinctual and emotional needs. It describes our sense of self-worth and self-esteem, which we experience as lovability. When we see what we value embodied in someone else, we love, admire, and appreciate them. In a natal chart, Venus strongly aspected to Chiron often reflects a perception of damage to our sense of self-worth. We fear that we will never be fully lovable and that we will be doomed to disappointment in relationship.

A tragic example of this is Marilyn Monroe, who was born with a close out-of-sign conjunction between Venus at 28° Aries and Chiron at 0° Taurus, both in the 9ᵗʰ house but within orb of conjunction with the MC. Most of her childhood was spent in foster homes and orphanages, and the perception of being unwanted and socially inferior left an enduring wound. She was never convinced that she was truly lovable. She felt bitterly disappointed by every man with whom she became involved because none of them could ever offer enough love to heal her wound. No matter how much they demonstrated their devotion, she never felt worthy of it. The more fame she acquired as a symbol of sexual desirability, the more the gap grew between her public image and her low self-esteem.

Another sad example is Michael Jackson, with Venus at 17° Leo in the 6ᵗʰ house opposing Chiron at 19° Aquarius in the 12ᵗʰ. His obsession with perfect physical beauty drove him to literally destroy his face with a succession of cosmetic surgical procedures, each of which left him feeling it still wasn't perfect. He seems to have equated an idealised image of beauty with lovability, perhaps – with Chiron in the 12ᵗʰ in Aquarius – reflecting the marginalisation of his Black family background at a time when racism in America was displayed in particularly brutal ways through segregation in schools and overt discrimination in housing, jobs, government services, and public accommodation. Michael Jackson's wound is ancestral, but he projected it onto his own physical body with tragic results.

With Venus-Chiron, our physical bodies can become a hook for the projection of an inner sense of damage. The medical term 'body dysmorphic disorder' describes a condition in which the individual's perception of their body is seriously distorted, focusing on flaws that are virtually unnoticeable or even non-existent. The term is often associated with anorexia, but it may also apply in situations where excessive cosmetic surgery is felt as the only way to correct perceived imperfections that are in reality symbolic of an inner feeling of injury and unlovability.

Audience: Might the feeling of not meeting a collective standard of beauty be justified? Does it always have to be subjective?

Liz: Yes, it might, and no, it doesn't. Humans can be horribly cruel to each other, and children can be particularly cruel if they perceive someone as an outsider. This behaviour might be due to social, racial, gender-based, religious, or economic differences, physical disability, or some other quality of differentness – including exceptional intelligence or a creative gift – which means the person doesn't meet the prevailing group standard of so-called 'normality'. Some collectives tend to be more intolerant than others. I would like to look more carefully later at the archetypal theme of the Scapegoat, which is closely connected with Chiron, and at the issue of why, as a collective, we humans always seem to need scapegoats, especially if we feel scapegoated ourselves.

Venus-Chiron is often literally scapegoated in early life because of external appearance. It usually isn't only subjective; Chiron needs an external trigger to activate the unfolding of the story, which is often a painful encounter with life's unfairness and with the human potential, which lies in every one of us, for ignorance, spite, and malice. Humans can be very frightened of differentness because it triggers each person's fear of losing the security of the group and having to experience the aloneness of genuine individuality.

Sometimes the extent of feeling wounded depends on whether we've received enough genuine support, love, and encouragement – which are not the same as pity or condescension – from family members and the early school environment. Sometimes a history of family wounds exacerbates the situation. And sometimes a parent who is too dependent on being socially acceptable can make things much worse by expressing disappointment in a child whose appearance doesn't fit social expectations.

Venus-Chiron never forgets such early wounds, which can form the foundation for an ongoing expectation of rejection and hurt. The challenge is to find enough insight, compassion, and self-value to move beyond the feeling of being a perpetual victim. Sadly, if we can't manage this, we may unconsciously create our own isolation by behaving in ways that are unlovable. Venus-Chiron, and Moon-Chiron too, may try to test loved ones in unpleasant ways to see whether they love us enough. This typical Chiron defence mechanism usually backfires badly.

Humans have always been prone to confusion about what constitutes genuine value. On this theme I would recommend that you read a poem by the German author Stefan George, written in 1907, called *The Antichrist* (*Der Widerchrist*). You can find it in various translations online as well as in print. It's eerily prophetic and is even more relevant today than it was when it was written. In Stefan George's chart, natal Chiron is at 0° 19' Aries in the 4th house in an out-of-sign trine to Venus at 26° 54' Cancer in the 9th. Chiron also forms out-of-sign trines to the Sun and Mercury, also in Cancer in the 9th. His understanding of this archetypal human problem was profound on both personal and collective levels.

In the poem, the Antichrist speaks to us in the first person, describing how he will offer humans something that looks and tastes like wine but isn't quite the real thing, and something that looks like gold but is really a fake; but they won't notice the difference. And as they become increasingly incapable of distinguishing what is of value from what is worthless, he will gradually enslave them. Here are a few lines from a translation by Jay Scott:

> There's no work of heaven I do not produce.
> It's off by a hair's breadth, but you are all fooled.
> Your senses have been overmastered.
> In return for what's rare and what's hard I create
> The simple – a semblance of gold from the clay.[32]

---

32 Jay Scott, *Der Widerchrist*, at satirist.org/poetry/text/me/antichrist.html. See also Stefan George, *Poems,* trans. & ed. Carol North Valhope and Ernst Morwitz (Pantheon, 1946).

From all this, I'm sure you can get a sense of how a Venus-Chiron synastry aspect might be expressed in a close relationship. The perceived beauty, charm, and lovability of the Venus person arouses desire, envy, and painful insecurity because an underlying feeling of irrevocable damage is triggered in Chiron. The Chiron person may idealise Venus but may also feel so much resentment that they become destructive, undermining the Venus person's sense of value to assuage a chronic expectation of being deemed unloved and unlovable.

Audience: So in some ways it doesn't matter which planet in the other person's chart aspects our Chiron – we will still feel the wound.

Liz: It matters in the sense that a specific quality or attribute in the other person constellates the wound. But it doesn't matter which planet it is in the sense that the wound will still be triggered. The specific nature of the planet may arouse envy in Chiron, as well as the urge to undermine or injure the other person in particular ways if we act blindly from the reflex of our pain. So yes, we will feel our own damage acutely – although often unconsciously – when in the presence of the other, whatever planet they are bringing to the relationship. Our own wound might not be in the same sphere as theirs, but the experience of irrevocable, unfair damage is an archetypal human experience.

Audience: Is there an upside with Venus-Chiron synastry?

Liz: There's always an upside. Instead of idealising perfection, Venus could learn from Chiron to appreciate those aspects of life that are cyclical and flawed rather than eternal and flawless. Any capable gardener knows that whatever we do, there will always be some blackspot on the roses and some slugs on the hostas. Venus is often attracted to Chiron as a kind of 'diamond in the rough', and the challenge for Venus is to appreciate the roughness as it is rather than trying to perfect it. And Chiron might begin to feel more valued and also more willing to do what Venus does best:

making the most of what's already there, however imperfect, by valuing it, enhancing it, and taking pleasure in it.

Fashion, home décor, and the cultivation of our own individual style, which all belong to Venus' domain, aren't mere vain frivolities, nor are they dependent on material wealth. They can nourish something valuable within us, as long as we don't become obsessive about them and lose our sense of humour. Individual taste, honestly expressed, can reflect our deeper values as much as, or perhaps even more than, loudly proclaimed ideological claims. The longing to create beauty that Venus symbolises isn't shallow or unnatural; it's archetypal. Through an encounter with someone's Venus, Chiron might discover its own individual sense of beauty and value.

Any thoughts about that square between King Edward VIII's Chiron and Wallis Simpson's Venus?

Audience: He would have been enchanted by her. Maybe by her wit and style, even though she was past her youth and wasn't conventionally beautiful.

Liz: Yes, that's a good summary of it, and 'style' is a highly appropriate word to use. Wallis' Venus is in Gemini, so although she wasn't beautiful by the standards of the time, her sparkle, wit, elusiveness, and stylishness must have fascinated him, as did her intriguing 'foreignness', since American women of her background weren't a usual part of his social world. Edward's natal Chiron is in the 7th house, trine his natal Venus. Trines may be less uncomfortable than squares, conjunctions, or oppositions. But they can also be more unconscious because the sense of pain isn't as acute, and pain tends to wake us up. Despite his popularity and his parade of mistresses, deep down he probably felt shy, socially inept, and unable to attract people based on who he really was rather than on the glamour of being the Prince of Wales.

We will probably never know what went on between these two people behind closed doors, not only sexually but also emotionally. It's likely that at various points Edward blamed Wallis bitterly for his isolation, the loss of his throne, and his separation from his family. His feelings of devotion may have been accompanied by deep resentment and a desire to hurt her. On the surface they appeared to be a close and devoted couple, and they created a world of endless socialising with all the trappings of luxury and sophistication. They entertained dignitaries from every nation and were known for their extravagant parties. The bond between them was indestructible, although it came at a very high price.

I'm sure that Edward sometimes made Wallis' life miserable in private with periodic bouts of whining, carping, criticism, sulks, and coldness, reflecting his Chiron in Virgo square her natal Venus. He was capable of sapping all the pleasure from situations where she wanted to enjoy herself. He may have also displayed a possessiveness that she found claustrophobic. It's impossible to know how the relationship might have developed if he had achieved his goal and managed to stay on the throne with her as his Queen. It seems as though a kind of fate was at work that concerned not only them, but also the entire royal family and its future and, due to the symbolic role of the Crown, the future of the nation.

Transits over synastry configurations

On 11 December 1936, the date of Edward's abdication, transiting Chiron was at 20° 44' Gemini, conjunct the Gemini planets in both their natal charts. It squared Edward's natal Chiron and made a close trine to his natal Saturn. It also formed an exact trine to Wallis' natal Moon-Chiron conjunction and a trine to her Aquarian Ascendant, and made an exact square to her natal Uranus. It had been hovering around the Gemini planets in both their charts for several months, throughout the period in which Edward tried to convince Parliament, the Church of England, and the royal family to sanction his marriage, and it continued to move over these Gemini planets through the summer of the following year.

Transits over a synastry aspect, especially if the transiting planet is the same as the one involved in the synastry configuration, often reflect a time when the deeper meaning of the synastry aspect manifests in external life. Edward and Wallis were born under one of the great outer planet conjunctions, the Neptune-Pluto conjunction in Gemini. Neptune-Pluto conjunctions occur roughly every 493 years, and they remain within orb of conjunction for around ten years. It's unlikely that anyone alive at the time that Gemini conjunction was exact – 1891 and 1892 – is alive today, and unless we discover the secret of immortality, it's unlikely that any of us will live to see the next one, exact in 2384 and once again in Gemini.

As the beginning of a new cycle, which takes nearly five centuries to unfold, each Neptune-Pluto conjunction heralds profound changes in the collective psyche, when social structures and values that have endured for half a millennium begin to collapse and die and new ones start to emerge in seedling form, fuelled by dreams of redemption and freedom from limitation and suffering. The Neptune-Pluto conjunction prior to the one under which Edward and Wallis were born was exact in 1398 and 1399 at 3-4° Gemini. This conjunction coincided in the West with the dawn of the European Renaissance, the end of feudalism, and the beginning of the erosion of the power of the Catholic Church. The conjunction of 1891 and 1892 coincided with the waning power of religion in the West and the rise of scientism. Edward and Wallis were deeply bound to an historical epoch in which the Gemini spheres of communication, political debate, education, and practical science acted as agents for social transformation, inspired by collective dreams of spiritual and cultural redemption through advances in knowledge.

This sounds noble and inspiring. But outer planet conjunctions can only be processed and given life through individuals. Some individuals become heralds for change of a positive kind. Some are trampled by collective movements they can't understand. Others, losing or never having known any sense of an individual self, and identifying with the archetypal figures and stories associated with these planets, act as avatars for the darker dimensions of the collective. Hitler was also born under this conjunction.

Transiting Chiron moved across the natal Neptune-Pluto conjunction in both Edward's and Wallis' charts at the time of the Abdication, suggesting that, due to their prominent public profiles, they might be perceived as – or perhaps actually were – harbingers or symbols of social change in both positive and negative forms. In Edward's time, no British king could marry a divorced woman unless it was a morganatic marriage. This law reflected entrenched, outdated collective attitudes toward not only marriage, divorce, and gender, but also the role of religion, the role of a nation's ruler, and the boundaries between personal and public lives. Many issues involving important public figures could, at that time, remain utterly secret. The incriminating Marburg Files which linked Edward with the Nazi regime were only discovered in Germany in 1945, and then only by accident, if that's the right word. But the conjunction heralded the development of new forms of communication and technological innovation.

The incandescent light bulb, for example, was invented by Thomas Edison in 1891 when the conjunction was exact, as was the Tesla Coil, invented by Nikola Tesla. This remarkable creation acted as a transformer, allowing the transmission of wireless electrical energy for point-to-point telecommunications, broadcasting, and electric power. On an altogether different front, the conjunction presided over the emergence of depth psychology and the analysis and mapping of the unconscious psyche. This extraordinary burst of human ingenuity, expressed in characteristic Gemini forms, ensured that, as the decades passed and the conjunction moved into its outgoing sextile – under which we are still living – such secrecy would become increasingly difficult.

The world is a very different place now, and the changes heralded by that late 19th-century conjunction in Gemini will continue to unfold, ripen, and eventually slide into decline until the next Neptune-Pluto cycle. It isn't surprising that the story of Edward VIII and Wallis Simpson continues to resonate today on many levels. We're only in the early stages of that cycle; the two planets haven't even reached their outgoing square, which will occur between 2061 and 2065 with Neptune back in Gemini and Pluto in Pisces.

Mars-Chiron aspects in synastry

Have any of you have experienced a relationship where your Chiron aspects another person's Mars, or vice versa?

Audience: Yes, I have, but I didn't notice it.

Liz: Did your Mars aspect your partner's Chiron?

Audience: Yes. They are conjunct. I left the relationship eight times. It was stormy.

Liz: But you didn't notice it? What *did* you notice? I'm not really poking fun at you, but sometimes when one feeds back to people what they've just said, it can sound quite bizarre. With your Mars involved, was it sexually very exciting?

Audience: Yes, and it remained so the entire time.

Liz: With any close Mars contact in synastry, including aspects to Chiron, sexual excitement can be an important component. The desire-nature of Mars isn't the same as the desire-nature of Venus. When we're attracted in a Mars way, there's something we want to conquer or win. For Mars, challenge is a potent aphrodisiac, and easy conquest can sometimes be a turn-off. Mars reflects an active, energetic desire that thrives on rivalry, competition, and pursuit. Mars doesn't have the reflective quality of Venus, who says, 'I find you beautiful. Am I beautiful in your eyes?' Mars can be passionate, and a Mars-Chiron synastry contact can arouse passionate feelings. We might wonder why Chiron can draw out that kind of passion.

But sometimes the unobtainable is more seductive to Mars than overtly reciprocal desire.

Audience: He is a musician, and much younger than me. He didn't speak English very well.

Liz: I'm not sure that Chiron's unobtainability is necessarily linked with a language barrier. Languages can be learned. But Chiron is deeply defensive and highly complex, and it can be extremely attractive to Mars because of its inaccessibility. Chiron's emotional firewalls can appear to Mars as an intensely desirable challenge.

Audience: He slipped through my fingers the whole time.

Liz: Yes, Chiron can thwart or elude Mars' passion. It isn't necessarily through lack of reciprocal desire, or the wish to hurt or frustrate. But there's a vulnerable wound that Chiron tries to protect, and Mars can be experienced as pushy and aggressive by the Chiron person. Even if Mars' desire is flattering, it may still be felt as an invasion or a threat, and Chiron can get defensive and reject or evade Mars' overtures, subtly or overtly. A lot then depends on how the Mars person reacts. Some people respond with great anger. But it might not always be easy to recognise or admit the anger.

Audience: That's true. I sometimes experienced lightning anger toward him. It was so fast that I didn't even notice.

Liz: In some Mars people, Chiron's resistance can trigger violence, especially if Mars already feels held back by difficult natal aspects. For example, if a person has a tense natal Mars-Saturn or Mars-Pluto aspect – or, for that matter, a tense natal Mars-Chiron aspect – and this configuration has been exacerbated by childhood abuse or violence, the person may unconsciously carry great rage and deep insecurity about their potency. If Mars is then blocked by a lover's natal Chiron, it may trigger all the childhood rage, and then the Chiron person may become the victim of, or the scapegoat for, a Martial anger which has far older roots.

Audience: I'd forgotten something that you just made me think of. I used to get so angry that I would actually shake him.

Liz: You seem to be forgetting quite a lot about this relationship. It's not surprising, as it seems some very dark and painful feelings were constellated in both of you. I think this may help to answer your question about what happens with Mars-Chiron cross-aspects. You may have edited parts of the relationship from your memory because it was clearly a hurtful and uncomfortable experience, not least because of what it revealed to you about yourself.

Mars-Chiron synastry contacts can sometimes provoke violence because Mars, especially in a person who feels painful insecurity about their potency, can't bear to be told it can't have something it badly wants. In myth Mars isn't known for his ability to compromise. I mentioned earlier the story of Mars, Venus, and Adonis. Mars can't tolerate Venus' love for the beautiful mortal youth Adonis, even though the war-god isn't exactly faithful himself, so he transforms himself into a boar and gores Adonis to death. This is a very Martial way of dealing with a rival, metaphorically and perhaps sometimes even literally – hence the French term, *crime passionnel*. As Joseph Stalin, who had Mars in Scorpio opposite Pluto and square Uranus, once said, 'No man, no problem'. But this kind of response, even when it's subtle, isn't very promising for the future of a relationship.

When I refer to 'potency', I'm not just talking about the sexual kind. I mean the self-confidence that allows us to believe we can get what we want from life and that we have enough courage and determination to see it through. When there's a history of frustration, the need to prove our potency can become intense and even obsessive. Desire and affirmation of potency are fused together in Mars because our ability to get what we want affirms our power as individuals. Our ability to win someone we desire is life-affirming. If we can conquer a reluctant prize, it confirms our potency.

It may be a gross generalisation, but I don't believe the act of rape is motivated by sexual desire. It's driven by rage and a craving for power, and it's an attempt to assuage intolerable feelings of impotence through humiliating and subjugating the victim. There are other forms of rape that aren't physical but involve emotional violation and control, and they are equally concerned with rage and power. Mars conflicts can also lie behind the destructive rivalry that infuses many relationships. Someone may seem especially desirable to Mars because they're attached to someone else, and this can sometimes be a repeating pattern in relationships. If we can win the desired object from the rival, it proves that we're potent.

Chiron can defend itself against Mars simply by withholding physical sex, or by a subtler kind of sexual and emotional withholding. Chiron can also sometimes become violent or cruel in an effort to pre-empt an anticipated injury, and undermining Mars' autonomy by encouraging helplessness can be a way of trying to wrench back control. Chiron's defences are rooted in a chronic fear of being wounded, humiliated, or victimised, especially if the fear is unconscious.

I should emphasise that it isn't always men who may display emotional or physical violence with difficult Mars-Chiron synastry aspects. Anyone can exhibit violence if this combination of planets in synastry happens to trigger difficult natal Mars aspects. You've been honest enough to admit your own violent feelings toward your lover. It's often easier with a trine or sextile between Mars and Chiron in synastry because there's more space for honest communication. The hard cross-aspects aren't entirely unworkable, and they don't always have to end badly. But they do require a lot of consciousness and self-honesty in both people, and a willingness to be vulnerable.

Let's not forget that Mars rules not only Aries but also Scorpio. Mars can have a long memory if there have been early experiences of feeling impotent and helpless. It doesn't always display the quick, fiery anger of Aries, which vanishes once it's vented; Mars is also capable of the brooding, vengeful resentment of Scorpio, which can reflect childhood feelings of humiliation, betrayal, and crushed pride. In ancient Rome, Mars was worshipped as the divine ancestor and guardian of the people because the city's legendary founders, Romulus and Remus, were the children of the war-god. In 42 BCE, Octavian, who later became the Emperor Augustus, defeated Brutus and Cassius, the murderers of Octavian's great-uncle Julius Caesar, at the battle of Philippi. Before the battle Octavian vowed to erect a temple and a massive statue to Mars Ultor, which means Mars the Avenger, if the god granted him victory. It took him decades but he kept his vow. The statue is still extant and can be seen at the Capitoline Museum in Rome. It's colossal and intimidating. You really wouldn't want to meet this deity on your own in a dark alley.

Both Mars and Chiron can display cruelty if sufficiently frightened and enraged. A well-publicised example of the ending-in-tears type of Mars-Chiron relationship can be seen in the charts of Johnny Depp and Amber Heard. The collapse of their relationship resulted in the public being inundated

Mars Ultor, c. 2 BCE. Musei Capitolini, Rome.

with an unending series of revelations of mutually violent episodes. The synastry between the two won't tell us who did what to whom; that's for Saturn's lawmakers to decide. But the charts don't offer a comfortable array of synastry aspects. There seems to be no recorded birth time for Amber Heard – the chart below is set for noon – but we can still look at the Chiron synastry.

Chiron in synastry, Example 2: Johnny Depp and Amber Heard

Left, Johnny Depp at the Berlinale Festival in 2020. Photo, Harald Krichel. Right, Amber Heard at the San Diego Comic-Con International in 2018. Photo, Gage Skidmore.

Johnny Depp has natal Mars at 3° Virgo in the 1st house but close to the cusp of the 2nd, sandwiched between Uranus at 1° Virgo in the 1st and Pluto at 9° Virgo in the 2nd. Pluto opposes natal Chiron at 15° Pisces in the 8th but Mars is too early in Virgo to oppose Chiron. We've already looked at Chiron in the 8th in Wallis Simpson's chart. Johnny's Chiron squares his natal Sun at 18° Gemini, forming a mutable T-cross involving Sun, Pluto, and Chiron.

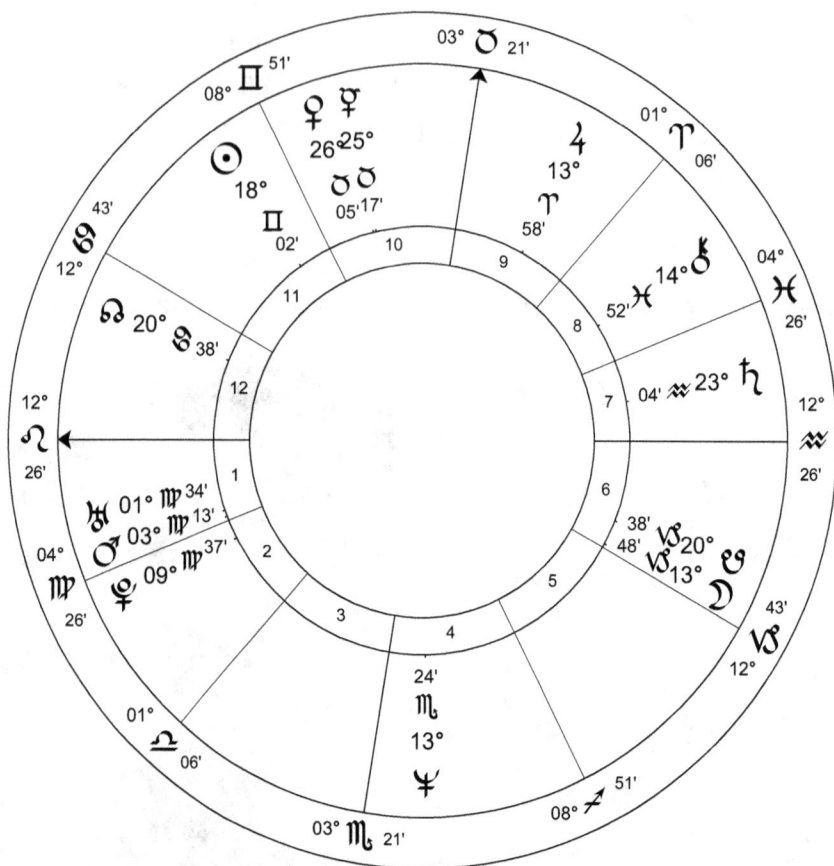

Johnny Depp
9 June 1963, 8.44 am, Owensboro, KY

Amber Heard's natal Chiron is at 11° Gemini. We don't know what house it's in, but it conjuncts Johnny's natal Sun, squares his natal Mars-Pluto conjunction, and squares his natal Chiron. Amber's Chiron squares her own natal Jupiter and opposes her natal Saturn, and these two planets obligingly join the mutable funfest and trigger Johnny's Uranus-Mars-Pluto configuration and also his Chiron. Thus Amber's Saturn-Jupiter-Chiron T-cross triggers Johnny's Sun-Pluto-Chiron T-cross.

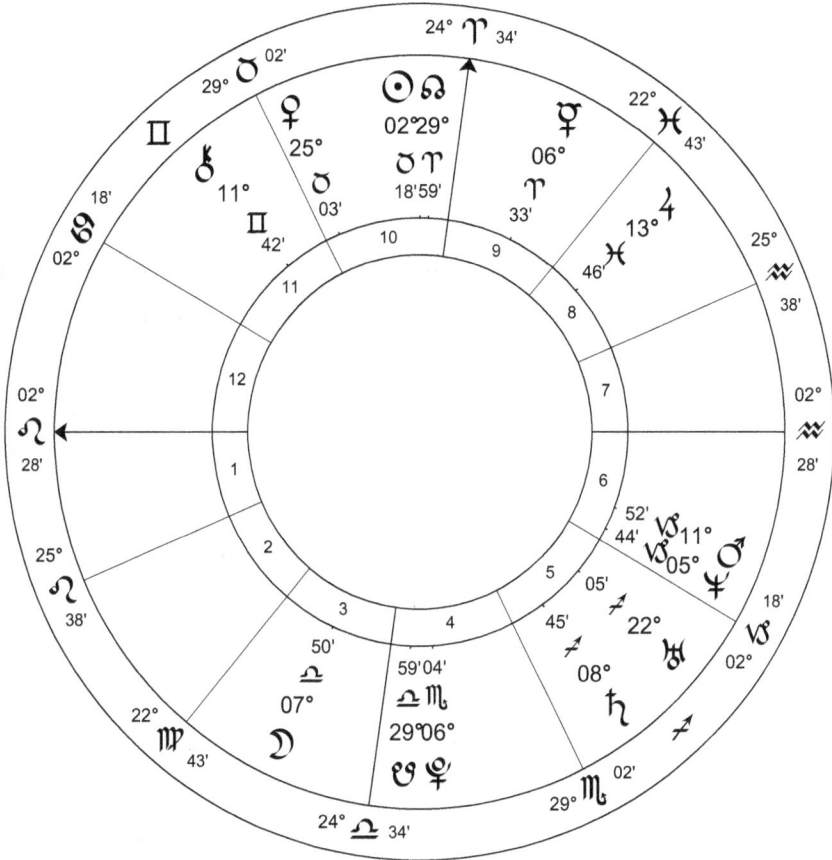

Amber Heard
22 April 1986, 12.00 pm, Austin, TX

We might well ask what drew these two people together. I've been focusing on the difficult Chiron exchanges, but of course there are other aspects that might reflect strong attraction and empathy, such as Venus in almost the same degree of Taurus in both charts. Among other potentially benign synastry aspects is a Jupiter-Chiron conjunction. I touched briefly on the Jupiter-Chiron trine between the charts of King Edward VIII and Wallis Simpson. Johnny has Chiron at 15° Pisces, closely conjunct Amber's Jupiter at 13° Pisces. Does anyone want to comment on this combination?

Jupiter–Chiron aspects in synastry

Audience: You said that Edward's Jupiter brought sparkle and fun to Wallis Simpson's Moon-Chiron. Would the same thing be true here?

Liz: I'm not sure 'sparkle' would be quite the right word because this conjunction is in watery Pisces, not in the airy realm of Gemini and Libra. But Jupiter seems to be able to lighten Chiron's load with optimism, generosity, and an injection of meaning, although a lot depends on how the Chiron person copes with being regularly cheered up. Sometimes we need our sulks and bouts of misery, even though we long to be free of them. But the creative potential of the aspect often balances or outweighs the difficulties, perhaps because both Jupiter and Chiron, sharing the hybrid centaur as a symbol, can bridge disparate realms of life.

Jupiter reflects our urge to find meaning, whether it's through Pisces' empathetic identification with others' feelings or Sagittarius' quest for greater understanding. We need to feel our lives mean something, and we seek it through making connections with what we perceive as a bigger, higher, or deeper universe. This makes us feel special – not in the way the Sun does with its focus on the development of the individual self, but by enlarging our horizons far enough to discover there is an intelligent and benign pattern in life that makes our apparently random experiences, whether of suffering or of joy, meaningful and of value.

When Jupiter and Chiron are in aspect natally, we may be inclined to think deeply about the meaning of human suffering: the reasons why it exists, whether it serves a larger or higher purpose, and how it could lead to greater understanding. Jupiter can offer a philosophical perspective to Chiron and constellate the Centaur's potential wisdom. The natal aspect can also reflect a need to avoid the pain through escape or oblivion – favourite Jupiterian routes out of a mess – and this combination in the birth chart, especially if it's a square or opposition, may also be related to drink and drug problems as well as a kind of footloose disengagement from any sort of commitment in life. In synastry it may do the same.

Johnny's Chiron in Pisces in the 8th suggests a deep and intractable wound around emotional intimacy, and a feeling of profound loneliness and disconnection from the emotional life of the family and the collective. Amber's Jupiter conjuncting his Chiron might reflect the healing potential of her empathy, which was probably a big attraction in the early stages of the relationship. When he was with her, he didn't feel so utterly alone, and her ability to reach him deeply, emotionally and sexually, might have given her the feeling that her own life was more meaningful. They might have followed the murkier Jupiterian routes of escape as well, but that isn't mutually exclusive of genuine empathy and understanding.

But it seems the difficult synastry aspects overwhelmed the potential of that conjunction. Amber's Saturn in Sagittarius, square her natal Jupiter, is also square Johnny's Chiron, so she may have struggled with bouts of depression and loss of faith that crushed not only her spirit but also his. Her Chiron conjunct his Sun might also reflect her envy of him, because his Gemini fluency and chameleon-like talent may have made her feel her own talents were mediocre at best and at worst, non-existent. Actors, if they are to be convincing and move us emotionally, can only draw on their own experience and their own inner world to bring to life the roles they are playing. Although we might not immediately associate Gemini with great emotional depth, this particular Gemini has Sun square Chiron and Pluto. And it's worth remembering the declaration of the American poet Walt Whitman, who had Sun in Gemini: 'I contain multitudes.'

Johnny Depp is a highly versatile actor who can play anything from comedy to tragedy to farce to horror. It's a very large umbrella that can encompass Captain Jack Sparrow's stylised antics in *Pirates of the Caribbean*, Dean Corso's spiritual corruption in *The Ninth Gate*, Ichabod Crane's comical but admirable integrity in *Sleepy Hollow*, Gilbert Grape's depressive misery in *What's Eating Gilbert Grape*, and Gellert Grindelwald's sociopathic destructiveness in *Fantastic Beasts*. Amber Heard, as an actress, doesn't appear to possess this kind of versatility. With Chiron in Gemini, she may feel her capacity for fluent self-expression is severely limited. Although she no doubt admired him, she may also have bitterly envied his talent as well as his fame.

Audience: Could I just ask something about Mars and potency? I have Mars in Pisces. Is there any way a Pisces Mars can find its potency?

Liz: Mars in Pisces doesn't lack potency. It's still Mars. But it might be a different kind of potency from the kind displayed by Mars in Aries or Mars in Capricorn. Try watching the film *Aquaman* some time. This is a superhero who draws his power from the sea. The plot might be silly and the acting wooden, but some of the visual imagery could speak to you about the immense potency of the element of water. And don't forget Poseidon, the Greek antecedent of the Roman Neptune, who was portrayed as a primal force capable of generating not only vast tidal waves but also earthquakes. He was envisaged as a giant bull with flaming eyes, living in the waterways beneath the earth, roaring and stamping and toppling cities.

Mars in Pisces discovers its potency through its receptivity to the collective psyche, and through serving as a conduit and champion for the emotional and imaginal needs of other people. This is not a 'weak' placement, although it's not always very good at clean, open warfare. It's more likely to lurk underwater and throw metaphorical dead fish at its opponents. Mars in Pisces may have had bad press in older textbooks because it isn't usually a rampant go-getter. It depends on the imagination to find its creative energy and impetus for action.

Mars in Pisces often can't act decisively on the basis of personal ambition or desire. There needs to be a feeling of inspiration, of emotions and imagination being stirred, to get it moving. It's not the easiest placement for handling direct confrontation if the conflict is personal. Justifiable anger on behalf of oneself isn't easy to acknowledge or express.

And difficult natal aspects to Mars can reflect a tendency to depression and a craving for escape from life. But Mars in Pisces will take on any opponent if there is a heartfelt cause to fight for.

This might be why Mars in Pisces is often happiest working in the arts or the helping professions, where imagination and empathy trigger energy and desire. The same thing applies to sexual passion. Treating sex like a tasty, satisfying meal might be fine for Mars in Taurus, but it doesn't work very well for Mars in Pisces. This Mars requires an imaginative, subtle, implied eroticism rather than blatant sexual overtures. Seduction, and being seduced, may be more fulfilling than obvious pursuit. A fine cinematic example of this is *The Age of Innocence*, made in 1993 and starring Daniel Day-Lewis, Michelle Pfeiffer, and Winona Ryder. It's based on a 1920 novel by Edith Wharton and portrays with moving delicacy an intense love affair that's never quite consummated but exists almost entirely on emotional and imaginal levels. I would recommend it to anyone who wants to gain some insight into Mars in Pisces.

Audience: A lot of people born in the 1960s have Saturn and Chiron together in Pisces opposing Pluto and Uranus in Virgo. When I've been involved with them as friends or lovers, my Mars lands on this configuration in their charts. I find it very hard to deal with because I feel so powerless.

Liz: Do you get accused of being manipulative or dishonest?

Audience: Yes, sometimes. Actually, a lot. But I don't try to be. It's just that I find it hard to be direct when someone is shutting me out or shouting at me. I just want to go away and cry.

Liz: The Uranus-Pluto-Saturn-Chiron configuration of the 1960s is a turbulent and difficult one, and you can get the flavour of it by looking at the huge upheavals and changes going on in society at the time. This was an us-against-them world. People born under the configuration carry a mini-version of that world's conflict and disruption within them, including the tendency of Chiron in Pisces to identify with the archetypal victim oppressed by dark powers that appear 'out there' as a cold, authoritarian Uranus–Pluto behemoth which crushes all heart and soul.

These dark powers may be projected onto powerful institutions like the police, the government, or international corporations. That doesn't imply a particular political affiliation. Depending on which side of the oppositions the ego identifies with, the destructive evil in the world can also appear as an amorphous army of shady, disgruntled, drugged-up Saturn–Chiron saboteurs and subversives determined to undermine law and order. This configuration contains its very own conspiracy-theory manufacturing plant. Of course, not everyone born in the 1960s displays such florid interpretations of reality. But traces of it can still pop up in personal relationships as well as in political views.

Since your Mars is involved, it might help for you to recognise this and not expect easy, peaceful relationships with people born under this configuration. The subtlety of Mars in Pisces can feel threatening to a person who is already braced for being manipulated and crushed by just about anyone, and the fact that you might genuinely empathise with the person and show them understanding might even disturb them more than overt demands. You have the ability to enter into another person's emotional world, so perhaps you might try to use that sensitivity to reflect on your expectations and understand that the rebuffs might not be as personal as you think. You will know perfectly well when you're being manipulative, and you may need to learn to avoid using this reliable weapon in the Piscean armoury. Feeling sorry for yourself isn't likely to be helpful, nor is covert resentment expressed as emotional blackmail or what used to be known as 'laying a guilt-trip' on someone.

People born into this generation group might arouse your desire because they embody a time of major collective upheaval and transformation which fascinates you and fires your imagination. They will never be easy conquests. The more you understand this, the easier it might be to navigate these relationships. With any planet aspecting someone else's Chiron, it's important to understand how complex the reaction is likely to be in the Chiron person. You may feel you're being gentle and subtle, but it might be read by Chiron as manipulative and dishonest. Think about what kind of ideal world the Chiron in Pisces generation longs for, and what kind of hurt and disappointment they feel.

Generation groups: Chiron in Pisces

Audience: The wound is in the disappointed longing to be one with everyone.

Liz: Yes, precisely. In Pisces' lost paradise, humans are all part of one living organism, and compassion and service are more important than personal fulfilment, lust for power, or material gain. But the world is never likely to oblige this dream, and the events of the 1960s cast a harsh spotlight on human greed, authoritarianism, and rejection of the imagination and the heart, as well as the equally human tendency to cling to the womb as long as possible and be cared for and looked after without any personal effort or responsibility. The anti-Vietnam War protests, the anti-racist protests, and the global student riots reflect the collapse of that ideal Piscean vision and the rage that erupted as a result.

A person born under this configuration isn't likely to instantly give you the emotional intimacy you desire. Mistrust in the fundamental decency of the human heart runs very deep in people with Chiron in Pisces. You're likely to experience behaviour that's sometimes hurtful, and you will need to learn to cope with it and not react as though you're a victim. Mars-Chiron synastry aspects by themselves, even without the involvement of Saturn, Pluto, and Uranus, aren't a good signature for naïve dreams about relationships in which every day is Valentine's Day.

Chiron reflects the sphere where humans are at their most complex. It stands between the personal and the collective and siphons the feelings of the latter into the former. Chiron's orbit cuts between Saturn, which forms the boundary of the personal world, and Uranus, which opens the gates to the collective psyche through the realm of ideas. Chiron symbolises the zone in which we experience our wounds as personal, but beyond this lies a vast reservoir of collective human suffering.

If Mars in your chart makes a strong aspect to Chiron in another person's chart, you'll need to find the resources to understand and cope with that complex duality of levels. Otherwise you might be better off finding someone simpler whose Venus is on your Mars and whose Sun is on your Moon, and with whom there aren't any prickly Chiron contacts. And if you ever do find such a person, I promise that you'll be bored to distraction because the element of magic and potential transformation will be missing. The element of potential healing may be missing too. But it will be a lot easier, which is what lots of people convince themselves they want.

Chiron in synastry, Example 3: Princess Margaret and Anthony Armstrong-Jones

Here is another example of a Mars-Chiron contact between two charts: the relationship of Princess Margaret and her husband Anthony Armstrong-Jones, Earl of Snowdon. Like the marriage of Johnny Depp and Amber Heard, it ended in tears. Obviously not all Mars-Chiron contacts reflect the kind of problems these two couples faced. Many other factors contribute to a relationship lasting or disintegrating, and difficult Chiron issues aren't the only signature of problems. And perhaps some relationships

Princess Margaret and Anthony Armstrong-Jones, Earl of Snowdon, ©Cecil Beaton/Victoria and Albert Museum, London.

are meant to teach us about ourselves and others but not to endure with a 'happy ever after' *dénouement*. We could learn from what happened with these two Mars-Chiron exchanges and see possibilities in how we might work more constructively with the aspect.

When she was twenty-two years old, Princess Margaret met and fell in love with Group Captain Peter Townsend, a Royal Air Force pilot fifteen years her senior. The feeling was mutual. He was in the midst of divorcing his wife at the time, although this wasn't because of his relationship with Margaret. It seems his wife had been unfaithful and he was the perceived 'innocent' party. But a marriage between Peter and Margaret was forbidden by the Royal Marriages Act of 1772 and the rules of the Church of England unless she received the consent of her sister Queen Elizabeth, because Peter was about to become a divorcé and Margaret was not yet twenty-five years old. The Queen withheld her consent and asked Margaret to wait until her twenty-fifth birthday, hoping that by then the heat would have gone from the relationship.

The heat didn't abate. The couple waited patiently until Margaret reached the appropriate age and could marry whom she chose. But she discovered that it wasn't quite that simple. She could marry Peter, but she was required to give up her place in the line of succession to the throne. Unlike her uncle King Edward VIII, she couldn't face relinquishing her position in the royal hierarchy to marry the man she loved, and she reluctantly ended the relationship.

I don't want to spend any time on Peter's chart, although if you're interested, you can find it on astro.com. But it's worth noting that there are no close Chiron aspects between Peter's and Margaret's charts involving Sun, Moon, Venus, or Mars. Margaret's Chiron in Taurus squares Peter's Jupiter in Aquarius and widely opposes his Mercury in Scorpio. His Chiron in Pisces trines Margaret's Jupiter in Cancer, an aspect whose benign possibilities we've already looked at. Although there are tricky Saturn contacts between Margaret and Peter, the relationship apparently didn't trigger the compulsive and painful dynamics typical of Chiron's hard aspects in synastry, and a marriage between them might have worked out quite happily. But perhaps 'happy' wasn't really at the top of Margaret's list of priorities. It seems that self-destruction might have been a more attractive option. Her marriage to Anthony Armstrong-Jones was a much darker matter altogether.

Margaret met Anthony three years after her separation from Peter Townsend, when she was twenty-eight years old. She didn't immediately fall in love with him as she had with Peter. But she needed to marry someone; twenty-eight was already 'on the shelf' by the standards of the

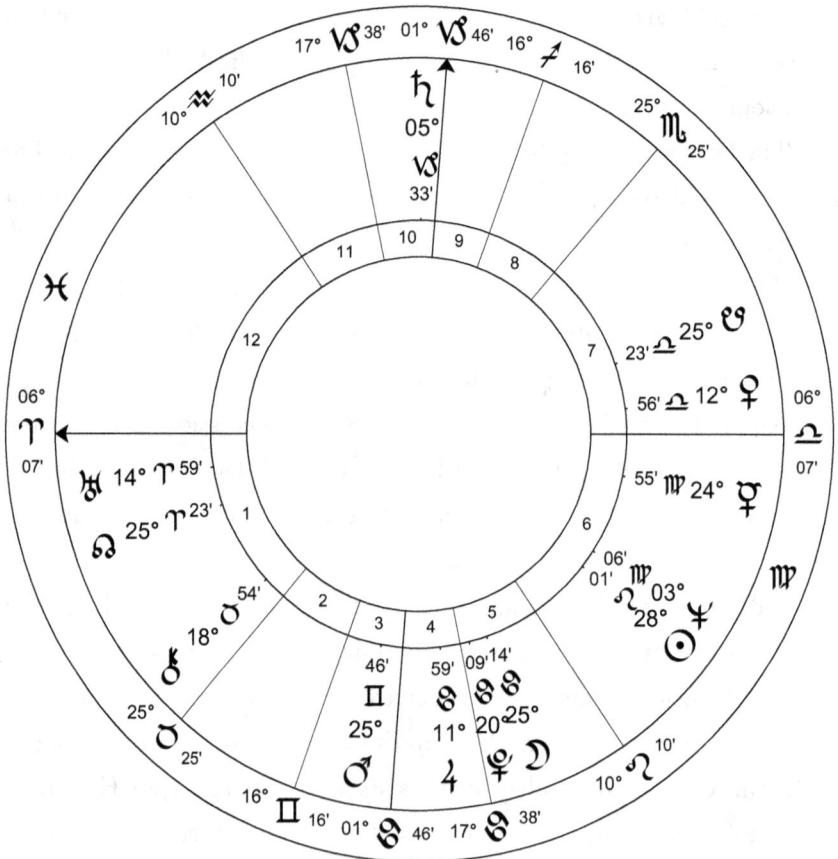

Princess Margaret
21 August 1930, 9.22 pm, Glamis, Scotland

time, and she desperately needed to move on from her heartbreak over Peter. Anthony's enigmatic, elusive nature and impressive creative talent intrigued her. He wasn't a divorcé, but he had a highly colourful past with a string of lovers of both sexes and a bohemian lifestyle that bore little resemblance to the social niceties and constrictions of royal life. He appealed to the imaginative, rebellious element in Margaret's nature.

After a long courtship that took place during her first Saturn return, they married when Margaret was thirty. He became Earl of Snowdon after the birth of their first child. Anthony initially appeared to adapt to royal life. This isn't surprising as he was so mutable, with Sun and Ascendant

Anthony Armstrong-Jones, Earl of Snowdon
7 March 1930, 6.15 am, London

in Pisces and Moon in Gemini, and he could be utterly charming and accommodating, at least on the surface. But the marriage gradually fell apart in the midst of violent quarrels and affairs on both sides, and ended in a bitter, acrimonious divorce. Afterward Margaret spiralled down into a haze of alcohol, drugs, and depressive episodes which eventually culminated in an unsuccessful suicide attempt.

Margaret's natal Chiron is at 19° Taurus in the 1st house, widely square the Sun at 28° Leo in the 6th. It squares Anthony's conjunction of natal Mars at 22° and Mercury at 25° Aquarius in the 12th house. He was born in the same year as Margaret and their natal Chirons conjunct. Both belonged to the same Chiron in Taurus generation, and both suffered from a profound lack of self-worth and a deep mistrust in the future of any promised security they were offered. Anthony's Chiron is earlier than Margaret's, at 10° Taurus, closely sextile her Jupiter in Cancer and trine her Saturn in Capricorn.

Audience: There's the Jupiter–Chiron aspect again. It seems to be part of strong attractions.

Liz: Yes, it does recur a lot in romantic relationships, although it's not an aspect that necessarily implies sexual attraction. I've seen it feature strongly in close friendships and productive working partnerships. It may reflect Jupiter's capacity to coax Chiron out of the pain and depression of the cave and into a brighter world where it's possible to laugh, see the bigger picture, and find some humour and optimism in life. But the hard aspects can trigger Chiron's resentment and envy toward someone who seems to have greater confidence or who might simply appear luckier. And the mythic Zeus isn't known for a spotless track record in moral rectitude. Jupiter might also offer Chiron a darker route out: 'Just try this pill/powder/drink/syringe/joint, and I promise you'll feel *so* much better.' I have no idea whether this scenario was relevant in this couple's case or in any of the other relationships we have looked at with Jupiter–Chiron synastry aspects. It's always a possibility.

The collapse of this relationship can't be attributed to hard Chiron aspects alone, although a good deal of the emotional violence and bitterness might. There are quite a few difficult synastry contacts between the two charts apart from Chiron. Margaret's grand cardinal cross involving Saturn, Uranus, Venus, Jupiter, and Pluto is directly lined up with Anthony's cardinal T-cross involving Saturn, Uranus, and Pluto in the same signs. Perhaps the most painful component in these overlapping and tense cardinal configurations is Margaret's natal Venus in Libra square her natal Saturn in Capricorn and closely square Anthony's natal Saturn, also in Capricorn. He exacerbated her innate propensity to feel lonely and rejected. These synastry contacts may have required a greater capacity for reflection and self-honesty than either of them was able or willing to pursue. They were too alike in their insecurities and defences, and ultimately drew the worst out of each other.

Each of them also had pragmatic motives in marrying. She needed a husband, and he needed status and money, and they both knew it. This could have made it harder for them to trust each other on the emotional level. The worldly element might reflect their natal Saturns in Capricorn. Although it doesn't always apply, there's an old saying about Capricorn: its motto is 'I use'. But the square between Margaret's Chiron and Anthony's Mars may have been a major contributing factor in both the attraction and the eventual rage and bitterness, not least because of the unconscious way in which they both dealt with the destructive feelings that kept bubbling up between them.

Audience: Would her Chiron square his Mars mean she rejected him sexually?

Liz: On the surface, it seems that he rejected her by taking other lovers and refusing to be pinned down even in simple things like explaining where he had spent his time on Monday evening. But on a deeper level she may have rejected his Mars in Aquarius nature, which doesn't like being confined and needs challenging intellectual companionship as well as breathing space to stir desire. Mars in Aquarius needs a friend as well as a sexual partner, and it doesn't respond well to intense emotional pressure. The more demanding Margaret became, the more elusive Anthony became. His freewheeling attitude toward sexual fidelity, his caustic wit, and his refusal to be caged probably threatened her sense of security, which was already terribly fragile.

She unleashed imperious demands, carping criticism, and emotional coldness in retaliation, and he responded with freezing disinterest and verbal disembowelment, the latter being a particular talent of natal Mercury-Mars aspects. Her demands were guaranteed to enrage a man whose greatest fear was of being locked in a box. He was a *puer aeternus* who couldn't bear being trapped by emotional needs, his own or those of others. She infuriated him by constantly testing him to ensure she wouldn't be wounded again. Perhaps his flagrant infidelities were in part an escape from her increasing efforts to control him. In the end she adopted his methods and engaged in a well-publicised affair with Roddy Llewellyn, who was eighteen years younger than her. Their relationship lasted for eight years and led directly to Margaret's and Anthony's divorce.

Margaret's mistrust was exacerbated by her earlier heartbreak. But she was already predisposed to expect rejection. It seems she always felt unloved, unlovable, and unworthy no matter how much love she was offered, reflected by both natal Chiron square Sun and Saturn square Venus. She compensated with a confident, theatrical persona that was partly real – she was a Leo with Aries rising, after all – and partly a defence against her lack of self-worth. Anthony treated her as she unconsciously believed she deserved to be treated. This raises the thorny question of how much choice is really involved concerning the people with whom we decide to share our lives.

Why did Margaret first attach herself to an unavailable and unsuitable man, knowing that sooner or later she would run into the intractable opposition of a code that ensured she could never marry him? Why, the second time around, did she choose someone who could never offer her the emotional stability, constancy, and safety she craved? Jung wrote that our complexes, if they remain unconscious, confront us as fate, and it does seem as though Margaret had a determinedly self-destructive need to be wretchedly unhappy in her personal life.

Margaret's natal Chiron is placed in the 1ˢᵗ house. The energy, originality, and revolutionary spirit of Sun in Leo and Aries rising with a 1ˢᵗ house Uranus in Aries had to live side by side with a gnawing feeling of being worthless and boring. Her wound lay in her perception of herself and her expectation of how the outside world would treat her. If we are to believe *The Crown* – and in its first two seasons it was probably quite accurate in its portrayals – throughout her life Margaret blamed her chronic discontent on the fact that it was her sister who became Queen. She felt she would have been better suited to the role. Unlike her father King George VI, she bitterly resented being the 'spare' and constantly projected her natal Chiron onto a sibling with Sun in Taurus who provided a convenient hook for the projection. The Queen, with natal Chiron in Aries, no doubt returned the favour.

Audience: Could it have worked out any differently?

Liz: I don't know. Perhaps the marriage really was doomed. Perhaps not. The ways in which Margaret and Anthony reacted to its disintegration were, in theory, in their own hands. But psychological awareness wasn't common currency at the time, especially in the circles in which they moved. I mentioned earlier that it's impossible to look at the behaviour of another generation or epoch and impose current insights, values, and expectations on it. And with all our purported increase in social awareness today, there is still a terrifying lack of self-knowledge even among the self-proclaimed enlightened. Social awareness isn't the same as psychological insight. The sense of life's unfairness can be palpable when we think of the lost possibilities and the tragedy of people who have doomed themselves to unhappiness because they didn't know any better. That's one of the conundrums we find in Chiron's cave, and hopefully we can learn from it.

Great expectations

Great expectations and their inevitable disappointment lie at the heart of Chiron's story. We expect godlike perfection from ourselves and from others. The mythic Chiron, as a divine being, takes his divinity for granted until he's wounded. We also expect godlike perfection from any planet that Chiron strongly aspects, in our own chart and in the charts of others, and we can't forgive ourselves or them for being less than divine. The experience of injury grows in the gap between who we are and what we expect from ourselves and from life. In the abyss between the two, a feeling of being irrevocably wounded arises. Mortality itself might be seen as a kind of inevitable wound, as no mortal creature can live forever. Everything in material form is doomed to eventual ageing and dying, even the stars themselves. But there are many people today who believe that if science could only find the right formula, we wouldn't have to age or die at all. And there is always the belief in an afterlife, which ensures that, even if the mortal body dies, we will still live forever.

There's always a gap, not only between Chiron's expectations of the world and the world as it actually is, but also between the expectations we have of ourselves and the individuals we really are. The world isn't as fair as we would like, and we are not as wonderful as we would like to believe we are. Jung spent a lot of time pointing out that individuation involved completeness rather than perfection, but we persist in confusing the two. Relinquishing immortality doesn't mean that we should stop striving to better ourselves and the world in which we live. But it might mean that we need to start from a place of greater humility, realism, and self-awareness. These attributes, rather than self-pity and bitter rage, may be an integral part of Chiron's healing.

It's important to be as conscious as possible of the nature of our expectations of life and of ourselves. You can see why, with Chiron synastry aspects, the perfection that we can't find in ourselves gets projected onto others, who are then inevitably doomed to fail us. Then the cause of the failure is blamed on the imperfect Other. If our Chiron conjuncts someone else's Moon, endless emotional warmth and unconditional support are perceived as the Moon person's dominant attributes because we haven't yet learned to nourish our own emotional needs. If they show anything less than perfect care, it can trigger great resentment and disappointment. If our Chiron opposes someone else's Venus, beauty and grace and sensuality appear to have achieved a state of perfection in the Venus person, because we haven't yet learned to value these qualities in ourselves. If only that beautiful person could love us, we would become beautiful and worthy. If only that nourishing, sympathetic person could hold and contain us forever, we would feel comforted and cherished and safe.

The projection of Chiron's ideals onto other people may be part of the reason why, in relationships, the Chiron person may feel worse over time and can eventually begin to spit out an accumulated fund of resentment and envy. Chiron may perceive superiority in the other person, who doesn't appear damaged. This can become a hateful experience because feeling inferior to others can be unbearable, even though we impose these feelings of inferiority on ourselves. It's very difficult to be in a relationship with someone whom we feel is better and more lovable than we are. We may fall in love with them for that reason, but we might also begin to resent them, because when we're around them, we feel inferior – not because the other person is actually trying to make us feel that way, but because we perceive them as whole and perfect when we ourselves feel so incomplete and damaged. And their pain may go unnoticed and undervalued because we're so preoccupied with our own.

Audience: How much easier is a trine than a hard aspect between two people?

Liz: It's easier to work with, although it can still be painful. The ease seems to come from Chiron's potential for compassion and wisdom being triggered by the other person. A feeling of affinity is less threatening than a conflict of values and perceptions. There may still be feelings of resentment and envy, but sympathy and understanding are easier to achieve. A trine or sextile from another person's planet can constellate the capacity for realism and acceptance that lies in Chiron as well as irritating the wound, making honesty easier to achieve in the relationship.

Audience: And in a natal chart?

Liz: Likewise in a natal chart.

Audience: So the expectation of perfection is still there, but living with the hurt and disappointment is easier.

Liz: Yes. But the profound transformation that can sometimes come out of the hard aspects isn't always achievable to the same degree with the soft aspects, because it just isn't painful enough to make us want to struggle for greater awareness. Like Chiron, we have to be *in extremis* before we're willing to relinquish our immortality. It's one of the great ironies of life that we won't do the hard work to become more conscious unless it hurts so much that we have no other option. Less emotional pain makes life happier and more comfortable. Greater suffering, if it doesn't destroy us or the people we're close to, can enlarge and transform us.

Not everyone is drawn to relationships with a lot of hard Chiron aspects between the two charts. Nor does everyone have difficult aspects to Chiron in the natal chart. Every person has an individual path, an individual *daimon*, and a unique journey. Some may appear easier and some may appear harder. There isn't any point in making comparisons or in envying or disparaging people who have a different road to travel. One road isn't more 'spiritual' or more 'pathological' or 'healthier' or more 'normal' than the others. Whatever comes into our lives, fair or unfair, everything depends on how we deal with it. One of Chiron's most important themes is our quest for the meaning of suffering and how we face and work with it. Although we might not find answers, it's asking the right questions that can make the biggest difference.

The transits of Chiron

I would like to say a bit more about Chiron's transits. Earlier I talked about Chiron transiting through Gemini and conjuncting the planets in Gemini in the charts of King Edward VIII and Wallis Simpson at the time of the Abdication. One way of viewing transits to natal planets is to see them as symbolic triggers or wakeup calls. Something within us, symbolised by the natal planet or angle, is constellated by an encounter or experience in the outer world, symbolised by the transiting planet. The natal planet has received its cue and is asked to come on stage and discover a new level of its nature through engaging with other characters. Over the span of a lifetime, that natal planet will have been in the spotlight many times, sometimes making a lightning-quick appearance if the transit is a fast-moving planet like Mercury or Mars, and sometimes participating in a series of scenes that last for years if the transit is a slow-moving planet like Pluto.

Exploring earlier experiences of transits over that natal planet can help us to understand the meaning of a current transit, because transits are always cyclical. The mode by which the planet is woken up is described by the transit, or by another person's natal or progressed planet. In this sense, synastry contacts have a lot in common with transits. The transiting planet or synastry contact is the catalyst; the natal planet is what we experience within ourselves, even if we persist in projecting it. Transits and synastry contacts portray the activation of a natal planet as a symbol of the unfolding development of the individuals we are in process of becoming.

Chiron transiting over a natal planet reflects the triggering of the natal planet through a painful or disillusioning experience. Any planet that transits natal Chiron, especially a slow-moving one, can trigger Chiron's sense of being unfairly wounded. This might not always be through disappointment in love. But relationships – including family bonds, friendships, work contacts, open enemies, and engagement with non-human entities – seem to be the main trigger for our emergence as individuals. Relationships provide the most challenging and most fruitful of all alchemical alembics.

We will all have a Chiron return at the age of fifty. We're likely to notice it because of the experience of the ageing of the body, which connects us with the archetypal theme of Chiron's relinquishing of immortality. Fifty is not considered old these days, but we might well begin to register the fact that we will not live forever. Some of us might manage two Chiron returns. We're unlikely to experience a third one unless, like Nicolas Flamel in *Harry Potter and the Philosopher's Stone*, we can get our hands on the Elixir. The deeper meaning of the first Chiron return doesn't literally describe the ageing of our bodies. But we will probably experience it on a physical level, although not necessarily through illness, simply because we're growing older. If we manage to reach a hundred and experience our second Chiron return, we are more likely to encounter its challenges through the increasing frailty of the body and the awareness that death is not that far away. But even at the first Chiron return, the awareness of physical vulnerability can begin to bite.

Sometimes this triggers a passionate determination to 'work' on the body and 'keep fit' to slow down the ageing process. Innovative diets and dietary supplements, repudiation of 'bad' habits, face lifts and Botox, and membership of the local gym are characteristic responses. So are efforts to renew youthfulness through a new romantic encounter with a younger partner. We can think of ourselves as in the prime of life at fifty, and perhaps rightly so. But we can't think of ourselves as youthful any more. The exit door is now just a bit closer than the entrance. The body in which we are incarnated may become a major preoccupation. But the real issue is often our perception of vulnerability on a deeper level, which is projected onto the body.

Chiron transits can be as subtle as they can be obvious. We will all have lots of opportunities throughout the Chiron cycle – its transiting squares, oppositions, trines, and sextiles as well as its return – to gain a deepening understanding of what Chiron's wound is about and how important it can be, not only for a sense of what our journey might really involve, but also for our capacity for compassion and our ability to let people close enough to see us as vulnerable humans.

If a transiting planet aspects natal Chiron, the same principle applies as with transiting Chiron aspecting a natal planet. But this time it's the moment for natal Chiron to move onstage. If a relationship is going through difficulties or we enter a relationship or end one under an important Chiron transit – either transiting Chiron to a natal planet or a transiting planet to natal Chiron – the themes of the relationship will be connected to the archetypal themes of wounding, bitterness and poison, healing, and the sacrifice of immortality.

Our engagement with the material world – money, home, work, physical health and illness, and all the other matters symbolised by the earthy houses – involves a form of relationship. The stirring of memories, family relationships and engagement with the family past, confrontation with deeper levels of the psyche, and all the other matters symbolised by the watery houses, also involve a form of relationship. Creative expression, the pursuit of an ideal, the outpouring of inspiration, our dreams of the future, and all the other matters symbolised by the fiery houses, involve relationship. So do the airy house spheres of our mental development, our education, our communication with others, our confrontation with the public, and our sense of social participation. In this sense all important transits, including those of Chiron, present us with an awakening triggered by relationship dynamics on one level or another.

Sometimes no recognisable concrete event takes place during a Chiron transit. We can wait in vain for something to 'happen'. Identifying what constitutes an event is a tricky business, since concrete happenings are usually only the visible tip of a very deep iceberg. For example, when does a relationship actually end? When the decree *nisi* comes through? When we move out of the marital home? When sexual attraction dies? When feelings of love and empathy ebb away? When we fall in love with someone else? These are all potential stages in an ending, and some may occur quietly and without any external happening, under the auspices of different transiting planets that suggest different dimensions of an ongoing process.

But even if no concrete event 'happens' during a Chiron transit, somewhere deep down the wound is constellated, even if we can't find an external reason that explains it. Chiron has a mysterious relationship with the physical body, which is suggested by his story. The mythic Chiron is associated with physical healing, and it's the animal side of the centaur that is wounded and poisoned. The astrological Chiron seems to be bound up with the health of the body, although not always in a literal sense. Chiron transits don't necessarily imply illness. But humans as well as animals may express their suffering through the body. We often treat our bodies like a faithful pack horse that must carry the emotional burdens we can't or won't deal with on the psychological level. Sometimes the load becomes too great.

It's not often that we have a chance to hear Chiron's most creative voice concerning this realm articulated by a public figure in a coherent and insightful way. I would recommend that you read some of the talks given by King Charles when he was Prince of Wales, offering his vision of what he refers to as 'integrated medicine'.[33] His involvement in this domain has been consistent throughout his adult life. In a paper he presented at the World Health Assembly in Geneva in 2006, he comments:

> In every treatment, the human attributes of compassion, empathy, touch and rapport are as vital to the art of medicine and healing as they are to the essence of humanity.'[34]

In another paper presented at the first annual conference of the Prince's Foundation for Integrated Health in 2009, he states:

> Human relationships, the human effect, personal care and continuity are, I believe, a crucial part of integrated care. The compassion that goes with them is an expression of values and humanity, and also the very act of healing itself.[35]

And in an article first published in the *Temenos Academy Review* in 2002, he refers to the urgent need to

> ...heal the mortally wounded soul that, alone, can give us warning of the folly of playing God and of believing that knowledge on its own is a substitute for wisdom.[36]

Not surprisingly, natal Chiron conjuncts the Sun in Scorpio in King Charles' chart. As with C. G. Jung and other individuals we'll look at briefly later, the mythic priest-healer who is also a wounded outsider might be seen as the archetypal background of King Charles' true vocation. The subtle relationship between body and psyche or, if you like, between body and soul, belongs to Chiron's realm. Understanding this is one of

---

33   These are available at www.princeofwales.gov.uk.
34   www.princeofwales.gov.uk/speech/speech-hrh-prince-wales-integrated-healthcare-world-health-assembly-geneva-switzerland.
35   www.princeofwales.gov.uk/speech/speech-hrh-prince-wales-princes-foundation-integrated-healths-first-annual-conference.
36   www.princeofwales.gov.uk/speech/time-heal-hrh-prince-wales.

the potential gifts of those who work with Chiron in creative rather than destructive ways.

Chiron on the angles in synastry

Audience: Could you talk about one person's Chiron on another person's angles? What does it do in a relationship?

Liz: The four angles of a horoscope aren't planets, and they're not dynamic characters in the story in the sense the planets are. They symbolise the four cardinal points of the Sun's daily passage through the heavens: rising in the east, culminating in the south, setting in the west, and reaching its nadir in the north. In their symbolism the angles also reflect the cardinal points in the Sun's apparent annual journey around the earth: the spring equinox as the Sun enters Aries, the summer solstice as it enters Cancer, the autumnal equinox as it enters Libra, and the winter solstice as it enters Capricorn. It's this correlation that leads to our traditional association of Mars and Aries with the 1st house, the Moon and Cancer with the 4th, Venus and Libra with the 7th, and Saturn and Capricorn with the 10th.

There are no mythic tales about personified angles, although they often have divine guardians. But the guardians aren't planetary gods. The Greeks associated the four cardinal points with the four Winds or *Anemoi*. They aren't heavenly bodies, but they enter and depart from the earth-world through these gateways. In Chinese lore, mythic beasts known as the Four Gods guard the four cardinal points. In Hindu myth the 'Guardians of the Four Directions' are similar. We can understand the angles better if we recognise that they themselves aren't divinities. They are gateways over which divinities preside, and through which they come and go between other worlds and this world. If a natal planet, including Chiron, conjuncts an angle, then it becomes a kind of gatekeeper for realms beyond the purely concrete one. But the angles themselves, and the houses derived from them, pin our natal planets to expression in particular spheres of life. Put another way, the angles nail us to earthly incarnation.

The cardinal points are also sometimes related in myth to different cosmic spheres, like the underworld or the spiritual realm. The associations with each cardinal point can differ according to the cultural context, and they don't always coincide with our astrological definitions in any obvious way. The place of the setting Sun, for example, appears in Greek myth as the blissful Garden of the Hesperides, an Otherworld full of golden apples, hidden in the distant West and protected by the Hesperides, the nymphs known as the 'Daughters of the Evening'.

In the myths of many cultures the West is associated with the gateway into the spiritual world. You might well ask what this has to do with our astrological interpretation of the Descendant as 'relationships'. I don't know the answer. Myths are comprised of symbols, and symbols are always paradoxical and open to many subtly linked interpretations, although they have a consistent archetypal core. Perhaps relationships open us up to the reality not only of other humans, but to dimensions of life beyond our own individual selves. Our small, self-absorbed existence, reflected by the domains of the first six houses of the chart, dies as we are changed through our encounters with others and catapulted into a wider consciousness.

Another example of the complexity of symbols is the north point of the chart, the IC or *immum coeli*. It's sometimes called the 'end of life' in older astrological textbooks. But we also associate it with home, family, roots, and the experience of father. It's the point of the Sun's nadir when the night is darkest, and also the point of the winter solstice, the shortest day of the year in the northern hemisphere. The old Sun 'dies' and at that moment the new, regenerated Sun is born, hidden in the darkness. The Romans worshipped this solar deity as Sol Invictus, the Unconquered Sun, because paradoxically, although the Sun dies each year at the winter solstice, it is reborn as the spark of new life and therefore lives eternally. I'm sure you can see the relationship between this ancient idea and the timing of the Christian story of Jesus' birth, which occurs just after the winter solstice. You can also see how the astrological definition of the IC as 'roots' and 'origins' might reflect the idea of a new individual emerging from the family matrix at birth and rejoining it at the 'end of life'. At the IC, we begin by having ancestors, but we end by becoming one with them.

In contrast, in Porphyry's *On the Cave of the Nymphs*, written in the 3rd century CE as a Neoplatonic interpretation of Homer's references to the 'soul gates' in the *Odyssey*, souls descend into physical incarnation at the north point or *immum coeli*, and ascend to their heavenly home after death at the south point, the MC or *medium coeli*.[37] This doesn't seem to bear any relationship to our astrological understanding of the MC as our vocation and place in the world. We might need to look more imaginatively at this angle and consider that entrance onto the world's stage, reflected by the 10th house, is our first real participation in the collective psyche. The subsequent two houses, the 11th and 12th, deepen this participation until, in the depths of the waters of the 12th house, we cease to be aware of ourselves as separate individuals at all. Like the Descendant, the MC suggests a kind of death as we move beyond our personal relationships and take up our responsibilities to the larger human family. The word 'vocation' comes from the Latin *vocatio*, meaning a 'calling' or a 'summons'. We are summoned to make a particular contribution to the world by a mysterious summoner that feels as though it exists beyond our personal selves.

The point of this long digression is that the angles, mythically and psychologically, appear as gateways between the hidden world of the soul and the physical world into which we are born. Angles don't have an intent of their own like a planet does. As gateways they describe the worldly structures and situations into which we are incarnated, through which we are embodied, and to which we are bound throughout life. The Ascendant reflects our embodied consciousness as we first emerge from the womb and

---

37 Porphyry, *On the Cave of the Nymphs*, trans. Thomas Taylor (Wentworth Press, 2016).

learn to contend with the world in which we find ourselves. The IC reflects the family matrix from which we have come. The Descendant portrays our encounters with others, friendly or hostile. And the MC describes the goals and ambitions that ground who we are in the larger world.

Natal Chiron in one person's chart will respond to an angle in another person's chart in the same way it does to a planet. It will usually display its characteristic spectrum of feelings: admiration, attraction, envy, hurt, need, defensiveness, and anger. But an angle is a different kind of trigger. The angles describe who we are in the world, rather than what we are inside. They're the stuff of which we're made during our sojourn on earth, like having red hair or brown eyes or sensitive skin. The active agent in this kind of synastry aspect is the Chiron person. But as with all alchemical reactions, both people may be changed.

Generation groups: Chiron in Capricorn

Let's take a hypothetical example: you have natal Chiron in Capricorn and you become involved with someone with a Capricorn MC. What kind of wound is reflected by Chiron in Capricorn? What is this sign's lost paradise?

Audience: Status. Success. Being seen as someone important in the eyes of the world.

Liz: Yes, sometimes all those things. But look deeper. Capricorn is subtler than simple worldly ambition. This is a Saturn-ruled sign, and Saturn is anything but simple. Deep down, however materially fixated the person might appear, Capricorn idealises the rule of law, the hierarchical structures that sustain life, and the qualities of persistence, commitment, and service that allow the person to make an authentic contribution to the world. If that means climbing the ladder of success and gaining material and social rewards on the way, it's a bonus. For Capricorn these rewards represent an inner sense of achievement in accord with an underlying respect for a deeper hierarchy, even if the person can't acknowledge it consciously. Chiron in Capricorn's lost paradise is a world that functions according to the requirements of the law. The wound lies in realising that humans are fundamentally lawless, chaotic, lazy, indifferent to the good of society, and devoid of real inner authority.

Definitions of the law can vary. Capricorns aren't always law-abiding in the conventional sense and might choose to bend or rewrite the rules according to what they deem to be 'right'. Capricorn rebels don't cause trouble simply out of boredom, mischief, or resentment. They do it because they hear the compelling voice of a different law. This law can be understood as divine or cosmic law, which might sometimes collide with earthly laws. Or it may be an idealised version of earthly law. The motive might be positive, but equally it might serve a much darker purpose. Yet it's still what the individual perceives as the law.

The law may also be interpreted as the orderly functioning of the cycles of the natural world. The mythic Kronos, the personification of divine law, presides over a Golden Age when humans live in harmony with the orderly cycles of the seasons that mirror the orderly cycles of the heavens. The physical body also has its own laws, which aren't always respected or fully understood by science and conventional medicine. A world in perfect harmony with the law – whether civic, cosmic, or natural – is Chiron's lost paradise, and the wound reflects disillusionment with the integrity of existing authorities and the loss of trust in laws and structures that serve no one except those at the top of the hierarchy.

Chiron takes roughly four to five years to transit Capricorn. It last moved through the sign between December 2001 and February 2005. Although some might think the people of this generation are still too young to fully reveal what they might eventually become, many members of this Chiron generation group have already made it clear that they have no faith in current worldly hierarchies and authorities. Perhaps one of the best representatives of this recent Chiron in Capricorn generation is Greta Thunberg. Although it seems her birth time isn't available, she was born with Chiron at 11º Capricorn conjunct the Sun at 12º Capricorn and, depending on her time of birth, possibly also the Moon. The Sun-Chiron conjunction forms sesquiquadrates to Uranus at 26º Aquarius and Venus at 26º Scorpio but makes no major aspects to any other planets.

Greta has challenged the global establishment on behalf of an ideal vision in which disregard for natural law and the wilful destruction of the planet can one day be eradicated. Although this vision of a perfect world may never be realised in any foreseeable future, given the nature of human greed, opportunism, and addiction to power, nevertheless she has proved to be a powerful force in waking people up to the damage they have done and continue to do to the planet. Diagnosed at a young age with Asperger's syndrome, obsessive-compulsive disorder, and depression, single-minded, short-tempered, rude, and even fanatical, she might not seem an obvious candidate to serve as a vessel for the archetypal role of the priest-healer.

Greta Thunberg at the European Parliament, 16 April 2019. Photo EU Archives.

Nevertheless, as a wounded outsider and a mouthpiece for the grievances of her generation group, she has already made an extraordinary difference and demonstrates, like King Charles, that Sun-Chiron can reflect a vocation to heal rather than just an unhealable wound.

Prior to its 21st-century transit, Chiron moved through Capricorn between February 1951 and January 1955. Do any of you remember what the world was like during the early 1950s?

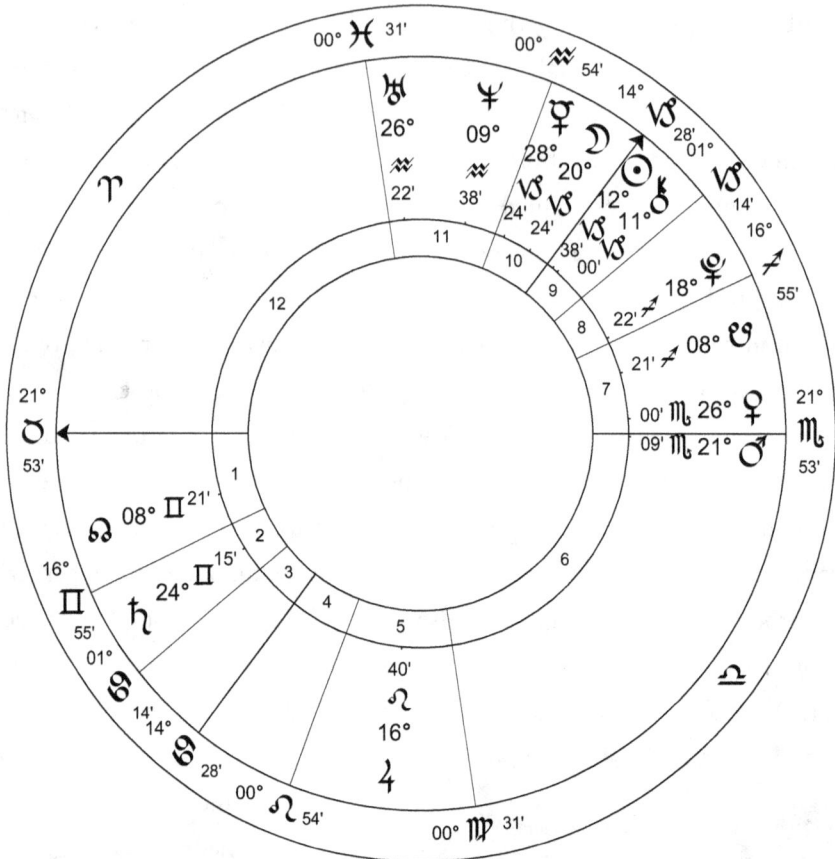

Greta Thunberg
3 January 2003, no time (chart set for noon), Stockholm, Sweden

Audience: It was the Cold War.

Liz: Yes, the Cold War was just beginning, although the Berlin Wall wasn't built until 1961. But nations began to polarise between extremes, politically and socially, and those in authority repeatedly misused their power. The post-war world was bleak and harsh for a long time after the war's official ending, and it seemed that no leader could be trusted. Europe was weakened and impoverished, cities were still full of bombed ruins, and by 1952, seven years after the end of the war, there were still nearly 200,000 displaced persons uprooted by the conflict. Food rationing, which had ended in most

European countries by 1950, continued in Britain until 1954. This period also presided over the foundation of the British Welfare State. On one level it promised to provide government support and protection to the people 'from cradle to grave'. But on another level it grew into a powerful 'Nanny State' with its own unelected hierarchies that created a different but equally harsh kind of oppression.

While Europe swung to the political left in repudiation of Hitler and Mussolini, in America the political right took power under Eisenhower and Nixon. Senator Joe McCarthy's political witch-hunts, at their height during this transit, displayed a shocking hypocrisy and abuse of authority that dominated the political and social values of the time. Public faith in leaders and institutions began to collapse, and no authority could be trusted because they always seemed to have a self-serving motive or a snout in the trough. The 'Baby Boomers' born into this Chiron generation aren't predisposed to swallow whole any political or social vision, however noble it might sound, if it smells of hypocrisy and the abuse of power. Chiron in Capricorn is attuned to the odour of corruption in hierarchical institutions and can easily feel victimised by perceived tyrannical father-figures everywhere.

In contrast, individuals with Capricorn at the MC – especially in maturity, since this sign, like good wine, often improves with age – tend to instinctively respect the rule of law and are comfortable with the steps required to climb the ladder, sometimes through adapting to the structures of existing institutions and sometimes through claiming a new form of authority themselves. The world out there, for a Capricorn MC, isn't always perceived as a friendly place, but it's all there is, so one has to make the best of it.

This can result in an impression of self-sufficiency and self-control which carries its own authority. It might not be how the person actually feels inside, but it's how the world perceives them and how they instinctively deal with the world. And in synastry it can trigger Chiron in Capricorn's terror of being controlled by controlling people. Respect and admiration are often mixed with envy, resentment, and mistrust. The envy may be directed at the Capricorn MC's worldly achievements, and if Chiron unleashes that envy, it can have a destructive effect on the other person's confidence in their work and their goals.

There are also creative possibilities. The realism and tenacity of a Capricorn MC, especially if the person has achieved a lot in worldly terms, could wake Chiron up to the fact that genuine authority isn't always oppressive, accommodation with existing institutions doesn't always require selling one's soul, and achieving goals doesn't always necessitate leaving a trail of bodies behind. Greed might not be good, but the satisfaction of conserving and enjoying the fruits of one's labour is entirely acceptable. But a lot of the time, Chiron may deeply resent and envy the Capricorn MC's ability to relate comfortably to a world that Chiron finds disturbingly menacing. Ironically, the horror of being controlled by corrupt authorities that seems such a prominent theme in Chiron in Capricorn's inner world can easily morph into a determination to control others in defence. The tyrant and the oppressed subject become interchangeable.

If natal Chiron conjuncts another person's IC, it may stir memories of the family past in both people and provoke family crises that might otherwise never have surfaced. If natal Chiron conjuncts another person's Ascendant, the other person's appearance and way of interacting with the environment provide the trigger for Chiron's ambivalent responses. When it's on another person's Descendant, it's their relationships and their way of relating to others. Since a conjunction with one angle means an opposition to the other, it's helpful to view each angle as half of an axis rather than individually. The meridian axis reflects our origins and the culmination of those familial roots in our vocation: the fruit at the top of the tree embodies the soil at its roots. The horizon axis reflects our interaction with our immediate environment and with the larger world: how we deal with others crystallises how we perceive ourselves in relation to them. A wise

Chiron can mentor and help to shape the other person's expression and development in the world. An unconscious Chiron may attempt to harm, control, or undermine the other person's confidence. Sometimes both can occur. Chiron is the active agent in the synastry aspect. We can't change the substance of our angles to satisfy a Chiron person's needs, but we can be powerfully affected in both harmful and positive ways.

In the synastry between Freud and Jung that I talked about earlier, Freud's Chiron in Aquarius conjuncts Jung's Aquarian Ascendant. Freud was impressed and fascinated by Jung from the time they met. He invited Jung to join him in his work, provided a framework of ideas and taught him theories and techniques, and supported him as his 'heir apparent' to eventually lead the psychoanalytic movement into the future. Initially Freud played the role of the wise mythic Chiron with a young Achilles, acting as a mentor and teacher. But he ended up angry, hurt, and resentful, and rejected Jung's ideas as soon as they began to deviate too far from psychoanalytic doctrine and moved increasingly toward an Aquarian vision of a collective human psyche which at its deepest level shared universal archetypal images that are as spiritual as they are instinctual.

Jung was the only Christian in Freud's inner circle, and this rendered him more acceptable to a collective in which endemic antisemitism made Freud's contributions always appear suspect. Jung's personality was more genial in social situations; he was better at posing as an extravert than Freud, who had a Scorpio Ascendant and could be awkward with people he didn't know and trust. Jung's developing ideas about the archetypes of the collective psyche collided head-on with Freud's more literal and instinctually based interpretation of the unconscious. Freud found Jung's Aquarian personality and vision threatening. Jung couldn't be anything other than what he was and reacted to his mentor's constraints by stubbornly continuing to develop his own psychological perspective. Jung's declaration of war finally came with the publication of *Symbols of Transformation* in 1912, and so they parted ways.[38]

Audience: But surely some of this is also due to Jung's Sun opposing Freud's Chiron, and his Neptune squaring it.

Liz: Yes, you're quite right – we can't really separate one thread from a whole garment. I talked earlier about the Sun-Chiron aspect in their synastry. But there are some threads in the garment that are recognisably Aquarian, especially Jung's ability to earn the liking and respect of all kinds of people at all levels of society, which reflected his perception of humans not only as individuals but as part of a single human family.

'Individuation' is in many ways a uniquely Leonine concept. And what one of Jung's colleagues referred to as his 'nature mysticism', which certainly made Freud uneasy, might be reflected by Jung's Neptune in Taurus square his Sun in Leo, with both these natal planets forming hard aspects to Freud's Chiron. In a letter to Jung about his disciple's growing interest in astrology, Freud warned him that he would be 'accused of mysticism'. But the theory of a shared collective psyche underpinned by universal archetypal patterns is distinctly Aquarian. *Liber Novus* contains several beautifully painted images of the Water-bearer in various guises, pouring the water of enlarged consciousness onto the earth, not just to help a single suffering patient, but for the benefit of society as a whole.

Generation groups: Chiron in Aquarius

Audience: Could you say more about Chiron in Aquarius?

Liz: How would *you* understand the nature of the wound when Chiron is in Aquarius? What does the Aquarian lost paradise look like?

---

38 The book was first published as *Wandlungen und Symbole der Libido,* with the English translation called *Psychology of the Unconscious.* For more on Jung's parting of the ways with Freud, see Liz Greene, *Jung's Studies in Astrology*, pp. 18-22.

Audience: There's a collision between Aquarian ideals and the world as it is.

Liz: There's always a collision between the ideal and the reality, whatever sign Chiron is in. Ideals vary according to the sign, but the collision has a certain inevitability about it, just as Chiron's wounding does in the myth. What does a perfect Aquarian world look like?

Audience: Human fellowship. A global human family.

Liz: Yes, that's a big part of it. An individual born with Chiron in Aquarius perceives the beauty and truth of human fellowship as well as all the darker elements in human nature that undermine it. These human failings are usually perceived by Chiron in Aquarius as greedy, unrestrained instinctual and emotional needs and the selfish desire for individual expression at the expense of others. The intolerant, bigoted, and self-centred proclivities in human nature are anathema to Aquarius because they divide and destroy people rather than uniting them.

It can help to think in simple astrological terms to understand what Chiron in a particular sign finds most threatening. Aquarius opposes Leo and squares Taurus and Scorpio, and these three apparently inimical signs symbolise everything that threatens the perfect Aquarian world. Taurean greed and possessiveness, Leonine egocentricity and vanity, and Scorpionic negativity and emotional obsessiveness appear as the three-headed Serpent in the Garden.

Aquarian ideals embrace equality, fairness, tolerance, and a belief in individual sacrifice for the greater good. Creating this kind of world also means thinking logically, since emotions cloud reason, which is why Aquarius is so often fond of technology, science, and social and political systems and theories. And let's not forget Saturn's rulership of the sign, reflected in an idealisation of the law – in particular, laws concerning how people should relate to each other as social beings, as well as laws defining scientific truths. Sociology and political science are uniquely Aquarian fields of study The perfect Aquarian world may even adopt scientism as the one true religion that can cure all the world's woes, and cutting-edge technology such as artificial intelligence which can replace flawed human blundering.

Audience: It sounds horribly cold.

Liz: Yes, it does. But don't forget that this is Chiron's idealised world, not a living world that a person with an Aquarian Sun or Ascendant or Moon would necessarily want to inhabit. And if Chiron makes hard aspects to other planets, that ideal vision will come into conflict with other dimensions of the personality. Having said that, it *is* a cold vision. Ouranos is the god of the starry heavens, and his domain is the boundless realm of space. It's pretty chilly out there.

From the perspective of the divine Centaur, it isn't cold. People are meant to be happy and fulfilled in a world where everyone is treated as an equal, superstition has been eradicated along with illness, addictions, and violence, and truth is defined through logic and scientific experiment. Sadly, these noble ideals don't tend to work in actual life, and not because people are so intractably selfish and awful. Chiron's Aquarian ideals fail because they are too exalted and godlike, too intolerant, and too lacking in recognition of the value of individual differences, needs, and feelings. As a result, the Chiron in Aquarius generation may feel embittered toward collectives because personal experiences, and often family history, seem to prove that humans are self-centred, intolerant, petty, greedy, and hypocritical, especially when they gather in groups.

Sometimes, as with Freud, there's an identifiable family background of persecution at the hands of a bigoted and intolerant group. Freud had very good reasons to mistrust the collective. But sometimes it's not as clear-cut. The ways in which a person can be perceived as 'different' can vary enormously. Chiron's pain isn't always explained or alleviated through identity politics. Each individual's suffering is unique and deeply personal as well as springing from collective roots. In some ways Chiron in Aquarius can find it harder than other signs to acknowledge the personal dimension of the hurt because in Aquarius' ideal world, it's the collective, not the individual, that counts.

Audience: That's all very true. I have Chiron in Aquarius and I do feel all of that. I don't trust groups. I'm interested in the connection between this Chiron placement and the events going on in the world at the time. I grew up in America, and it seems to me that the late 1950s were a bland, smug time, with not a lot happening in terms of big events.

Liz: I'm not sure how bland it really was. And 'big events' aren't necessarily required to generate a sense of wounding. It can come from the slow drip of small hurts and disillusionments over a long period of time. During this transit the Cold War was approaching its height, with the undercurrent of paranoia that inevitably accompanied it. Although the American economy was booming, the sense of impending doom and disaster was sometimes quite acute, even though nothing 'happened'. The blandness you speak of, encapsulated in 1950s fashion with its fussy, stylised sentimentality, might be seen as a defence against a deep fear that the destruction of society was imminent. The kind of slow-cooking fear that was prevalent during that time can drive people into escaping into the fiction of an overly bright, sentimentalised, and sanitised world.

Although Joe McCarthy fell from power in 1954, he went on speaking publicly against the 'subversive' elements in society until his death in 1957. And 'McCarthyism' showed disturbing resilience as a socio-political perspective and was still very much alive and well when you were growing up. Interestingly, McCarthy belonged to the previous Chiron in Aquarius generation; he was born in 1908, with natal Chiron at 18° Aquarius in the 11th house square natal Sun in Scorpio in the 7th close to the cusp of the 8th and opposing natal Moon in Leo in the 5th. His paranoia resonated with the collective paranoia of the time, which might partly explain why his values lasted far longer than he himself did.

During the late 1950s, collective scapegoating focused on those individuals considered marginal and therefore potentially subversive to the 'American dream': artists, intellectuals, Jews, Blacks, Hispanics, native Americans, immigrants, and the low-income underclass. Anyone 'different' might be an enemy intent on subverting democracy, even if they weren't a communist. As a result there was immense pressure to be 'normal' and to 'belong'. This period marked the beginning of the Civil Rights Movement as a response to the gross inequalities and hypocrisy hidden beneath the prosperity. It's almost as though society was turning on itself and chewing off its own leg. It would have been a deeply painful time for anyone who didn't buy into or embody the 'American dream', for whatever reason. I wouldn't say this was a bland time in the nation's history. This is a generation group that can easily understand Groucho Marx when he declared, 'I refuse to be a member of any club that would have me.'

Audience: Would you say that Chiron can show us the pathway between the ego and the Self?

Liz: No, I don't think I would say that. I'm not sure what you mean by ego and Self, since these terms are used differently by different schools of psychological thought. My own feeling is that every factor in the natal chart can help illuminate a pathway to the development of an authentic individuality. There isn't any one planet that signifies this; it's the whole of the natal chart and the whole of the individual's choices in life.

Certainly Chiron's wounds can impel us to face our vulnerable humanness as well as our potential for envy and destructiveness. We might discover that we hunt scapegoats because we secretly feel so inferior ourselves, and then we might have to do something about that inner problem. But this is only one of many gateways pointing toward what I would understand as a sense of Self. The Sun can provide a gateway through the discovery of our potential as unique individuals, and Venus can provide one through discovering what we value most. For Mercury, knowledge and the communication of it may provide a gateway. For Saturn, the development of self-sufficiency and the struggle to manifest one's abilities in the world can offer a gateway. No planet is more important than any other planet in the chart because they all relate to each other whether they are in direct aspect or not.

It's problematic to take any psychological model and try to impose it on the chart. Although psychological models are immensely useful in understanding chart dynamics and vice versa, each has something the other lacks. They can't be made to fit exactly. It's not helpful to say, 'This bit of the chart is the shadow, here's the anima, here's the animus, that planet is the id, that one is the superego, that one is the pathway to the Self.' We need a sense of the interaction between planets and elements, and also of the impact of family and social environment on the natal chart. And most of all, as life progresses, our fulfilment as individuals, and perhaps as a collective too, may depend on our understanding of ourselves and our individual efforts and choices.

Chiron in synastry with the outer planets

Audience: You haven't said anything about Chiron and the outer planets in synastry. What about someone's Chiron conjunct someone else's Pluto?

Liz: Yes, I was working my way toward that dimension of Chiron in relationship. Chiron's response to the outer planets in another person's chart can be reflected by both powerful attraction and powerful fear. But the outer planets don't respond in personal ways as the inner ones do because they aren't personal.

Chiron stands at the gateway to the collective realm of the outer planets and serves as a mediator between our individual lives and a domain that by its nature threatens the integrity of individual values and choices. The outer planets aren't malefic. But they're not concerned with our individual needs, aspirations, desires, hopes, and fears. They seem to symbolise the great cyclical movements of the collective psyche that underpin major changes in human consciousness and in society. Individual values and needs might or might not accord with these vast impersonal currents.

People with a personal planet in strong aspect to an outer planet in the natal chart are already plugged into the collective realm, often unwillingly. They may struggle to find a way to combine their own development with an insistent and sometimes compulsive vision of what the world could be and is already becoming. They're sensitive to collective shifts and changes whether they wish it or not. Even trines and sextiles can be challenging. These aspects require us to hold on to our own values while embracing and providing vehicles for the inevitable changes heralded by the outer planet.

We've seen some examples of this earlier today, although I didn't focus on it. In Freud's chart, natal Sun conjuncts Uranus in Taurus. In Jung's chart, natal Sun in Leo squares Neptune in Taurus. Each man had a different vision of the psychology of the future, but 'vision' is the operative word. Both felt impelled to try to change how humans perceive themselves; they were 'called' by a future they sensed was coming and felt the need to participate in its birth. This impetus wasn't rooted solely in personal aspirations. They had a strong wind at their backs. Both men managed, imperfectly and with difficulty, to hold the ground between personal and collective by acting as avatars for a collective vision of change mediated through personal experience and personal values. Not everyone can manage it that creatively, and not everyone is called to do it on such a large stage. Even if they do manage it, they're still likely to feel like aliens who have accidentally been dropped like ET into a world of 'normal' people who can't see, feel, or imagine the reality of that other realm.

Some people are destroyed by these collective currents if they haven't been able to find firm ground to stand on as individuals. A tragic example of this is the English singer and songwriter Nick Drake. Outside the specialised domain of the music world, most people have never heard of Nick Drake. His songs blend exquisite poetry with folk, jazz, classical, and blues motifs to generate a unique sound that has continued to influence the work of songwriters over nearly five decades. Not surprisingly, a lot of musicians have 'borrowed' his style and chord progressions without acknowledging the source.

Nick Drake was born in 1948 and committed suicide in 1974 at the age of twenty-six. In his natal chart, the Sun conjuncts Uranus in Gemini in the 12th house, opposite Jupiter in Sagittarius in the 6th. Cancer is on the Ascendant and its ruler, the Moon, is in Scorpio in the 5th house, conjunct

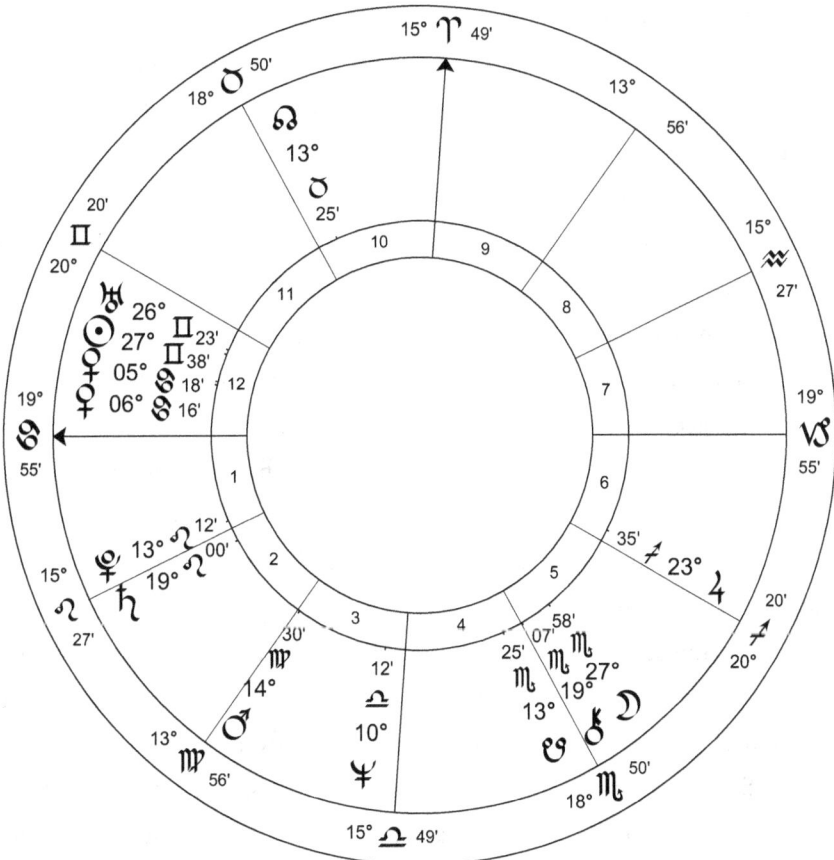

Nick Drake
19 June 1948, 7.15 am, Rangoon, Myanmar

Chiron and square Saturn. Chiron is square Pluto in the 1st house as well as forming an exact square to Saturn in the 2nd, suggesting not only intense loneliness and lack of self-worth, but also an acute receptivity to the survival instinct in the collective psyche with its potential for darkness and destructiveness.

Nick Drake was deeply introverted. Although he had a few good friends, he seems to have avoided any kind of sexual relationship. He loathed and feared public appearances and interviews. Partly because he couldn't and wouldn't satisfy the public need for showy onstage performances, and partly because his musical vision didn't fit into the *zeitgeist* of his time, his three recorded albums never achieved much recognition in his lifetime. It's only since his death that acknowledgement has gradually been given to the importance of his music. Reclusive and chronically depressed, he spent the last two years of his life on antidepressants, hidden away in his parents' house. He has been referred to as a 'doomed romantic', but he was rather more than that. His music was ahead of its time and effortlessly blends joy and sorrow, frivolity and melancholy, with unusual combinations of chords and subtle lyrics that give a voice to the profound ambivalence of life, not only for his own generation but also to the generations that followed.

The visionary nature of Uranus conjunct the Sun can't be held responsible for Nick Drake's suicide. Nor can the melancholy of Moon conjunct Chiron in Scorpio square Saturn, or Chiron in Scorpio square Pluto, painful though these aspects are. The filmmaker Steven Spielberg was born with a similar combination of Moon conjunct Chiron in Scorpio in the 5th house square Saturn and Pluto in Leo, with an opposition between natal Sun in Sagittarius and natal Uranus in Gemini. Both charts have Cancer Ascendants. Rather than retreating from an intolerable world, Steven Spielberg has gone from strength to strength creating films that portray the dark tragedy of war and of his family's Jewish background alongside the childlike wonder and terror of an Otherworld populated by resurrected dinosaurs, killer sharks, magical archaeological objects, and extra-terrestrials with superpowers. His many films have given joy, sadness, insight, and inspiration to more than one generation.

I can't explain why one of these immensely gifted individuals failed to cope with the darkness in life and the other transformed that darkness into a constant inspiration for creative work. Of course the charts are not identical. We could spend the next hour listing the differences. Is it because the natal Suns are in different houses, with Nick Drake's Sun, along with Uranus, Mercury, and Venus, in what was once known as the 'house of self-undoing'? Is it because Steven Spielberg's mother was more conscious than Nick Drake's? Is it because Nick Drake's Venus conjunct Mercury in Cancer

Steven Spielberg
18 December 1946, 6.16 pm, Cincinnati, Ohio

in the 12th square Neptune in Libra reflects an impossible idealism in love, while Steven Spielberg's Venus conjunct Jupiter in Scorpio in the 5th square Pluto suggests a tougher, grittier, yet more optimistic approach to love? Maybe all of the above. But I suspect the answer doesn't really lie in the natal chart, no matter how hard we look for it.

We might try to blame our mothers if natal Chiron conjuncts the Moon and squares Pluto. We might also try to blame and even scapegoat a social, racial, religious, or national group, which is what Slobodan Milosevic, with Moon conjunct Chiron and Pluto in Leo in the 4th house, did on a grand scale. He was born and spent his early years under the Nazi occupation of the Balkan states, and his mother and father both eventually committed suicide. His death in prison in 2006 is now officially attributed to heart disease. But at the time, the International Criminal Tribunal for the Former Yugoslavia, responsible for charging and incarcerating him, initially declared that he had committed suicide by self-medicating. Because he had been alone in his cell, rumours also circulated that he had been murdered. Whatever the circumstances of his demise, it seems that the collective darkness reflected by that natal Moon-Chiron-Pluto conjunction eventually subsumed him.

Although we might need to look beyond our personal anger and pain to the collective suffering that lies beneath, when Chiron aspects the inner planets – in our own or someone else's chart – we're still in a world we recognise, living in a society where we can see clearly enough what has gone wrong. But the outer planets can have a disturbingly faceless quality because they symbolise the future of the collective, not the personal present or past.

If Chiron aspects Uranus, Neptune, or Pluto in the natal chart, the outer planet may be projected onto what is perceived as a vast threatening external power, such as a nation, a government, the financial establishment, the armed forces, global corporations, or the terrifying power of the mob. I mentioned this propensity earlier when we looked at the opposition of

Saturn and Chiron in Pisces to the Uranus-Pluto conjunction in Virgo during the 1960s. Or we can feel as though we've been taken over by compulsions we don't understand, and sometimes, as in Milosevich's case, we are.

Here's a more optimistic example of natal Chiron involved with an outer planet in the natal chart – in this case, two outer planets – where the individual managed to transform the threat of the collective into a vision of potential healing on a global scale. This is the chart of Pope John XXIII, born Angelo Giuseppe Roncalli and known to history as the 'Good Pope'. Natal Chiron is at 19° Taurus in the 4th house, at the centre of a large stellium. It conjuncts Neptune at 14°, Jupiter at 19ª, and Pluto at 28° Taurus. Pope John, who occupied the papal throne for only five years, was unlike any Pope who came before or after him because he tried to modernise the Catholic Church in his lifetime by reaching out to, rather than condemning or attempting to convert, people of different religious persuasions.

John, unlike many religious leaders, was genuinely ecumenical. He seems to have believed sincerely that every human being suffers and merits pastoral care, regardless of their background or system of belief. He worked tirelessly to establish relations with the Greek Orthodox Church, the ancient enemy of Rome. During the Second World War, while still a papal nuncio, he made immense efforts to save Jewish refugees from the Nazis, in contrast to his superior, Pope Pius XII, who, justifiably or not, became known as 'Hitler's Pope'. John played a major role in gaining the support of the Catholic Church for the establishment of the State of Israel. After he became Pope he engaged in dialogue with the Communist countries of Eastern Europe and worked to reconcile the Vatican with the Russian Orthodox Church. He was deeply traditional in his beliefs. But he was a profoundly compassionate man who tried to live the *imitatio Christi* rather than just preaching it. He recognised suffering as a shared human experience, and its mitigation lay beyond the doctrines of any specific religious doctrine.

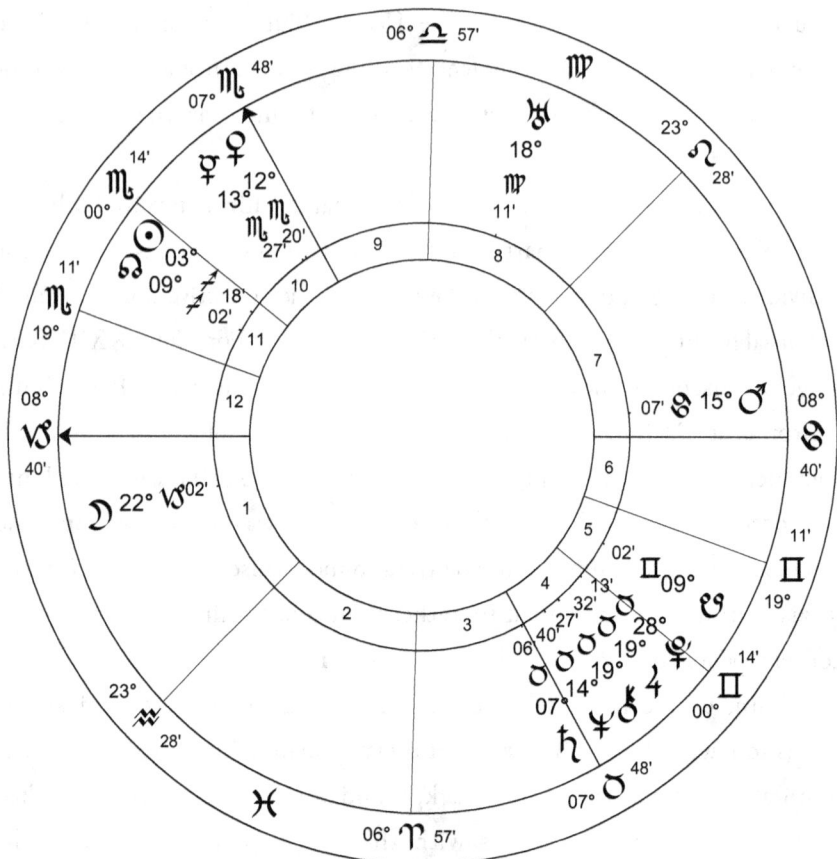

Pope John XXIII
25 November 1881, 10.15 am, Sotto il Monte, Bergamo, Italy

As an example, this is his statement about the Church's treatment of the Jews. It was published in the *Catholic Herald* in 1965 under that Uranus-Pluto conjunction in Virgo opposing Saturn and Chiron in Pisces which we looked at earlier today.

We are conscious today that many, many centuries of blindness have cloaked our eyes so that we can no longer see the beauty of Thy chosen people nor recognise in their faces the features of our privileged brethren. We realize that the mark of Cain stands upon our foreheads. Across the centuries our brother Abel has lain in blood which we drew, or shed tears we caused by forgetting Thy love. Forgive us for the curse we falsely attached to their name as Jews. Forgive us for crucifying Thee a second time in their flesh. For we know not what we did.[39]

Chiron conjunct Neptune in John's chart apparently opened the gates not only to an awareness of collective suffering but also, because it's Neptune, to the eternal human yearning for redemption and return to a divine source. Jung was also born under Neptune conjunct Chiron in Taurus, and his psychology is deeply concerned with a form of spiritual redemption, although he articulated it in more neutral terms. Chiron conjunct Pluto seems to have driven John into an honest confrontation with the depths of human darkness and cruelty, as well as the capacity for cleansing and transformation. John's statement about the Church's treatment of the Jews reflects a painful realisation of the nature of scapegoating.

Traditional Catholic doctrine provided him with a strong and unwavering framework, which isn't surprising with so many planets in Taurus and a Capricorn Ascendant. He certainly wasn't a friend to women who favoured birth control or abortion, and the idea of same-sex marriages or women priests would hardly have met with approval. But Chiron in aspect to Neptune and Pluto allowed him to move beyond the narrow confines of religious exclusivity and recognise the universal pain of being human.

If we take these observations and apply them to the experience of Chiron in one chart aspecting an outer planet in another person's chart, what kind of response can we expect?

Audience: Would the other person be the one who opens the gates to these experiences of universal suffering and darkness?

Liz: Yes, although it's rarely either intentional or conscious. Meeting an outer planet in the guise of another person can be uncomfortable because

---

39   Pope John XXIII, 'Our Eyes Have Been Cloaked', *Catholic Herald*, 14 May 1965.

the outer planet person seems to hold so much power. Even if they're unaware of it – which is usually the case – they appear to carry the force of an entire collective, and they can seem frightening as well as fascinating. Chiron may perceive an archetypal force in an ordinary individual who can't understand why they arouse so much fear. The Chiron person may be mesmerised like the proverbial rabbit in front of the headlights. This isn't always conducive to an easy or honest exchange. Chiron fears being injured, overwhelmed, and even annihilated by the other person, however vulnerable and ordinary that person might feel themselves to be.

The person whose outer planet is involved in the aspect may begin to feel a heightened connection with their generation group and its values, fears, and aspirations. That also might not be comfortable, but it could be immensely creative because it can help the individual to tap into deeper collective patterns that change and enlarge their way of seeing life.

Audience: What about Chiron and Uranus? I can understand collective suffering with Neptune and Pluto, but I'm having a hard time connecting suffering with Uranus.

Liz: Uranian vision may be a gift, but there's a high price tag. There is a disturbing work by the late-19th-century French symbolist painter Gustave Moreau depicting the mythic Titan Prometheus chained to his rock. Moreau was born with Sun in Aries in the 11th house square Uranus in Capricorn in the 8th. In the painting, he replaced the usual motif of Zeus' eagle with a pair of vultures, expressing his pain and disgust at the world of art critics and an ignorant public that tore into the work of visionary artists and repeatedly failed to understand it. The divine fire that the mythic Titan stole is shown in the painting as a small ovoid of light hovering just above Prometheus' head. The fire is the artist's vision, which isolates him from society and earns him condemnation, contempt, and sometimes even the label of madness. Seeing too much and too far can be the source of loneliness and suffering because the ideal world will never be manifested without humiliating compromise and irrevocable damage.

I'll give you an example of the interaction between Chiron and the outer planets in synastry, but be warned: it's a very dark and frightening example that can teach us a lot about the bitter fruits of unconsciousness. Earlier I mentioned the chart of Josef Mengele, Hitler's 'Angel of Death', with natal Chiron at 4º Pisces in the 9th house. Hitler was born under the Neptune-Pluto conjunction in Gemini at the end of the 19th century which we looked at earlier, and this conjunction, with Neptune at 1º and Pluto at 5º Gemini, completely unaspected in Hitler's 8th house, forms close squares to Mengele's Chiron.

Mengele was mesmerised through his own unconscious wound, which Hitler played on and used to his own advantage. With Chiron in the 9th, Mengele's bitterness and disillusionment toward conventional religious doctrines opened him up to a different and vastly more destructive kind of doctrine. Together these two men formed a terrifying conduit of collective darkness which neither man wished to or could control. Mengele was Hitler's puppet, enacting on a practical level the barbaric vision of someone who in turn was the puppet of collective forces that had found the perfect vessel.

Audience: That's horrible. It makes the outer planets sound like evil forces, and Chiron is like a place where infection can get in.

Liz: Hitler and Mengele *are* a horrible example, but the outer planets aren't evil. They just aren't personal, and it's hard for us as individuals to relate to such overwhelming movements in the collective psyche without either being trampled by the current or sacrificing our humanity to join it. Pluto reflects the collective survival instinct. In order to preserve the life of a species, a collective, a family, or an individual, Pluto must weed out and destroy anything that might threaten life. There's nothing intrinsically evil about that. It's what surgeons do when they remove a tumour or a hopelessly diseased organ so the patient can survive. But if this instinct isn't mediated through individuals conscious enough to reflect and discern where to draw the line, the tumour and the diseased organ can be perceived as an entire population.

We need to learn to be mediators for the outer planets, not victims of them or unthinking mouthpieces for them, as Hitler and Mengele were. What happened in Nazi Germany has happened in other guises throughout history, and on a much smaller and less overtly horrific scale it's happening all the time everywhere in every petty act of spite, vindictiveness, and scapegoating we display in our daily lives. Trolling someone on social media and trying to destroy them simply because they don't agree with you or because you secretly envy them is only different from these mass movements in size, method, and global impact, not in its essential nature.

It's humans, not planets, who behave in destructive ways if they're deeply unconscious. All through this seminar I've been trying to talk about how vulnerable we are to our own potential destructiveness and to the destructive aspects of the collective psyche if we don't face and work with our unconscious wounds as individuals. And you're right about Chiron: it can certainly be a place where infection gets in unless we understand that vulnerability.

Chiron in myth is a seer, a musician, a teacher, and a healer. He's good and wise, and he's wounded and poisoned because he underestimates the force of a collective on the rampage. In the end he is released from his suffering, and his power as an archetypal figure remains immortal even if he himself is not. I'm not a Catholic and so the doctrines of the Church don't really resonate with me, but individuals aren't doctrines. Pope John XXIII is an excellent example of how the poison can be transformed into something creative that heals rather than destroys. Freud and Jung are also examples, and in his own sphere, so is Steven Spielberg, and so is Nick Drake, despite his tragic end. These are people who have suffered but who have also helped to bring wisdom, beauty, compassion, understanding, and even humour to the darkness. Most of us will never be called to make such grand contributions. But we can do the same thing in small ways in our own individual lives.

Part Three

Chiron in the Family

Unlike our lovers and partners, we don't choose our families. Some might say we don't choose our lovers and partners either, although we would like to believe we do. But the role of unconscious complexes and the hidden pull of the *daimon* toward individuation may be doing most of the choosing. Some might also say that the soul does choose the family into which we incarnate, according to what might need to be learned or developed or contributed in a particular lifetime. The family might also be viewed as an alchemical vessel in which the formation of individuals is the goal of the process, and the interaction between family members is like the meeting of chemical substances in a sealed alembic: all are changed.

While these perceptions might or might not be true according to our individual worldview, nevertheless our families often feel like a fate imposed on us. We're compelled by ties of blood to interact with people whom we might otherwise avoid if we met them at a party, yet who have the power to wound us deeply, just as we have the power to wound them. Tight Chiron synastry aspects are a regular occurrence in families, as are particular natal Chiron signs, house placements, and aspects that repeat over many generations. I'm often left with the feeling that an inherited wound may be symbolised by this constant repetition, with each successive generation facing the task of finding a little more insight and a pathway out of the cave.

Natal Sun-Chiron aspects in the British royal family

Let's take as an example the British royal family. They are no different from any other family in terms of the frequency of Chiron synastry aspects and the frequency of hostile collisions as well as loving loyalties between family members. But they're subject to expectations, rules, restraints, and traditions that most of us cannot even begin to imagine. They live in a fishbowl from which, despite efforts to 'never complain, never explain,' the difficult family dynamics that the rest of us manage to keep private are often leaked to the media for everyone to see, especially when a disgruntled family member decides to air all the dirty linen.

King Edward VIII did precisely that. In 1951 he published a memoir entitled *A King's Story*,[40] presenting the reasons for his abdication in a way that deliberately made his family appear heartless and cruel. He received an advance of £500,000 from his publisher, which today would be worth £12,526,495.00.[41] Not surprisingly, he was accused of writing the book not only out of spite, but to supplement what he deemed to be an undeservedly meagre income from his family, who wouldn't allow him to live in the style to which he had once been accustomed. In 1956 Wallis Simpson continued the assault with her own memoir, *The Heart Has Its Reasons*. This book reveals her claim that she had offered to withdraw from her relationship with Edward to save his throne, but he had refused to be parted from her.[42] Thus she wasn't the wicked, manipulative seductress portrayed by the press. It was the heartless royal family who wouldn't accommodate Edward's noble and unwavering desire to be with the woman he loved.

It would be impossible to look at the entire astrological history of the British royal family in one seminar, nor would many astrologers be interested in such a detailed examination. And there are too many

---

40   Edward, Duke of Windsor, *A King's Story* (G. P. Putnam's Sons, 1951).
41   Calculation for 22 November 2022, from The Bank of England online Inflation Calculator.
42   Wallis, Duchess of Windsor, *The Heart Has Its Reasons* (Book Clubs, 1956).

centuries to cover and too many family members, and we don't always have birth charts for earlier generations. I would like to focus on specific factors involving Chiron, which in many ways is the wrong way to approach the interpretation of any natal horoscope. A chart is an organism in which every component interacts with every other. But focusing solely on Chiron in a small number of charts may still prove illuminating.

I've selected a handful of the royal family's charts from modern times. We can look first at natal Chiron placements, especially one recurring pairing in a variety of different aspects: Sun-Chiron, which seems to repeat with unusual frequency down the generations. Then we can look at some of Chiron's synastry aspects between the charts of family members. If you want to explore these charts further, you can find them online at astro.com.[43]

- Queen Elizabeth II: natal Chiron at 28° 01' Aries in the 3rd house, in an out-of-sign conjunction with natal Sun at 0° 12' Taurus.

- King George VI, her father: natal Chiron at 23° 54' Libra in the 12th house, sextile natal Sun at 21° 55' Sagittarius.

- Elizabeth Bowes-Lyon (Queen Elizabeth the Queen Mother), her mother: natal Chiron at 19° 10' Sagittarius in the 6th house, trine natal Sun at 11° 09' Leo.

- King George V, her grandfather: natal Chiron at 18° 50' Pisces in the 12th house, square natal Sun at 12° 26' Gemini.

43   Since this seminar was first given, deaths and marriages have occurred in the royal family which have altered the positions, titles, and relationship dynamics of many family members. Prince Philip, Duke of Edinburgh, died in 2021, Queen Elizabeth II died in 2022, and her son Charles, who was Prince of Wales at the time of the seminar, is now King Charles III. His eldest son William married Kate Middleton in 2011 and is now Prince of Wales; his younger son Prince Harry married Meghan Markle in 2018 and is now Duke of Sussex; and Camilla Parker-Bowles, who became Duchess of Cornwall in April 2005 when she married Charles, is now Queen. I have edited the relevant titles and added new members to bring this section up to date.

- King Edward VIII, her uncle (whose chart we looked at earlier): natal Chiron at 16° 16' Virgo in the 7th house. Chiron forms no aspect to natal Sun.

- Prince Philip, Duke of Edinburgh, her husband: natal Chiron at 13° 23' Aries in the 9th house. Chiron forms no aspect to natal Sun.

- Princess Margaret, her sister: natal Chiron at 18° 54' Taurus in the 1st house, square natal Sun at 28° 01' Leo.

- King Charles III, her eldest son: natal Chiron at 28° 13' Scorpio in the 5th house, conjunct natal Sun at 22° 25' Scorpio.

- Princess Anne, the Princess Royal, her daughter: natal Chiron at 15° 37' Sagittarius in the 2nd house, trine natal Sun at 22° 02' Leo.

- Prince Andrew, Duke of York, her second son: natal Chiron at 27° 38' Aquarius on the cusp of the 8th house, in an out-of-sign conjunction with natal Sun at 0° 0' Pisces.

- Prince Edward, Duke of Edinburgh, her third son: natal Chiron at 14° 49' Pisces in the 5th house, conjunct natal Sun at 20° 17' Pisces.

The late Queen, her father, her mother, her grandfather, her sister, and all her children have a natal Sun-Chiron aspect. Four of them (the Queen, Charles, Andrew, and Edward) have conjunctions; one (her father) a sextile; two (her grandfather and her sister) a square; and two (Anne and the Queen Mother) a trine. On this list, only Prince Philip and King Edward VIII lack a natal Sun-Chiron aspect, and neither of them was crowned as monarch.[44]

The monarchs preceding King George V, the late Queen's grandfather, also carry the Sun-Chiron signature. It repeats with disturbing consistency from King George I down to the present King Charles III, with only two exceptions.

---

44 Edward VIII became King the moment his father died, but he abdicated before he could be formally crowned.

- King George I (the first Hanoverian monarch): natal Chiron at 19°
  15' Capricorn quincunx natal Sun at 17° 10' Gemini.

- King George II, his son: no aspect between natal Chiron and
  natal Sun.

- King George III, his son: natal Chiron at 5° 17' Gemini conjunct
  natal Sun at 13° 20' Gemini.

- King George IV, his son: natal Chiron at 19° 54' Leo opposition
  natal Sun at 22° 31' Aquarius.

- King William IV, brother of King George IV:[45] natal Chiron at 28°
  Leo 13' in an out-of-sign opposition to natal Chiron at 6° 25' Pisces.

- Edward, Duke of Kent, fourth son of King George III and father of
  Queen Victoria:[46] natal Chiron at 12° 05' Pisces trine natal Sun at 9°
  53' Scorpio.

- Queen Victoria: natal Chiron at 28° 34' Pisces in an out-of-sign
  sextile to natal Sun at 2° 07' Gemini.

- King Edward VII, her son: no aspect between natal Chiron and
  natal Sun.

Many earlier monarchs, such as Henry IV, Henry VI, and Henry VII,
and even William the Conqueror (King William I), also have a Sun-Chiron
contact. Even Oliver Cromwell, the Lord Protector who ruled the country
during the interregnum between the beheading of King Charles I and the
accession of King Charles II, had a Sun-Chiron sextile. But historically,
the charts of earlier Kings and Queens don't have the aspect with the same
frequency as those from George I onward. The appearance of the aspect in
the charts of earlier rulers might be understood as random in accord with

---

45 King George IV died without any legitimate children, so his brother succeeded him.
46 Edward, Duke of Kent, was never crowned King. His daughter Victoria succeeded
to the throne as the niece of William IV because there were no other legitimate children
before her in the line of succession.

statistical probability. Out of any group of people, a certain percentage can be expected to have the aspect. But from George I onward they are too consistent to be random. Would anyone like to offer a comment on what this might mean?

Audience: I don't know enough about the history of these people to comment. But I wondered whether the aspect appears in the chart of the United Kingdom.

Liz: It's a good question, and one that I also wondered about. But it doesn't. The birth chart of England, usually dated to the crowning of William the Conqueror in 1066, has no aspect between Sun and Chiron, although William himself, first King of England, has a square between Sun in Libra and Chiron in Capricorn. The chart for the United Kingdom, dated to 1801, also has no aspect between Sun and Chiron. It seems that the aspect began to pick up steam after the arrival of the first Hanoverian monarch, which occurred after the death of Queen Anne in 1714.

George I, a German prince of the Electorate of Hanover, took the British throne because there were no other legitimate Protestant heirs. George's mother Princess Sophia was the granddaughter of King James I (who had Sun quincunx Chiron) and was Queen Anne's second cousin. Sophia had become Electress of Hanover through marriage and would have become Queen of England herself as she was next in the line of succession after Anne. But both women died in 1714 and the crown passed to George. It's all rather confusing. But this was a period when a great many babies died stillborn or very young, and not every monarch enjoyed the luxury of an heir and a spare. We could speculate about why the family signature began to accelerate with the arrival of the Hanoverian dynasty, but it really would be pure speculation.

Now let's look at a few more contemporary royal family charts.

- Princess Diana, first wife of King Charles III: natal Chiron at 6° 28' Pisces in the 3rd house, trine natal Sun at 9° 40' Cancer.

- Queen Camilla, second wife of King Charles III: natal Chiron at 2° 31' Scorpio in the 4th house, in an out-of-sign square to natal Sun at 23° 47' Cancer.

- Prince William, Prince of Wales: natal Chiron at 25° 17' Taurus in the 5th house. Chiron forms no aspect to natal Sun.

- Prince Harry, Duke of Sussex: natal Chiron at 8° 33' Gemini in the 5th house. Chiron forms no aspect to natal Sun.

Interestingly, neither William nor Harry has a natal Sun-Chiron aspect, although Charles' first and second wives both do – Princess Diana has a Sun-Chiron trine and Queen Camilla has a Sun-Chiron square. Let's look at William's and Harry's wives' charts, and at their children's charts as well.

- Katherine, Princess of Wales, William's wife: natal Chiron at 18° 03' Taurus in the 10th house, trine natal Sun at 19° 12' Capricorn.

- Meghan, Duchess of Sussex, Harry's wife: natal Chiron at 22° 35' Taurus in the 11th house. Chiron makes no aspect to natal Sun.

- Prince George, eldest son of Prince William: natal Chiron at 13° 15' Pisces in the 3rd house, sesquiquadrate natal Sun at 29° 59' Cancer.

- Princess Charlotte, daughter of Prince William: natal Chiron at 20° 20' Pisces in the 10th house. Chiron makes no aspect to natal Sun.

- Prince Louis, youngest son of Prince William: natal Chiron at 0° 19' Aries at the IC. Chiron makes no aspect to natal Sun.

- Archie Mountbatten-Windsor, son of Prince Harry: natal Chiron at 4° 18' Aries in the 12th house. Chiron makes no aspect to natal Sun.

- Lilibet Mountbatten-Windsor, daughter of Prince Harry: natal Chiron at 12º 13' Aries in the 8th house, sextile natal Sun at 14º 21' Gemini.

Although she isn't a family member by blood, Kate has the family signature of Sun-Chiron, in her case a close trine, although William, her husband, has no aspect between them. Meghan has no Sun-Chiron contact; her natal Chiron in Taurus trines Venus in Virgo but makes no aspect to any other personal planets. Prince George, who is next in the line of succession after his father Prince William and his grandfather King Charles, has a sesquiquadrate between Sun and Chiron. Princess Charlotte, daughter of Prince William, has no Sun-Chiron aspect. Louis, younger son of Prince William, has no Sun-Chiron contact. Archie, son of Harry and Meghan, has no Sun-Chiron contact. Lilibet, daughter of Harry and Meghan, has Sun sextile Chiron. It seems that the frequency of Sun-Chiron contacts in the younger generations of the family has begun to slow down and revert to statistical probability.

We could go on with the children of Anne, Andrew, and Edward, and all their grandchildren. But I think this list illustrates the point. How would you understand this Sun-Chiron aspect running down through so many generations of the family?

Audience: They aren't really free to be themselves. They're held back by their upbringing and the roles they have to play. Their relationships have sometimes been ruined and their real views silenced. Could that be a kind of wound?

Liz: Yes, it could certainly be seen as a wound. I have no doubt that for most of their lives, every one of these Sun-Chiron people, regardless of the type of aspect, has suffered through feeling their individual potentials were unfairly blocked and their lives painfully limited by the position that history thrust upon them. But at the same time, Sun-Chiron might also point to a special collective role which, while hurtful to the expression of individuality, could provide a symbol of healing and integration for the nation. The Sun symbolises our vocation, and whether they like it or not, these people have been 'called'. Some are better equipped to carry their role than others, some voluntarily choose to uphold it, and others reject it or attempt to change it.

The archetypal priest-king

The symbolism of sacred kingship is archetypal, and written references to it date back to ancient Mesopotamia. It's undoubtedly older than that and vanishes in the mists of prehistory. Every ancient culture developed its own mythology around the archetype, whether the individual on whom it was focused was called a king or queen, a chieftain, a warlord, a tyrant, an archon, an emperor or empress, a *lucomo*, or a *pontifex maximus*.[47] This mythic theme presents the chosen individual as a mediator or agent for the divine on earth. The anointing with oil at the time of the coronation of a King or Queen of Great Britain is a living tradition that has ancient antecedents. Although the anointing symbolises the worldly power the deity confers on the monarch as a vessel, it also symbolises the ruler as the sacred Scapegoat who suffers for the people.

The archetypal king or queen is also a priest, a seer, and a healer, and we can immediately recognise Chiron, priest-king of the Centaurs, in this figure. I'm not suggesting that any member of the modern royal family consciously identifies with the archetype, although historically some

---

47   The ancient meaning of 'tyrant', from the Greek *tyrannos*, didn't connote then what it does today. A tyrant was an absolute ruler. Some were cruel and voracious, some were benign and devoted to the service of the people, and some were both. From the word we get *tyrannosaurus rex*, whose name means 'king of the ruler lizards'. *Lucomo* is the name given to the Etruscan priest-kings who governed the twelve Etruscan city-states before the advent of the Romans. The Latin term *pontifex maximus* means 'great bridge-builder'. It is now applied to the Pope but was originally used by Roman emperors to indicate their role as intermediaries between the people and the gods.

earlier kings like Henry IV and Henry VII, who both had Sun-Chiron aspects, certainly did. They 'knew' they had been chosen by God even if their accession to the throne meant the imprisonment and murder of the previous incumbent. The idea of sacred kingship was embedded in the medieval worldview. But some modern royals have taken the symbolism more seriously than others, not as a means to absolute power but as a necessary responsibility in return for the position and privileges they enjoy.

Queen Elizabeth II devoted her life to the task of service to the nation and fulfilled it with grace, dignity, and humility. It seems she instinctively understood the importance of the symbol without believing she personally *was* the archetype. To the extent that any member of the royal family finds the demands of the archetypal role intolerable, they are likely to rebel against it.

Audience: What does this say about the ones who don't have the aspect, like Edward VII?

Liz: I'm not sure. I don't think lack of a Sun-Chiron aspect means that the person would be a bad or incompetent monarch. But perhaps it means the painful experience of a sacred burden requiring great personal sacrifice isn't part of the individual's sense of self.

King Edward VII, fondly known as 'Bertie', didn't have a Sun-Chiron aspect. His natal Sun is at 17º Scorpio in the 10th house, sextile Mars in Capricorn in the 1st, square Neptune in Aquarius in the 2nd, and trine Uranus in Pisces, also in the 2nd. Like everyone else, Bertie's chart has a natal Chiron, which in his case is at 2º Leo in the 7th house. It trines Mercury in Sagittarius and sextiles natal Moon at the end of Virgo. His marriage to Princess Alexandra of Denmark wasn't a love-match but it seems to have been harmonious, no doubt helped by Alexandra's decision to tolerate her husband's many affairs.

Bertie inherited the throne from his mother Queen Victoria but didn't inherit her obsessions. While Prince of Wales he was known as the 'playboy prince'. But once he became king, he took his public duties very seriously. Many people were surprised that he handled the job so well. He was liberal in his thinking and unafraid of showing it. He established close friendships and working relationships with several Jewish people, an act frowned upon at a time when 'polite' antisemitism was the norm in most social circles. He was an affectionate parent. He was determined to enjoy his privileges and indulged himself thoroughly without feeling unduly hampered by a guilty conscience. He was also known for his droll wit. While still Prince of Wales and waiting patiently, decade after decade, for his chance to rule, he remarked about his mother Queen Victoria:

> I don't mind praying to the Eternal Father, but I must be the only man in the country afflicted with an eternal mother.[48]

King Edward VII. Bromide postcard print c. 1900.

Although he made many mistakes, Edward VII was greatly loved, and in his relatively short reign proved capable of dealing with the challenges of his role astutely, honestly, and conscientiously while remaining charming, accessible, and human. He wore the royal mantel responsibly but lightly, apparently oblivious to Shakespeare's declaration in *Henry IV*: 'Uneasy lies the head that wears a crown.'

---

48 www.imdb.com/name/nm0454371/bio.

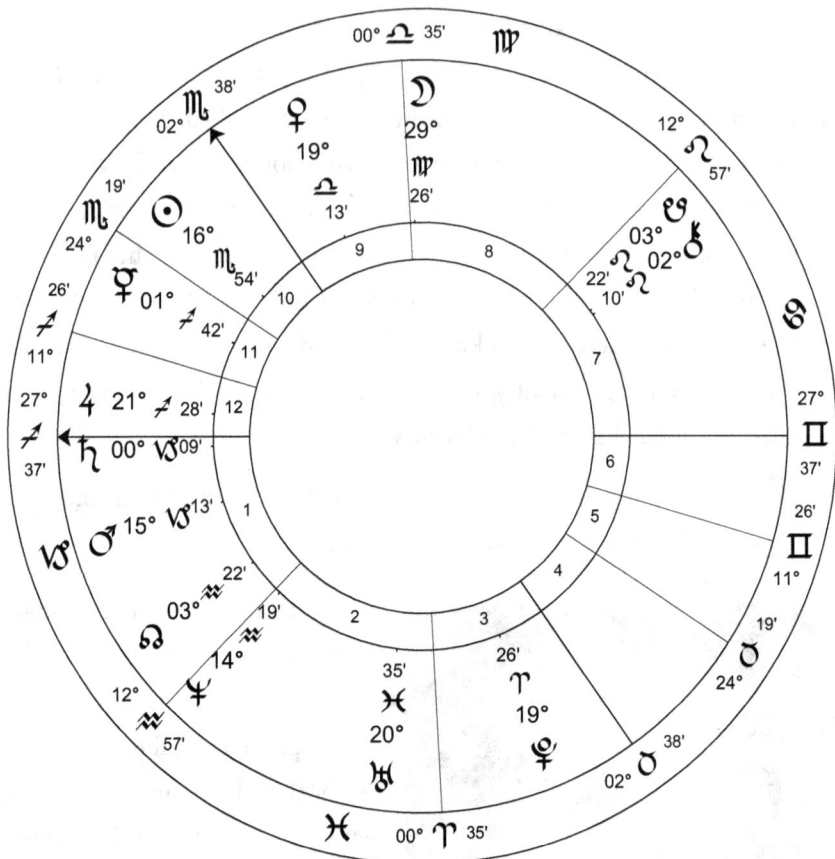

King Edward VII
9 November 1841, 10.48 am, London

Sun-Chiron as a vocation

We looked at some of the dimensions of natal Sun-Chiron aspects earlier in the seminar. The Sun is concerned with the movement toward individual fulfilment and individual destiny. It is our vocation in the deepest sense, what we are 'called' to become and contribute, although this might not necessarily be reflected in how we earn a living in the mundane world. Sun-Chiron aspects reflect a sense of damage to the confident expression the Sun, usually triggered by early experiences that thwart or undermine our aspirations and exaggerate what we perceive as our failures and deficiencies. But Sun-Chiron's wound can also point to a meaningful pattern of development that requires suffering and sacrifice. We may feel called upon to utilise our inner pain as a source of understanding and offer some form of service, teaching, or healing. The unhealable wound becomes a necessary experience that unlocks humility, depth, and compassion for others as well as for oneself.

Four more examples of this creative expression of Sun-Chiron are worth noting. We've met it already in Jung, Greta Thunberg, and King Charles III. James Hillman, with Sun and Moon conjunct Chiron in Aries, was a Jungian analyst who created his own school of 'archetypal psychology' and wrote a number innovative, challenging books that are remarkable in their depth and insight. I've quoted him several times during the seminar. Marie Curie, with Sun in Scorpio trine a Moon-Chiron conjunction in Pisces, was a Polish-French physicist and chemist. She won two Nobel prizes for her pioneering work on radioactivity and radiography. Although she was the first woman to become a professor at the University of Paris, she was denied membership in the French Academy of Sciences because she was female.

The Welsh writer Arthur Machen, with Sun conjunct Chiron in Pisces, began his long life during the reign of Queen Victoria and died during the reign of King George VI. His work deserves to be far better known. He produced elegantly crafted stories and novels steeped in his own unique mystical vision, focused on spiritual suffering and the painful collision between human awareness and the hidden and often dangerous depths of the invisible world. Finally, the French-American astrologer and composer Dane Rudhyar, with Sun in Aries opposition Chiron in Libra, created visionary work, inspired by both Theosophical and Jungian models, which has had enormous influence on several generations of astrologers.

All these people, in very different ways, made the convoluted depths of human suffering their vocation. Although the archetypal priest-king is a vessel for the divine, the individual is an ordinary mortal who will sometimes make terrible mistakes, become ill, experience love and hate, suffer grief and loss, endure failure and enjoy success, grow old and frail, and die like everyone else. The operative word here is 'vessel'. Vessels may sometimes never know in their lifetimes the archetypal role they are called to carry, and they can never be immortal or perfect because they are human conduits, not gods. And sometimes the most effective vessels are those who have been deeply damaged by life.

Chiron synastry in the royal family

Now let's look at some synastry aspects involving Chiron in the charts of some of the royal family members I mentioned earlier.

- The late Queen Elizabeth II's natal Chiron in late Aries conjuncts her son Charles' Moon in early Taurus.
- Prince Philip's natal Chiron in Aries opposes his son Charles' Venus-Neptune conjunction in Libra.
- Charles' natal Chiron in late Scorpio conjuncts his mother Queen Elizabeth's Saturn in Scorpio.
- Charles' natal Chiron opposes his late wife Diana's Venus in Taurus, squares her Moon in Aquarius, squares her Mars-Pluto conjunction in early Virgo, and squares her natal Chiron in early Pisces.
- Charles' natal Chiron opposes his son William's Venus-Chiron conjunction in Taurus.
- Diana's natal Chiron in Pisces opposes Charles' Saturn in Virgo.
- William's natal Chiron conjuncts his mother Diana's Venus.
- William's natal Chiron squares Diana's Moon in Aquarius.
- William's natal Chiron conjuncts his brother Harry's natal Moon.
- William's natal Chiron opposes his grandmother Queen Elizabeth's Saturn in Scorpio.

- Camilla's natal Chiron in Scorpio opposes her husband Charles' Moon in Taurus.

- Harry's natal Chiron in Gemini exactly conjuncts his brother William's Mercury.

- Harry's natal Chiron in Gemini conjuncts his stepmother Camilla's Mars.

- Meghan's natal Chiron in Taurus conjuncts her husband Harry's Moon.

- Meghan's natal Chiron opposes Queen Elizabeth's Saturn in Scorpio.

- Meghan's natal Chiron opposes Charles' Sun-Chiron conjunction in Scorpio.

- Meghan's natal Chiron conjuncts William's Venus-Chiron conjunction.

- Meghan's natal Chiron opposes Camilla's Jupiter in Scorpio.

This is not a complete list. They are all tight Chiron synastry aspects, and there are a lot of them. But they're typical of many close-knit family groups. We might speculate *ad nauseam* about who does what to whom; I'm sure you will all have your own thoughts about each of them, and I've talked about many of these Chiron combinations earlier in the day. But a couple of examples might help to illustrate the kind of relationship dynamics so typical of Chiron.

The relationship between King Charles and his father Prince Philip was particularly tense when Charles was young. Philip's Chiron at 13° Aries in the 9th house opposes Charles' Neptune-Venus conjunction at 13° and 16° Libra respectively in the 4th house. It seems that Philip found the sensitive, visionary, romantic, and artistic dimensions of his son's personality disturbing and difficult to understand, and felt Charles needed 'toughening up'. He implemented this by sending Charles to Gordonstoun, an independent school in the remote northeast of Scotland which Philip himself had attended as a boy and which at that time was known for its rigour, encouragement of athletic prowess, and harsh disciplinary practices.

Predictably, Charles was miserable at Gordonstoun. He was lonely and incessantly bullied, described his time there as a 'prison sentence', and referred to the school as 'Colditz in kilts'.[49] Philip later admitted that sending Charles there had been a mistake. But his decision was not based on deliberate cruelty or callousness. He loved his son deeply and no doubt genuinely believed that as he himself had benefited from his time there, Gordonstoun would give Charles a bit more of the grit and resilience Philip felt he would need as a future monarch.

But we could also look more deeply and consider the possibility that Philip, who had suffered greatly from his own turbulent and unstable childhood, not only wanted the best for Charles but also unconsciously envied and resented his son's aesthetic gifts as well as the fortunate circumstances that ensured Charles had an attentive family around him and a childhood with the kind of stability and comfort that Philip himself had been denied. This is also an example of Chiron in a synastry aspect with an outer planet: Philip's Chiron exactly opposes Charles' Neptune, and the element of mysticism in Charles' nature may have been deeply unsettling to a pragmatic man who, with Chiron in the 9th house, struggled to sustain his own religious faith. We always need to keep in mind that Chiron can be both destructive and creative in relationships, and resentment and envy aren't mutually exclusive of love.

Sometimes events as well as personal feelings or actions can be reflected in Chiron's wound. For example, Prince William lost his mother Diana when he was fifteen. She obviously didn't set out to abandon him. But when she died he must have felt abandoned nonetheless. His

---

49 Colditz is a medieval castle near Leipzig which during the Second World War became a German prisoner-of-war camp set up to house incorrigible Allied officers who had tried to escape from other camps. It was dramatically portrayed in the 1955 film *The Colditz Story*.

exact natal Chiron-Venus conjunction in Taurus on Diana's natal Venus may reflect his experience of loss, grief, and anger at her death and the circumstances in which it happened, as much as it might hint at difficulties in their relationship. And of course everything depends on how each of the individuals involved handles the Chiron synastry.

Charles' Sun-Chiron conjunction in Scorpio opposing Diana's Venus in Taurus and square her Moon in Aquarius and her Mars-Pluto conjunction in Virgo, and Diana's Chiron in Pisces opposing that natal Mars-Pluto conjunction as well as Charles' Saturn in Virgo, were certainly reflected in a deeply unhappy marriage. Neither of them felt they were being seen, understood, or valued. Each of them had something the other one envied bitterly. And both experienced extreme anger and disappointment. But there aren't any real villains here, nor any neatly defined victim or persecutor – just two people who, for various reasons, were unable to cope with their pain, resentment, and envy in a constructive way, and who became increasingly hurtful toward one another as a result. External circumstances, including family interference, contributed to their difficulties. The marriage was manoeuvred if not actually arranged by family members rather than based on any deep mutual affinity. Charles was prevented from marrying the woman he really loved. And he and Diana hardly knew each other when they married. It isn't surprising that Chiron would display its least attractive face.

The marriage between Meghan and Harry, which appears to be more of a love match, involves a close Moon-Chiron conjunction in Taurus across the charts. Moon-Chiron synastry contacts, as we've seen, are common in romantic relationships as well as in families. We might surmise that Harry's empathy for Meghan's perceived vulnerability and unstable family background allows him to feel needed and able to express his own needs more freely. But we might expect Harry to trigger more ambivalent feelings in Meghan, whether we hear about it or not. Harry's Moon is placed at the IC. The response of Meghan's Chiron to this lunar placement, and the impact of that response on him, are directly related to his home, family, and roots. Earlier today the question came up about one person's Chiron on an angle in another person's chart. This is a very literal example of how it can sometimes work out.

The Moon-Chiron conjunction between Harry and Meghan also suggests that he perceives in Meghan many of the qualities he needed and depended on in his mother, reflected by his Moon conjunct Diana's Venus in Taurus. Chiron in Taurus is not the same as Venus in Taurus, but it can still provide a hook for projection. The same affectionate aspect of Moon and Venus that occurs between Diana's and Harry's charts also occurs between Harry and William. But their synastry aspect is complicated by William's Chiron in exact conjunction with his own natal Venus and conjunct Harry's Moon, and by Harry's Chiron in exact conjunction with William's Mercury in Gemini. Earlier we looked at some of the ways Mercury-Chiron aspects in synastry can be expressed.

The complex dynamic involving Chiron between Meghan, Harry, William, and Diana (and her memory) also extends to other family members such as Charles, Camilla, and Kate because so many of them have Chiron in Taurus or Scorpio. Chiron in Scorpio has a profound mistrust of emotional exposure and a constant expectation of betrayal by those who are closest. Hopefully over time, greater understanding might develop and a less fraught dimension of these Chiron exchanges might emerge. But Scorpio and Taurus are fixed signs and aren't known for their flexibility. Both have very long memories.

Several younger members of the family belong to the same Chiron in Taurus generation, including not only Meghan and William but also Kate, William's wife. Princess Margaret, from an earlier generation, also has Chiron in Taurus. Would anyone like to comment on Chiron in Taurus as a generation group?

Generation groups: Chiron in Taurus

Audience: The wound is around feelings about security, and also self-worth. Maybe there's a lot of anxiety about stability.

Liz: Yes, fear of instability might be a big part of it, although in the case of the royal family this fear probably isn't focused on the material world. Meghan's background suggests that material as well as emotional security might have been in short supply. For William, Kate, and Princess Margaret, material security doesn't seem to be an issue. But you mentioned self-worth, and I think that's far more relevant to all of them. Chiron in Taurus generations struggle to develop a solid sense of self-value independent of whatever role they're called upon to play in the world, whether it's a princess or a plumber. Some lines from a song from the 1920s, inspired by Edward VII's popularity before he became King, encapsulates the problem of being identified with a superficial image:

> I danced with a man
> Who danced with a girl
> Who danced with the Prince of Wales.

What is your real value as an individual if all anyone sees is your public face?

Part Four

Chiron in the composite chart

Now I'd like to look at Chiron in the composite chart as the symbol of an incurable wound in a relationship – something that both people must learn to cope with because it won't go away. It helps to think of the composite as the psychological map of a real entity that expresses a unique individual life. This relationship entity has its own development pattern and its own qualities, which will not be identical to the birth charts that make up the composite. Wounding in the context of a relationship as a discrete entity may seem to be a rather strange idea. Composite charts themselves are a rather strange idea because they're based on midpoints rather than on observed heavenly phenomena. But they appear to be helpful and revealing anyway. In the end, the only criteria we can use to judge the composite is whether it works.

The wound in the relationship

Every relationship has a sore and vulnerable place where there seems to be something that can't be healed and must be accommodated and understood. We might view it as a distillation or a paradigm of the combined hurts of the two individuals who create the relationship, as though an alchemical reaction has taken place and each person's wound combines with the other one's to produce a new entity. There is some obstruction or area of suffering in a relationship which is not necessarily the same obstruction or area of suffering that's portrayed in the individual charts of the two people.

When we're in the relationship, we feel and experience this composite wound, but it's very hard to grasp and work with because it might not reflect how we feel about ourselves as individuals. The wound only emerges when we're with the other person, not when we are alone or with someone else. Composite planets don't describe me or you, and they don't portray the back-and-forth interaction of psychological dynamics that's reflected in the synastry between two charts. The composite is created between two people, built on the midpoints of each pair of planets and angles – Sun and Sun, Moon and Moon, Chiron and Chiron, and so on – in the two birth charts.

When we consider an unhealable wound in a composite, we're looking at something that is built into the structure of the relationship. But it isn't coming from either individual specifically. It seems to arise from the interweaving of the two people's individual stories and family histories. There's a quality of fate about it, or something that feels very like fate. A composite can't discuss its feelings or explore itself through psychotherapy. The entry point where we can begin to work with it is through the synastry between the composite and each individual birth chart. That might sound complicated, but it basically involves exploring the aspects between the composite and each individual chart in the same way we would explore the synastry aspects between the charts of two individuals.

Composite Chiron will probably form different aspects to the planets and angles in each individual chart, so the relationship as an entity will have a different impact on each person. It's one of the reasons why, when people try to discuss their difficulties in relationship counselling, two entirely different portrayals emerge which aren't explicable through synastry aspects alone. And it gets even stranger. Composite Chiron seems to partake of the history of the couple before the relationship begins. One of the things I've noticed about composite Chiron is that it points back to patterns that are common to both people's history, and even to their families' histories. The wound isn't due to any particular individual's choices or mistakes. It's part of the inevitable unfolding of a story that began before the relationship developed and perhaps even before the two individuals were born.[50]

For example, Chiron's wound in a composite might be connected with the fact that one or both people have been married before. That's a common Chiron dilemma in composite charts. Former relationships are not, of course, necessarily wounds in themselves. But both people in the new relationship may have to deal with the awkward presence, physical or emotional, of a difficult, invasive, or needy ex-partner, or the legitimate but sometimes burdensome demands of children from a former liaison. Sometimes the memory of a beloved deceased partner may haunt the new relationship, a theme that Daphne du Maurier used to great effect as the basis of her novel, *Rebecca*. There may be financial responsibilities from earlier relationships that handicap the present one. Or the couple may have to face the challenge of an elderly, ill, or demanding parent who constitutes an interference, willing or not, in the lives of both people. This kind of situation isn't necessarily destructive, and it can be creative for both people. But it may still feel like an incurable wound.

Sometimes composite wounds are more internal. Both people may have experienced early deprivation or the loss of one or both parents, or they were subjected to similar experiences of abuse or scapegoating. Both may bear emotional scars resulting in mistrust and the expectation of disappointment. Composite Chiron points to an issue from the past that can never entirely be escaped. It highlights a place where something painful must be faced honestly, accepted, and worked with by both people in the relationship. Whether these wounds can be healed depends on how we define 'healing'.

Audience: What happens when it sits on itself?

---

50 For more on this mysterious dimension of the composite chart, see Liz Greene, *Relationships and How to Survive Them*, Part One: The Composite Chart (CPA Press, 1999, e-book version 2013).

Liz: That sounds either impossibly acrobatic or vaguely obscene. Do you mean composite Chiron conjunct natal Chiron in one of the charts?

Audience: Yes, composite Chiron conjunct one person's natal Chiron.

Liz: This will always happen when two people are born quite close together or fifty years apart and have natal Chirons within orb of conjunction in the same sign. If composite Chiron conjuncts one person's natal Chiron, it will also conjunct the other person's Chiron. A great many relationships of every kind – romantic, familial, friendly, creative, work-related – occur with natal Chirons conjunct, so it isn't an unusual occurrence. If you remember the example I showed you earlier in the seminar, Princess Margaret and Anthony Armstrong-Jones have Chiron in the same sign because they were born in the same year and their natal Chirons are within orb of conjunction. Although we didn't look at their composite chart, composite Chiron will inevitably conjunct both their natal Chirons.

When two people are born with Chirons conjunct, their experience of wounding, reflected by Chiron's sign, will be related to the same damaged ideal. The specific arena in which each of them experiences it, and how it impacts other dimensions of the personality, might not be the same because Chiron may be in a different house in each chart and make aspects to different natal planets. But both people belong to the same Chiron generation and will experience a similar kind of collective suffering. There may be deep empathy between them because they're embittered, disillusioned, fearful, and needy about the same things, and they may perceive the same failings in human nature and in society. There can be an unusual degree of empathy and understanding.

But it can also go the other way. One person might project all the difficult Chiron feelings and behaviour patterns on the other person, who gets to be the scapegoat; or both may project Chiron and accuse each other of doing precisely what they themselves are doing without realising it. A great deal depends on how each natal Chiron connects with other natal planets and with each other's planets in synastry. If the two natal Chirons are closely conjunct, then composite Chiron will form the same aspects to the natal planets in both charts as each natal Chiron does. There's always a possibility that one or both people might defend themselves against too much vulnerability in a relationship. Although the potential may be deep compassion and understanding, defensiveness around Chiron's wound may result in savage attempts to protect what the person doesn't want to face. Then it can be very difficult because the wounded may become the wounder.

Audience: Can you set up a composite for yourself and anything, like an institution or a country? Would there be any point in looking at composite Chiron in that kind of relationship?

Liz: Yes, there's certainly a point if it's an important issue for you. Composite Chiron in the chart of an institution or a country doesn't reflect a wound in the sense of human feelings of pain and scapegoating. But we can think in terms of something that has damaged the development of the entity, or where some part of it hasn't been able to develop properly because of a past event that occurred early in its development. It's interesting to look at natal Chiron in a nation's horoscope, always providing we can find a birth date and time. Some nations, like France and Germany, are virtually impossible to chart because their origins are shrouded in an ancient past and they've had several different incarnations. Some astrologers working with mundane astrology look at separate charts for each successive incarnation, reflected in the different forms of government. The chart for the French Revolution, for example, reflects the birth of the modern French Republic, but not the France of King Louis XIII. Other national charts, such as the US or Israel, have a specific date of birth, and Chiron's placement in these charts can offer a lot of insight into the psychological dynamics of the collective entity.

Chiron in the birth chart of the US is at 20° Aries in the 4th house, opposing Saturn in Libra in the 10th, square Pluto in Capricorn in the

2nd, and square Mercury in Cancer in the 8th. I will leave it to you to contemplate the possible meanings of this complex configuration in cardinal signs. This natal Chiron placement points to complex issues involving roots and origins, collective attitudes toward parenting, home, and the land, and relationships between individual states, indigenous peoples, and immigrant groups that form part of the nation's family. Composite Chiron between a nation's chart and your own might reflect a similar past injury or blockage that could impinge on your ability to live contentedly in that country if composite Chiron forms difficult aspects to your natal chart.

Although we can't attribute human emotions to Chiron in non-human entities, these entities can still be damaged by the collective, by past history, and by unfair events that happen in the outer world. A country can have an inheritance that is particularly painful because its foundation rests on bloodshed and suffering. That early wound may affect the development of the nation for both good and ill because it has left scars. Chiron in the birth chart of Israel, for example, is at 21º Scorpio in the 2nd house, in close opposition to the Sun at 23º Taurus in the 8th. This shouldn't come as a surprise. Israel as a nation arose as a form of recompense and healing for the atrocities of the Holocaust, ancient ties to the land, and a much longer history of constant persecution and suffering. Soon after Israel's birth, several neighbouring nations vowed to annihilate it, and this threat is ongoing. We might view this aspect as an unhealed wound in the fabric of the nation. And we might also think about what I said earlier about Sun-Chiron as a vocation and consider what creative insights and contributions this nation, as an 'outsider', might have to offer to other nations.

Nations have composites with other nations too, and I'm sure any historian would get a great deal of much needed insight from exploring these kinds of links without feeling they have to adopt a political stance. And national leaders, democratically elected or not, have composite charts as well as synastry with the nations over which they preside. We should always prepare to be surprised by what we find if we explore these dimensions of the collective psyche, because the insights these charts reveal might not always accord with our particular political perspectives.

Chiron in the composite, Example 4: Elvis Presley and Colonel Tom Parker

Let's look at an example of composite Chiron in a relationship. This is the composite chart of Elvis Presley and Colonel Tom Parker, his mentor and business manager. I have also included the two birth charts.

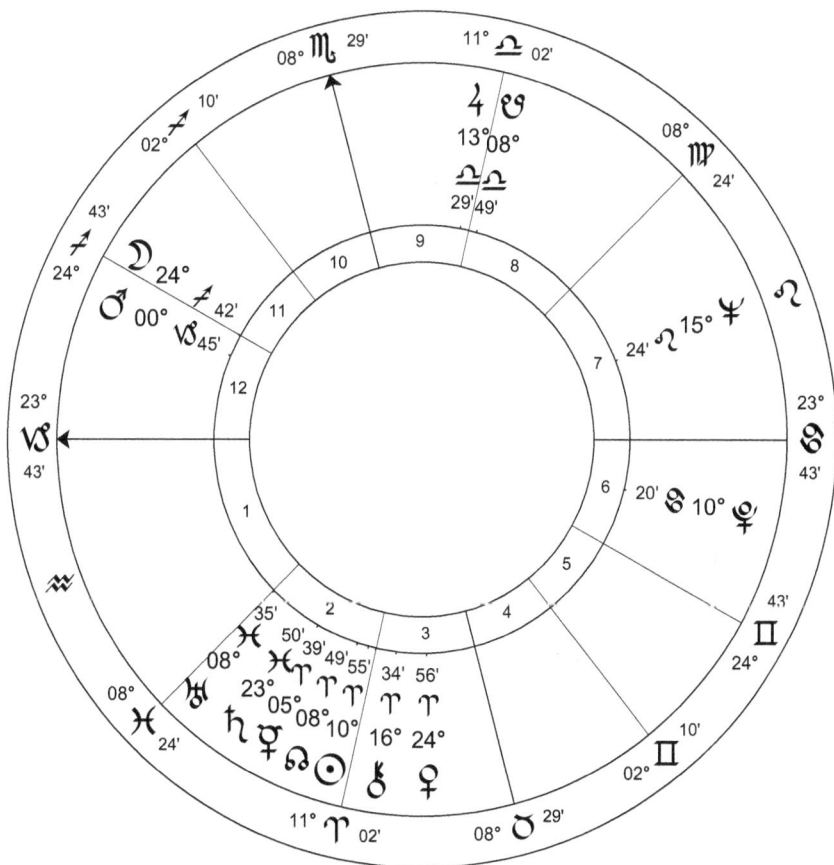

Composite chart of Elvis Presley and Colonel Tom Parker

It might seem, with the stellium of planets in the composite 2nd house, including Saturn, the chart ruler, that this relationship was all about money. On one level that's certainly true – it made both men eye-wateringly wealthy. But the 2nd house isn't just about material issues. It also concerns values and talents. Also, there's a strong emphasis on the 3rd house, with the Sun right on the cusp and a Chiron-Venus conjunction in the 3rd. This pairing of two remarkable individuals wasn't a romantic relationship, but it was close, intense, turbulent, and lasted until Elvis' death and beyond. Tom Parker is sometimes credited with 'creating' Elvis, and he seems to have been a kind of surrogate father as well as a kingmaker. He's also been

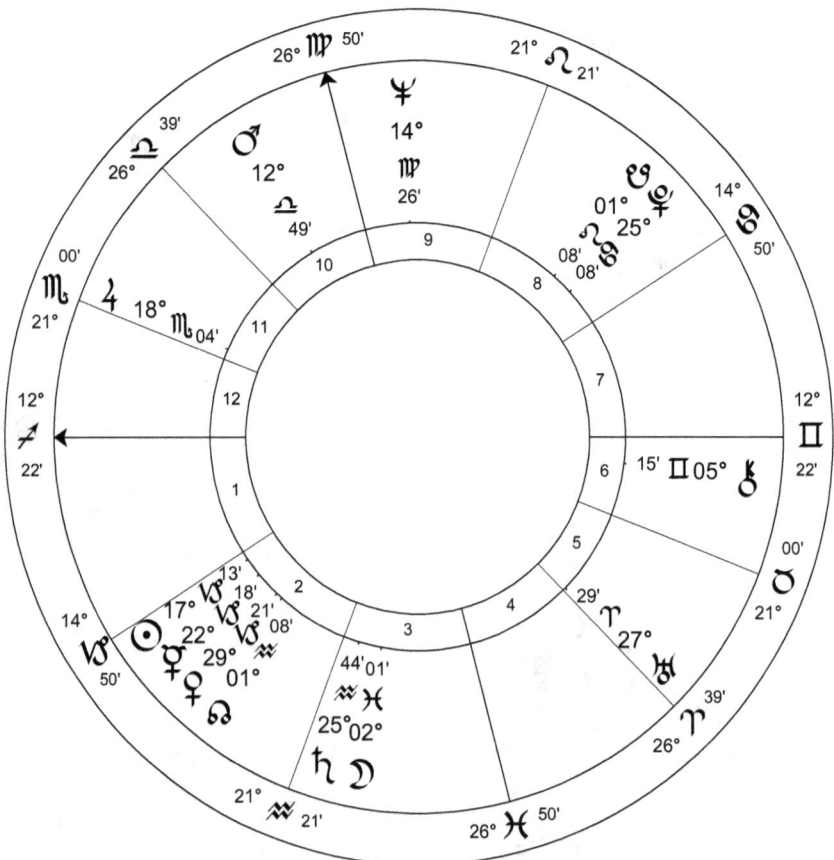

Elvis Presley, 8 January 1935, 4.35 am, Tupelo, Mississippi

accused of being Elvis' destroyer, and there may be some truth in that too. But if so, Elvis colluded in his own destruction.

Elvis met Parker in 1955, when he was just twenty. Parker was an illegal immigrant from the Netherlands who claimed he had been born in West Virginia. Like many people with Mercury in Gemini, he must have been very clever at mimicking accents to get away with that porkie. By the time he and Elvis met, he had carved a promising place for himself in the music world by managing two well-known country singers. Elvis had already made his first recordings for Sun Records, performed at various local concerts, and made appearances on local TV shows. But he was still only a regional celebrity. A

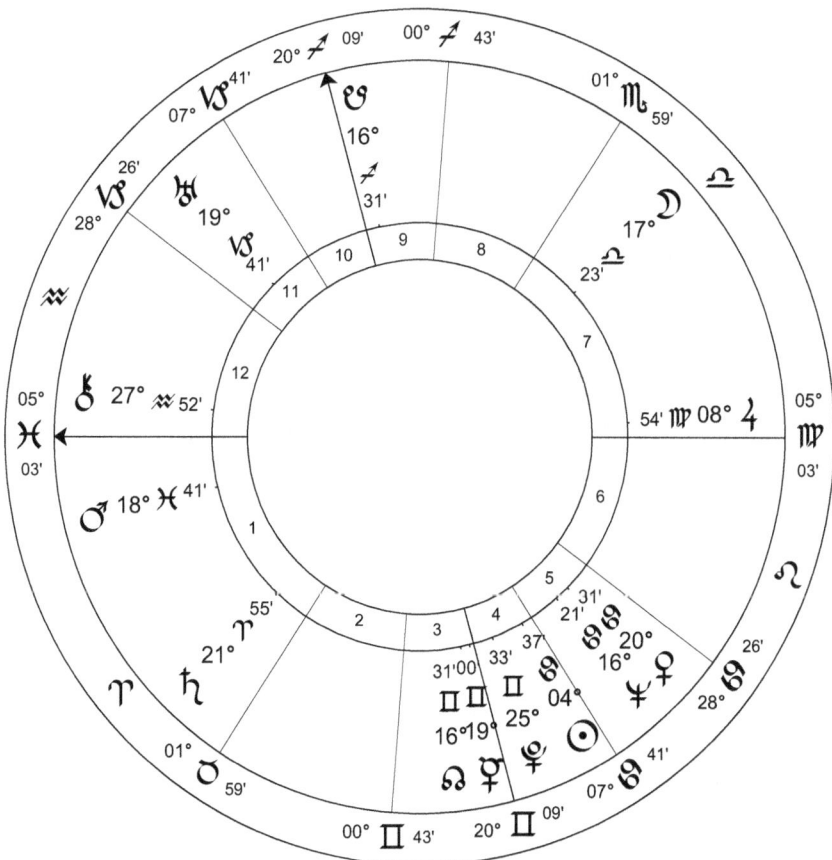

Colonel Tom Parker, 26 June 1909, 11.00 pm, Breda, Netherlands

Elvis Presley and Colonel Tom Parker on the set
of a Hollywood film, 1969.

promoter and DJ called Bob Neal had been managing him, but Neal felt Elvis was capable of a great deal more and introduced him to Parker, who was purported to be the best promoter in the music business.

Elvis was impressed by Parker's acumen in arranging lucrative concerts that reached a wider audience. He retained Neal as his manager but appointed Parker as his 'special advisor'. Due to Parker's efforts, in January 1956 Elvis made his first recordings for RCA. Among these was his first big hit, *Heartbreak Hotel*, followed by *Blue Suede Shoes*. Also through Parker's machinations he made his first appearances on national television. Soon after, he terminated Neal's contract and hired Parker as his manager. And the rest, as they say, is history.

When you're trying to view three charts at once, it can feel overwhelming and it's easy to get information overload. Let's focus primarily on Chiron. In Elvis' natal chart, Chiron is at 5° 15' Gemini in the 6th house, square a Moon-Saturn conjunction in the 3rd house. Chiron also trines Mars in Libra in the 10th and trines natal Venus at the end of Capricorn in the 2nd. How would you understand natal Chiron in Gemini?

Audience: Maybe he felt wounded in his intellect. Or in his everyday life and habits, since it's in the 6th. He was addicted to drugs most of his life, wasn't he?

Liz: Yes, he was, but let's try to get a sense of what the wound might really feel like, and then look at the ways in which it could be expressed. Drug addiction can certainly be a possible response to Chiron's sense of injury, but it's not the wound itself. What does Gemini's lost paradise look like?

Audience: A world where everyone can say whatever they want. A place of freedom. Open communication and all the knowledge you want made available, and schools where children are taught real information and not just a censored selection of other people's ideas, and where they can talk about their own ideas.

Liz: Yes, very well put. You should be a campaigner for Gemini rights.

Audience: I'm a Gemini.

Liz: Of course you are. For Elvis, that ideal world was crushed before he ever had a chance to discover its existence. Or perhaps it had never existed. Tupelo, Mississippi in the late 1930s wasn't exactly a place where a shy and lonely boy from a deeply troubled and impoverished background was likely to find much of what you've described. But as he grew older, Elvis discovered that he had determination as well as talent. The popularity he achieved through his music went at least a little way toward assuaging his unhappiness.

I would understand Chiron in Gemini as a wound to self-expression. Elvis had no idea how to communicate what he felt inside. This might have been partly triggered by his parental environment and partly by the kind of schools he attended. He was mediocre in his schoolwork and his teachers regarded him as 'average'. Music was his only real channel of expression, but he failed his music exam and was even told by one teacher that he had no aptitude for it. He couldn't read music and learned to sing and play by ear. By his own declaration he was also very shy, and as a boy he was bullied by his schoolmates and called a 'mama's boy', which I suppose he was. Eventually he learned to disguise the shyness by wearing flashy clothes, growing sideburns, and dressing his hair with rose oil and Vaseline. Music was the only thing that gave him a real voice.

The squares between natal Chiron and Moon-Saturn in the 3rd house suggest an early life of hardship and loneliness. Saturn in the 3rd echoes the pain of Chiron in Gemini and underlines the difficulties he experienced in communicating. The Moon in the 3rd in Pisces describes a rich imagination and a fluency in non-verbal ways of expressing himself, but it's constrained by both Saturn and Chiron. This Chiron-Saturn-Moon configuration has a terribly isolated and stifled feeling.

His father has been described as shiftless and lazy. Elvis had an older twin who had died stillborn, and his mother never got over it; she became obsessively overprotective of her remaining child. She was chronically depressed and was addicted to various kinds of painkillers and sleeping pills as well as alcohol. She died of heart failure when Elvis was twenty-three. By that time he had already achieved fame. And he had familiarised himself with his mother's medications long before and was already addicted to them himself.

Colonel Tom Parker, who was born Andreas Cornelis van Kuijk, was twenty when he emigrated to the United States in 1929. He began his working life in his new homeland by selling toffee apples at carnivals. His climb to fame and fortune included many episodes that might be termed 'shady' if not downright criminal. He managed to escape the consequences most of the time. But after enlisting in the American military he deserted, got caught, and ended up first in solitary confinement and then, after a breakdown, in a mental hospital for two months. He was more careful after that experience.

Parker controlled virtually every aspect of Elvis' life, from his marriage to Priscilla to his appearances in musical films such as *Love Me Tender*, *Jailhouse Rock*, and *King Creole*, and he helped himself to half of Elvis' money in return. He tried to wean Elvis off drugs for a time, but his efforts were unsuccessful, perhaps because he simply didn't know how – there were no fashionable celebrity clinics available at the time where 'The King' could dry out. Eventually Parker gave up trying. The two began to quarrel with increasing frequency and nearly parted ways in 1973, but they carried on anyway. Parker remained his manager until Elvis' death in 1977, and he continued to collect royalties from Elvis' estate until his own death in 1997 at the age of 87.

Natal Chiron in Parker's chart is at 27° 57'Aquarius in the 12th house, conjunct his Pisces Ascendant and trine natal Mercury and Pluto in Gemini and Sun in early Cancer in the 4th house. He was a loner and an outsider, and his departure from his homeland is shrouded in suspicion and mystery. But he seems to have coped with it by reinventing himself with a new name, a new nationality, a new home, and eventually a new surrogate family, perhaps because the trines made it easier for him to carry, and even capitalise on, the painful feelings of being marginalised and homeless.

Parker's Chiron is in close conjunction with Elvis' natal Saturn and in an out-of-sign conjunction with Elvis' Moon. We've already explored the synastry conjunction between Saturn and Chiron in the charts of King Edward VIII and Wallis Simpson, although that one is in Libra. How would you understand this conjunction?

Audience: Maybe it's similar. The two planets are in Aquarius. Elvis and Parker were both outsiders, so maybe their shared loneliness made them protective of each other. Also, Elvis' Moon is on Parker's Ascendant and trines his Sun. So there was a lot of emotional empathy.

Liz: I think that's all true, and it may account for a large part of the mutual tolerance they exhibited toward each other. Both men could be utterly vile in their behaviour, but still they carried on. Parker's Chiron is on Elvis' Moon as well as on his Saturn. We looked at that synastry contact earlier as well. The Moon tends to feel empathy and protectiveness toward Chiron. But Chiron can feel envious and resentful toward the Moon as well as emotionally dependent, and Parker had no qualms about dominating

Elvis' personal life in ways that were often damaging and destructive. He even demanded the right to choose Priscilla's wardrobe and hairstyle, which – as she has a Sun-Uranus conjunction and a Scorpio Moon – wasn't well received. Yet it was a binding relationship that only ended with Elvis' death. Even afterward, Parker never ceased to use Elvis' undying popularity to bolster his own declining years.

Now let's consider composite Chiron. It's placed at 16° 34' Aries, conjunct composite Sun and composite Venus in the 3rd house. Composite Chiron is also trine composite Neptune in Leo in the 7th and composite Moon in Sagittarius in the 11th, forming a grand trine in the element of fire. What do you make of this?

Audience: I'm having a hard time getting my mind around understanding a composite. I know it isn't a person. But I keep wanting to see that grand trine as lots of creativity and imagination but with something very painful at the core.

Liz: Don't worry, what you've said makes sense. A relationship can be imbued with creativity, imagination, and innovation as the core of its existence. Do you remember what kinds of themes came up when we were looking at Sun-Chiron in a natal chart? There's often the sense of a special destiny that comes from a feeling of being irrevocably wounded. The pain provokes a need to transform the wound into a meaningful purpose in life.

Perhaps the same thing applies here. This relationship circles around a central core – if you like, the solar 'self' of the relationship – focused on the expression and communication of innovative creative ideas, but with a wound at its heart that makes the impetus to expression troubled and urgent. We might think about the Greek deity Hephaistos, the smith-god, who was permanently crippled after being thrown from Mount Olympus to the earth. His immense creativity, fuelled by his wounds, impelled him to fashion all the beautiful objects and magical implements that gave the other gods their special powers. A relationship as an entity might not have human feelings, but it can reflect a mythic theme.

We could also say that this composite describes a powerful sense of destiny that would stir the aspirations of both people as well as energising the creative imagination in both. There are overlaps between the grand fire trine in the composite and the fire placements in the two birth charts. Elvis has a Sagittarius Ascendant which trines composite Mercury, Sun, and Chiron in Aries and also trines composite Neptune in Leo. Parker has natal Saturn in Aries conjuncting composite Venus-Chiron in Aries and trine composite Moon in Sagittarius.

Neither man has fire as a dominant element in the natal chart, but it seems as though the relationship itself provided the fire that energised them both. Something happened when they got together that brought all the potential inspiration out of them both. I've seen this kind of pattern with other composite charts. The relationship may constellate qualities, behaviour patterns, and choices, sometimes positive and sometimes negative, that neither person would ordinarily find easy to express on their own.

Both men suffered from painful feelings of isolation and loneliness. Parker was a trickster in his dealings with the world, but he was a Cancer with a Pisces Ascendant and at times he must have found the isolation bitterly hard. The difficulty in communication and self-expression suggested by Elvis' natal Chiron in Gemini square Saturn-Moon in the 3rd house is echoed by composite Chiron in the 3rd. Parker's chart doesn't have this kind of 3rd house emphasis. But his natal Saturn in the 1st house opposing Moon in Libra in the 7th echoes Elvis' Moon-Saturn conjunction with its feelings of loneliness and abandonment. And Parker's natal Mercury-Pluto conjunction, although it can be voluble on the surface, is often too mistrustful to express deeper thoughts and feelings.

Despite their isolation – or perhaps because of it – both men were driven by a strong desire to make their mark on the world. This might be reflected in Elvis' chart by his natal Mars in Libra in the 10th house square Sun in Capricorn in the 2nd, and in Parker 's chart by his 1st house Saturn in Aries, which often tries to compensate for feelings of powerlessness by wielding power over others.

The composite conjunction of Sun-Chiron in Aries opposes Elvis' natal Mars in the 10th and squares his Sun in Capricorn in the 2nd, triggering his ambition, his desire for wealth, and his longing to be seen as someone innovative and ground-breaking in the eyes of the world. Composite Chiron also conjuncts Tom Parker's natal Saturn in the 1st house and opposes his natal Moon, triggering Parker's fear of being rejected and abandoned as well as stirring a powerful desire to be an Aries crusader and innovator.

There are many other contacts between composite Chiron and the planets in both natal charts, as well as a lot of strong links between other composite planets and the natal planets of both men. I've already mentioned the way in which the composite grand fire trine links with planets in fire signs in both natal charts. Another important link is composite Ascendant at 23° Capricorn conjunct Elvis' natal Mercury-Sun-Venus conjunction in Capricorn in his 2nd house. One way to view this is that Elvis' need to ground his talents in concrete form gave the relationship its shape by constellating the composite Ascendant – the specific way the relationship would be expressed in the outer world. Elvis' musical talent brought it to life, and in turn the relationship made him very wealthy and helped to give him a sense of worth.

Audience: What about when composite Chiron squares or opposes someone's natal planets?

Liz: We've just seen an example of this in composite Chiron opposing Tom Parker's natal Moon and squaring Elvis' natal Sun. It acts as a trigger for the natal planet through friction and conflict, and in this case also triggers the tension between Parker's Libra Moon with its need for constant companionship and Elvis' Capricorn Sun with its desire to achieve its goals as a solo performer.

Composite Chiron will usually show a mixed picture in relation to the planets in two natal charts. Every relationship, if has any depth at all, is likely to contain some painful conflicts. They come with the relationship kit. I've been focusing on some of the positive dimensions of composite Chiron in the charts of Elvis and Parker, but there are some very unpleasant aspects too. As well as conjuncting Parker's natal Saturn and opposing his Moon, composite Chiron in Aries squares his Venus-Neptune conjunction in Cancer and his natal Uranus in Capricorn, triggering a natal grand cardinal cross of Saturn, Venus-Neptune, Moon, and Uranus. The push-pull quality of Parker's way of relating, swinging from control to neediness and excessive idealism to cool detachment to the expectation of rejection and back again, was kicked into life by composite Chiron. It's not surprising that his treatment of Elvis was so erratic, and that he felt control was the only way he could ensure Elvis would stay in the relationship and never abandon him.

Every aspect composite Chiron makes to the natal charts is relevant. If the relationship lasts long enough, every aspect will reveal itself sooner or later. But it helps to get a sense of what will shout loudly and what will hum softly in the background, by thinking in terms of major themes rather than a simple list of planetary contacts. It's no different from working with the synastry between two charts. There will usually be a mix of easy and hard synastry aspects, and we need to get a feeling of which themes will dominate regularly and which themes may only surface when natal or composite planets are triggered by transiting planets. When composite Chiron makes hard aspects to natal planets, the inbuilt wound in the relationship will challenge and possibly even injure the expression of the natal planets it aspects. It will also kick these planets into further development and can sometimes inspire a highly creative response.

Earlier I talked about the kind of wound from the past that might be reflected by issues like children from an earlier partnership, or a difficult prior relationship that has left bitter scars and still reverberates emotionally. The relationship as an entity, portrayed by the composite, doesn't set about being unpleasant. It doesn't try to hurt people. It isn't a human being. Composite Chiron doesn't wilfully try to undermine or injure anyone. But some form of shared suffering that exists in the past of both people can pose a big challenge to them, and they may then react in constructive or destructive ways.

A composite chart can't sit down and reflect on its problems the way a human being can. Nor can it confront us and say, 'Look, I'm really upset because you're always ignoring me.' We can't ask a composite to go into analysis and become conscious of its complexes. It's up to the two individuals to explore the times when echoes from the past may impinge on the present. This kind of awareness and honesty, which doesn't depend on understanding astrology, could generate a more creative outcome from Chiron's hard aspects to the natal charts. A composite doesn't enjoy the freedom to choose, but as humans, to some extent we do.

Composite charts can be deeply unsettling because in theory, we could calculate our composite chart with every human being who has ever existed. The composite is a map of abstract potential. I have a composite chart with every one of you here today, as well as with every human, dead or alive, who has ever been born. So do all of you. For that matter, we all have a composite with every cat, goat, dinosaur, and earthworm ever born, although getting their birth charts might be a bit tricky. Unless a relationship actually comes into being, these infinite composites remain theoretical. They exist in the same realm as imaginary numbers.

Composite charts have no concrete reality until two people get together and create a living relationship. Then the composite takes form and incarnates between them. Prior to this, it exists only on the level of possibility. The moment two people actually engage with each other, or an individual forms a relationship with an institution or a country or even with a deceased person whose creative work exercises a powerful influence on their own development, the human energy brings the composite alive. The relationship which previously existed on a theoretical level now has life in it, and part of that life involves awakening the place in the composite where something from the past reflects an unhealed injury of some kind. Past hurts born out of life's vicissitudes are part of every human relationship, and every composite chart has a Chiron.

The question of orbs

Audience: Do you use the same orbs in synastry and in the composite that you do in the natal chart? You seem to be using 10° orbs.

Liz: Yes. With a composite I work with a 10° orb for oppositions, squares, and conjunctions, a 6° orb for a sextile, and a 2° orb for minor aspects like a quincunx or sesquiquadrate, just as I would do with a natal chart. The reason I use large orbs is that they seem to work. When a planet makes only one aspect and the orb is 10°, it's often so obvious in its expression that it becomes very difficult to insist that no aspect exists between them. I also use these orbs for out-of-sign aspects, which many people don't consider aspects at all. As with all these issues, you must experiment and form your own conclusions. From my own astrological experience I've learned to take wide orbs seriously, but of course it could be argued that one sees what one sees best oneself. The same could be said of all the different approaches and techniques in astrology.

With synastry and composites, as with natal aspects, it seems that the closer the orb, the more intense and compulsive the exchange. If we find very tight orbs such as the exact conjunction between Prince Harry's Chiron and Prince William's Mercury, we know that the tension is likely to be experienced in an intense and compulsive way. The attraction, the possibility of injury, the vulnerability, the envy, the compassion, and the potential of healing are so strong that we become aware of the dynamic very early in the relationship and can't help but follow where the aspect leads.

In close relationships, it can be very difficult to handle tight orbs because it's hard to find any breathing space. We have to struggle to get some perspective. The same applies to close orbs in a natal chart. It isn't easy to move far enough away from the compulsiveness of the aspect to get a sense of what it's about because it's in our face all the time. When we find a 10° orb in synastry between Chiron and another planet, there's more flexibility. The two people might not even recognise the possibilities of the aspect until they have got so far into the relationship that they can't easily get out again. Then the wide orbs become noticeable. The longer we're involved with someone, and the closer the involvement, the more those wide orbs make themselves known over time.

Part Five

Chiron and the Scapegoat

The ancient ritual of the Scapegoat

I mentioned earlier that I wanted to look more closely at the archetypal theme of the Scapegoat because it's so relevant to the astrological Chiron, natally and in synastry. This theme might make a fitting conclusion to our seminar. The story of the Scapegoat appears in ancient Hebrew tradition and is described in Leviticus. The Hebrew word for the Scapegoat – לַעֲזָאזֵל (*azazel*) – was understood in later Christian thought to be the name of a demon or a fallen angel, reflecting the idea of the goat as an evil bearer of the sins of the community. The goat in Christian iconography is often associated with Satan, who is portrayed with a goat's horns and hoofs. This iconography has carried through into modern times in the association of the goat with black magic. But in the Hebrew tradition, the goat itself isn't evil. It's a holy sacrifice, a blameless creature given the job of carrying human evil so the community can begin another year free of sin and guilt.

Two goats were involved in the early Hebrew ritual. One goat was sacrificed to the Lord and the second goat was driven into exile in the desert. Both were sacred, chosen creatures blessed by God to be the sacrifice. Driving the goat into the wilderness to die symbolised the cleansing of the community. The ritual took place each year as part of the ceremony of Yom Kippur, the Day of Atonement, the holiest day in the Jewish religious calendar. Yom Kippur usually occurs in late September or early October, close to the autumnal equinox when the Sun enters Libra.

Audience: Is that significant?

Liz: I'm not sure whether the timing has significance. I suspect it did once upon a time, although the meaning may be forgotten now. Rosh ha-Shanah, the Jewish New Year, begins around the time of the autumnal equinox, followed by Yom Kippur. The New Year must begin with a spiritual clean slate. A great many religious rituals of all persuasions tend to occur near the equinoxes and solstices, and perhaps were originally linked to them. Christmas occurs around the time of the winter solstice, as does Hanukkah, the Jewish Festival of Lights; Easter occurs at the time of the spring equinox, as does Passover, and the Feast Day of St John the Baptist occurs at the summer solstice. Four of the eight Celtic festivals or 'sabbats'– Samhain, Beltane, Imbolg, and Lughnasa – are very ancient and are related to the agricultural cycle, occurring roughly a week after the Sun's entry into the four fixed signs of the zodiac. The other four, practised today by many modern pagans – Ostara, Yule, Mabon, and Litha – coincide with the equinoxes and solstices.

Some of the symbolic connections between religious festivals and the solar cycle are clear. Easter occurs on the Sunday following the first full Moon after the spring equinox when the Sun enters Aries, the sign of new beginnings. Christmas occurs just after the winter solstice when the old Sun dies and the new Sun is secretly born in the darkness. The Jewish New Year occurs at the autumnal equinox when balance is achieved between darkness and light, and the ancient ritual of the Scapegoat followed immediately afterward. From a Christian perspective, Jesus might be viewed as the ultimate Scapegoat. But the theme of a surrogate who carries sin or evil for others is universal, reflecting its archetypal nature, and it exists outside of Abrahamic cultures. In Celtic lore, the Scapegoat was a designated human 'sin-eater' who consumed a ritual meal to spiritually absorb the sins of a deceased person whose soul would otherwise wander unredeemed in outer darkness.[51]

In ancient Greek ritual practice, following the belief that natural disasters such as plagues or earthquakes were a sign of the gods' anger, the perceived transgressions of the entire community were loaded onto one individual, deemed an appropriate 'sin-bearer' or *pharmakos*.[52] In archaic Greece, this sacrificial victim may have been the king himself as the embodied link between the godhead and the people, offered up in times of great crisis. In later centuries, an individual was chosen from among the people. The hapless victim was ritually beaten and, if they survived, driven out of the community. This Scapegoat was often chosen because of a physical deformity or disability, or because of having previously committed a crime, or simply because of perceived 'differentness'. It's a disturbing archetypal pattern, but it seems that communities have always felt some chosen individual, especially holy or especially hated or both, should carry the collective burden of evil.

Chiron isn't a literal scapegoat in Greek myth. He isn't driven out of the community carrying the sins of others; he's wounded by accident while trying to do something helpful. But in a deeper sense, this is exactly what happens to him. He is a sacrifice, inadvertently expiating the savagery and violence of his fellow centaurs as well as the arrogance and carelessness of the hero Herakles. He must bear the poison of the Lernaean Hydra and, alone among the deities, he is the one who must relinquish his godhead

---

51 On the tradition of the sin-eater, see Hilda Ellis Davison, ed., *Boundaries and Thresholds* (Thimble Press, 1993); Bertram S. Puckle, *Funeral Customs* (T. Werner Laurie Ltd., 1926).

52 The word may be related to *pharmakon*, which can be both a poison and a healing agent. On the Greek *pharmakos*, see Walter Burkert, *Structure and History in Greek Mythology and Ritual* (University of California Press, 1982); Todd M. Compton, *Victim of the Muses: Poet as Scapegoat, Warrior and Hero in Greco-Roman and Indo-European Myth and History* (Hellenic Studies Series 11, Center for Hellenic Studies, Harvard University, 2006).

for Prometheus, who really did breach divine law but manages to get away with it.

The Scapegoat in the family

An important dimension of Chiron's wound is the feeling that we have been scapegoated, unfairly victimised, or punished for something that isn't our fault. Sometimes the family history underpinning Chiron's wound reveals a literal version of this, especially if earlier generations have suffered collective atrocities such as slavery, persecution, or genocide. But sometimes scapegoating has a more personal history. As a child, the person may have had to carry the shadow side of the family psyche so that everyone else could walk away feeling morally superior and blameless. Family scapegoats are often individuals who begin to display the sense of an individual self from a very early age. They may threaten the unconsciously established assignment of roles and relationship alliances inherent in family dynamics, especially in an enmeshed family.

The scapegoated child can be a potential awakener who threatens to break open the cocoon of the family's wilful unconsciousness. Sometimes the child becomes the 'identified patient' who displays symptoms of what is interpreted as mental illness, and who must carry the conflicts buried deep in the family psyche. This tragic dimension of family scapegoating was explored by the psychiatrist R. D. Laing, who went as far as insisting that people labelled as schizophrenics were carrying the madness and suffering not just of the family, but of their entire collective. Although Laing's work is not considered acceptable within the mainstream psychiatric establishment, he may have had a point.

Family scapegoats are sometimes gifted children who become the targets of parental or sibling envy. They might be spirited, rebellious children who display attitudes that challenge the family status quo. They may also be children who appear lacking in ability according to the expectations placed on them by the family. Examples of this are the dreamy, imaginative child of a scientifically inclined family; the withdrawn, introverted child of extraverted, popular parents; the highly sensitive child born into a military family; or the artistic child of parents focused solely on the money-making potential of a family business. Not only enviable talents, but also a lack of talent or inclination for a particular family aspiration, can result in scapegoating.

Sometimes family scapegoating focuses on physical differentness such as a disability or perceived exceptional attractiveness or unattractiveness, or – very commonly, although often unacknowledged – a resemblance to an earlier family scapegoat. Great Aunt Violet went off the rails and eloped with a drug dealer, became an addict, had an abortion and a breakdown, and then committed suicide, and one ever speaks of it. If we happen to resemble poor Violet in appearance or manner, we may be scapegoated without ever understanding why.

Fairy tales like *Cinderella* abound with family scapegoats, often portrayed as unwanted orphans or stepchildren. The external focus for scapegoating can be just about anything, but the inner mechanism is the same: the goat must be driven out of the community carrying everyone else's sins. Identification with the archetypal Scapegoat lies at the heart of the astrological Chiron. But it's not a good idea to identify with an archetype. It destroys the possibility of individual development and individual values, and it tends to end badly.

The pattern of scapegoating in families is often passed down over many generations. Parents who scapegoat their children have usually been scapegoated themselves, or their own parents were; and these scapegoated children may grow up to be virtue-signalling scapegoaters hunting down someone else whom they feel should be punished for what they believe was once done to them or their family or collective. Sadly, these people may be genuinely idealistic and entirely unconscious of the ambiguous roots of their opinions and actions.

Audience: So does Chiron's placement show whether there has been scapegoating?

Liz: I think I would put it differently. Chiron's placement shows where we feel scapegoated. There's usually a trigger, but the impact of the trigger also depends on one's own perceptions. Quoting the late Queen once again, recollections may vary. Chiron *always* feels victimised, and it's hard to know how much is objective and how much is subjective. Sometimes destructive parental or peer group behaviour is so painfully obvious that there isn't any question about it. But sometimes it's far more ambiguous. The same experience may affect different children in very different ways.

The question of individual perception and how we interpret what has happened to us is critical in working with Chiron. Archetypal patterns, as James Hillman said, are lenses through which we view reality, and if we keep wearing Chiron's spectacles rather than those of other planets, we will always see ourselves as victims. And we may also need to consider whether a person who constantly feels scapegoated may behave in ways that provoke rejection from others. We're back to the issue of how we may sometimes create our own circumstances according to how we act in life, which depends in turn on what we perceive.

Audience: It sounds as if you're saying there isn't really any scapegoating, only people who feel they have been scapegoated. Surely that isn't the case. Scapegoating goes on all the time, but it sounds as if you're excusing it or saying it's purely in the mind of the victim.

Liz: I'm not saying that at all. Please try to listen, rather than reacting without thinking and immediately putting words into my mouth. You're giving us an excellent example of what I've just been talking about. I'm sorry if I've inadvertently put my finger on a wound. But please don't misinterpret or reinterpret what I've been saying.

Of course scapegoating goes on all the time, and it's brutal and inexcusable. It's not 'just' in the mind of the victim, and there is no justification for it. Sometimes we need to find the courage to avail ourselves of the law to right a wrong. But for your own sake there might be a better way of understanding what has happened to you, or to anyone else with whom you empathise, than simply returning the hatred fivefold and becoming a scapegoater yourself. If we want to work with Chiron in constructive ways and not get stuck howling in that cave full of bitterness and poison, it won't help to look only at the ugly reality of other people's behaviour. We might need to look at our own behaviour too. Scapegoating reflects the dark side of human nature, and only an incredibly naïve or deluded person would claim it's all purely subjective. But as Jung put it in *The Undiscovered Self*, 'None of us stands outside humanity's black collective shadow.' We might need to explore the ways in which we perpetuate the pattern rather than bringing about genuine change and healing, inner or outer.

I'm not suggesting minimising the pain, turning the other cheek, or pushing everything under the carpet. But we can become so stuck in hating and blaming that we see culprits everywhere, often in the wrong places, and fail to recognise that we might also be looking into a mirror. Becoming a scapegoater because you have been scapegoated is easy and seductive. It can even become addictive. But it won't do anything at all to help anyone else's pain, let alone our own. We just risk becoming the very thing we hate.

Any group within a general population – racial, religious, economic, social – may be scapegoated because they appear 'different'. They're often accused of causing social, political, and economic crises they have nothing to do with. Historically they have been blamed for the spread of disease, or they become the focus of conspiracy theories. The great challenge for any individual identifying with such a group is to avoid becoming a scapegoater seeking someone else to persecute. And that requires being able to distinguish what we perceive from what has actually happened.

Our individual perceptions affect not only how we experience our own wounds, but also the ways in which we interpret history. We can rewrite the past according to our personal grievances or we can make the effort to find enough detachment and balance to see the subtlety and complexity of Chiron's myriad colours as they tint human history. With sufficient unconsciousness, hatred, and envy, any current 'victim' movement, however justified it might seem in external terms, can facilitate the scapegoat becoming a scapegoater if we polarise and fail to distinguish reality from our own emotional responses. Then people unconsciously become the very thing they're opposing, and the cycle goes on and on into the future with no healing at all.

It would be misleading to associate Chiron with specific collective events such as pandemics, wars, or economic crises, in which there are always so many blameless victims. No planet 'makes' these events happen. The planets reflect our ways of perceiving, responding to, and interpreting events, and our responses in turn shape present and future events. If a collective is relatively unified in a particular response, it can change history for the better. But without individual reflection, it can also change it for the worse.

The dimension of the psyche that Chiron symbolises in the individual and the collective will respond to painful events with a particular mind-set, which initially is that of the archetypal Scapegoat. This mind-set might eventually transform into a wiser, more realistic, and more compassionate perspective. The impotent, poisoned centaur can reclaim his wisdom in the act of sacrificing his immortality. But the poisoned wound, accidentally inflicted, begins the story. Chiron reflects how we react as individuals and as a group when we feel unfairly victimised and scapegoated, which, sooner or later, for one reason or another, every one of us is.

Conclusion

Feeling helpless and enraged in the face of malign and unfair forces over which we have no individual power is characteristic of Chiron's response. We may feel victimised, but we may also seek victims – partners, parents, children, peers, governments, politicians, authors, racial or gender or national or economic groups – in order to feel more potent in the face of life's unfairness. We can see this dynamic with the greatest clarity in the relationships in which Chiron plays an important part.

If we really want to make a difference in the world, we need to begin in the hidden part of our own back garden or the alcove in the basement that no one ever sees. Chiron in love is also Chiron in pain. With some effort, self-honesty, humility, genuine communication, and a willingness to go through Chiron's stages from injury and rage to the acceptance of mortality, each of us might, within the individual sphere in which we work and live and in the relationships that matter in our lives, make a genuine difference.